SIGN LANGUAGE

Reading Flannery O'Connor's Graphic Narrative

MERCER UNIVERSITY

MERCER UNIVERSITY PRESS

Endowed by

TOM WATSON BROWN

and

THE WATSON-BROWN FOUNDATION, INC.

SIGN LANGUAGE

Reading Flannery O'Connor's Graphic Narrative

RUTH REINICHE

MERCER UNIVERSITY PRESS | *Macon, Georgia*

2020

MUP/ H984

Published by Mercer University Press
1501 Mercer University Drive
Macon, Georgia 31207

9 8 7 6 5 4 3 2 1

Books published by Mercer University Press are printed on acid-free paper that meets the requirements of the American National Standard for Information Sciences—Permanence of Paper for Printed Library Materials.

Printed and bound in Canada.

This book is set in Adobe Garamond Pro.

Cover/jacket design by Burt&Burt

ISBN 978-0-88146-740-6
Cataloging-in-Publication Data is available from the Library of Congress

Contents

Acknowledgments

I want to thank Charlie Scruggs for the idea of looking at the 1940's *New Yorker* cartoons and for knowing how to inspire me to complete the dissertation process. Thank you to Avis Hewitt for introducing me to O'Connor studies. Heather Mayo and Erin Overmeyer both patiently walked me through creative art processes when I needed instruction. Thank you for all you have contributed to my education and to art education in your public-school classrooms. I want to thank my friend and fellow O'Connor scholar, Rebecca Karnes, for uncomplainingly listening to my theories. Thank you to my book club: Samantha, Andy, Lauren, Jon, and Charlie who read O'Connor books exclusively the year I wrote my dissertation. Most of all, I want to thank my family, Sarah, Josh, Evi, Amos, Rebecca, David, Bob, Martin, and Mike for listening to me talk about O'Connor for eight long years. All of these people have provided the contextual support for this work. As I read these names, I realize that, for better or worse, these people are my community. Thank you all.

Preface

As I read Flannery O'Connor's *Wise Blood* for the first time, I could not shake the feeling that I was virtually walking through an art gallery and viewing a carefully constructed series of painted canvases. The forward flow of the narrative seemed to halt and, in my mind, a complete picture formed. W. J. T. Mitchell defines this type of stylistic event as gesture: the "moment when thought becomes visible, tangible, or palpable, staged and framed as *form*." He goes on to say that these moments become "something to be held and to hold us in mutual prehension" (Mitchell, *Preface*, xxi). O'Connor, preceding a reading she gave at Hollins College, Virginia, on October 14, 1963, describes the creation of such gestural moments in "A Good Man Is Hard to Find."

> I have decided that it is probably some action, some gesture of a character that is unlike any other in the story, one which indicates where the real heart of the story lies. This would have to be an action or a gesture which was both totally right and totally unexpected; it would have to be one that was both in character and beyond character; it would have to suggest both the world and eternity. The action or gesture I'm talking about would have to be on the anagogical level, that is, the level which has to do with the Divine life and our participation in it. It would be a gesture that transcended any neat allegory that might have been intended or any pat moral categories a reader could make. It would be a gesture which somehow made contact with mystery.[1] (Votteler)

Intrigued, I began first to isolate, and then to determine what was actually happening textually during these pictorial pauses which I was convinced must occur more than once in each of her novels. Did these pictorial moments require a reading that was different from that which is usually required by novelistic text? It was O'Connor's last and unfinished novel that determined how I would conduct this research.

---

[1] Votteler, Thomas. *Contemporary Literary Criticism: Excerpts from Criticism of the Works of Today's Novelists, Poets, Playwrights, Short Story Writers, Scriptwriters, & Other Creative Writers: 013.* Detroit: Gale Research Inc. 1979.

In 2009, while working in the archives in the O'Connor Collection at Georgia State College, I came across ten pages in the unfinished *Why Do the Heathen Rage?* that focused my studies of O'Connor's pictorial technique. In those ten pages, the main character of that novel, Walter Tilman, constructs a visual/graphic narrative using photographs. He thoughtfully, though comically and ineptly, arranges objects and people in each photograph, evaluating and reevaluating the effect of his visual message. Adding the series of photographs to the letter he is writing creates a kind of sign language that exists outside of, or in spite of, Walter's linear narration. Suddenly, it all became clear to me. I had a new perspective from which to evaluate the dual narratives that I had noticed in *Wise Blood*. The rhetorical strategy employed by Walter Tilman using photographs to create a pictorial or visual metanarrative that coexists with the linear narrative of the story is Flannery O'Connor's method of construction in her novels. My project then became to read the pictorial moments as visual text, as pieces of art, and to see where they led me.

Introduction

Sign Language

Reading Flannery O'Connor's Graphic Narrative

...a gesture that makes contact with mystery...[1]

The problem is posed for the modern artist in an insane manner, as a choice between the senility of academic rules and the primitiveness of natural gift: with the latter, art does not yet exist except in potentiality; with the former, it has ceased to exist at all. Art exists only in the living intellectuality of the habitus.[2] Jaques Maritain

Art makes the invisible visible. Art reveals truth. "Art is selective," Flannery O'Connor writes, "and its truthfulness is the truthfulness of the essential that creates movement."[3] Art captures a world in action. To gain perspective, to clarify her vision as an artist, O'Connor, using words as her medium, positions herself as if she were "standing a foot away from an impressionistic painting, then gradually [moves] back until it comes into focus."[4] This movement—"backward and forward"—is essential for O'Connor. "When you reach the right distance," she writes, "you suddenly see that a world has been created—and a world in action—and that a complete story has been told, by a wonderful kind of understatement. It has been told more by showing what happens around the story than by touching directly on the story itself."[5] The physical movement described by O'Connor replicates the cerebral movement required of the artist. Jacques Maritain, in his essay "Art and Scholasticism," writes, "It is indeed true that there is no nec-

[1] Flannery O'Connor, *Mystery and Manners* (New York: Noonday Press, 1969) 111.

[2] Jacques Maritain, *Art and Scholasticism with Other Essays* (Minneapolis, MN: Filiquarian, 2007) 44.

[3] O'Connor, *Mystery and Manners*, 70.

[4] Ibid., 79.

[5] Ibid.

essary progress in art, that tradition and discipline are the true nurses of originality."[6] An artist, according to Maritain, does not move forward unless she moves backward. To create this backward and forward movement in her texts, Flannery O'Connor constructs a textual gallery of "speaking pictures," visual texts that occur within the framework of her novels and short stories. These pictures, painted with words, assume the forms of *tableaux vivant*, photographs, and cartoons. Just as a speaker of sign language punctuates her narrative with signs that are at once pictures and words, O'Connor punctuates the narratives of her novels with moments or pauses in the forward motion that are somehow framed—in a mirror or in a window, for example—and that also are at once pictures and words. These pictorial moments not only occur in the reader's present, but because of the way they are stylized, they are simultaneously open windows into the historical world of the mid-twentieth century, a look backward into the classical past, and a veiled look into the mystery of a Divine Plan. Examination of the chronological development and refinement of Flannery O'Connor's pictorial technique presents a new perspective in interpreting her work. The pictorial pauses in her narrative text enable a reader to see "the whole world, no matter how limited his particular scene. For [the writer], the bomb that was dropped on Hiroshima affects life on the Oconee River, and there's not anything [he] can do about it. People are always complaining [O'Connor adds] that the modern novelist has no hope and that the picture he paints of the world is unbearable."[7]

"People without hope do not write novels"[8] nor do they read them is the way O'Connor answers those who complain about modern writers' depictions of the fallen world. Hope virtually materializes in O'Connor's work when she uses pictorial pauses to raise the veil between reality and the Divine and to provide for her readers a "sense of mystery deepened by a contact with reality," in essence, to view the invisible world in tandem with the real world.[9] The pictorial moments, i.e., pictures made using the medium of words, illustrate a marriage between the literal and the visual, between the body and the spirit, between the finite and the infinite.

[6] Maritain, *Art and Scholasticism*, 49.
[7] O'Connor, *Mystery and Manners*, 77.
[8] Ibid.
[9] Ibid., 79.

O'Connor's pictorial technique evolves as she moves from the undergraduate cartoons to the unfinished novel, *Why Do the Heathen Rage?* In the cartoons, the pictorial is framed and literally expressed by stark lines and dots. The visual text is accompanied by a defining caption of written text. O'Connor's cartoons reflect influence by cartoonists that she studied, particularly those in the *New Yorker* magazine. In *Wise Blood*, some of the cartoonish grotesques remain, but she places them in familiar compositions of classical tableaux or in ritualistic montage, creating jarring juxtapositions. In *The Violent Bear It Away*, O'Connor's pictorial pauses adopt the characteristics of the snapshot moment. In the mid-twentieth century, every photograph taken by a photographer, professional or amateur, was accompanied by its negative. These negatives made it seem like there was in existence some parallel universe which was the inverse of the one in which the photo existed. O'Connor's textual photographs are laden with significance and meaning and are fashioned in both negative and positive space. The idea of using tattoo as a pictorial medium and the human body as the canvas first occurs in the manuscript of *Why Do the Heathen Rage?* A minor character, a farmhand named Gunnels, wants a photograph of the tattoo on his back that happens to be a Byzantine Christ. In O'Connor's story "Parker's Back," this character is given a voice of his own. In this, her last short story, the pictorial frame disappears, images are permanently imprinted on the human body, and, for the first time, O'Connor requires one of her peculiar prophets to navigate the treacherous waters of marriage. The marriage of Parker and Sarah Ruth is the marriage of the literal and the visual made actual. Violence, of course, ensues.

Working in images and framed pictorials opens O'Connor's narrative in ways that are, certainly, particular to her style, but also that reflect the explosion of visual text that was occurring around her in mid-twentieth century America. She and her fellow Moderns left the mimetic "theories of the eighteenth century," particularly those perceiving art as a "copy—and hence inevitably an imperfect copy—of reality" behind. For these artists and writers, the true means "of representing reality was not to represent at all, but to create a portion of reality itself"—"an independent object with the same degree of 'thingness as objects in the world.'"[10] For Flannery O'Connor, participating in the Modern undertaking, making this art, creating this

[10] Wendy Steiner, *The Colors of Rhetoric* (Chicago: University of Chicago Press, 1982) 17.

"portion of reality itself," this adjusting of the "outer and inner worlds," is a deeply human endeavor. It does not transcend the world. It does not

> reside in an angelic mind; it resides in a soul which animates a living body, and which, by the natural necessity in which it finds itself of learning, and progressing little by little and with the assistance of others, makes the rational animal a naturally social animal. Art is therefore basically dependent upon everything which the human community, spiritual tradition and history transmit to the body and mind of man. By its human subject and its human roots, art belongs to a time and a country.[11]

Early on, the young O'Connor found Jacques Maritain to be a guide or mentor in the narrative "painting" of her stylized literary landscapes. In her introduction to the collection of Flannery O'Connor's letters, Sally Fitzgerald writes of finding the young writer's underlined copy of Maritain's *Art and Scholasticism* and postulates that "it was from this book that [O'Connor] first learned the conception of the 'habit of art,' habit in this instance being defined in the Scholastic mode, not as mere mechanical routine, but as an attitude or quality of mind, as essential to the real artist as talent."[12] Maritain defines for the reader exactly how this "habit of art" would manifest itself:

> Operative habits reside chiefly in the mind or the will.... Habits are interior growth of spontaneous life...and the only living (that is to say, minds which are perfectly alive) can acquire them, because they alone are capable of raising the level of their being by their own activity: they possess, in such an enrichment of their faculties, secondary motives to action, which they bring into play when they want.[13]

[11] Maritain, *Art and Scholasticism*, 77.

[12] Flannery O'Connor, *Letters of Flannery O'Connor: The Habit of Being* (New York: Farrar, Straus, & Giroux, 1979) xvii.

[13] Ibid. Fitzgerald continues her Maritain reference: "The object [the good of the work] in relation to which (the habit) perfects the subject is itself unchangeable—and it is upon this object that the quality developed in the subject *catches*. Such a habit is a virtue, that is to say a quality which triumphing over the original indetermination of the intellective faculty, at once sharpening and hardening the

It is in this endeavor, this pursuance of the "habit of art," that O'Connor begins to create her particular version of pictorial text, resulting in a stylized text which tests the "modern notion of 'expressive form' or the functionality of art.'"[14] An analysis of O'Connor's "habit of art" and how it develops into the particular pictorial text that is singular to O'Connor must begin with the worlds created and framed in the captioned cartoons that were published weekly in her college newspaper, *The Colonnade.*[15] These "speaking pictures" represent a beginning point in O'Connor's development as a creator of pictorial text.

DOCUMENTING THE DEVELOPMENT OF O'CONNOR'S PICTORIAL TEXT

In chapter 1, I will show how the cartoons created by Flannery O'Connor from 1942 to 1945, her undergraduate years at Georgia College for Women, serve as a beginning point in the analysis of the development of her particular style and purpose in creating pictorial text. The "speaking pictures" in the form of her captioned cartoons offered the young cartoonist a platform from which to exercise her singular voice in the same way that her pictorial text does in her later fiction. An analysis of the cartoons reveals a definite agenda of pictorial statements involving: abstract, simplistic, stereotypical characters; the tensions that exist between men and women; the tensions between both women and men and their illusions; the presence of violence at the base of all human interactions; and the exploration of the landscape between desire and desirability. In this chapter, I will pay particular attention to composition within the frame of the single-panel cartoon, as it is one of the pictorial elements that is carried forward into the framework of the novel. Another important influence on the undergraduate cartoons is the *New Yorker* magazine and its group of featured cartoonists, whose work O'Connor studied week after week with the arrival of each new issue. "I like cartoons," she wrote. "I used to try to do them myself, sent a batch every

point of its activity, raises it in respect of a definite object to a maximum of perfection, and so of operative efficiency. Art is a virtue of the practical intellect."

[14] See note 9 above.

[15] O'Connor's oil paintings would also make an excellent point of analysis from which to launch the study of her pictorial text. Since the paintings are not available to scholars, the cartoons will have to suffice.

week to the *New Yorker*, all rejected of course. I just couldn't draw very well."[16] She learned her lessons well and then, like any artist, defined and redefined what she was taught, and went on to develop her own signature style.

The virtual art gallery of pictorial texts that exist between the covers of *Wise Blood* will be the subject of chapters 2 and 3. In her first novel, Flannery O'Connor, maintains her voice as a cartoonist. In chapter 2, I will examine how she draws Enoch Emory and Hazel Motes as cartoon characters, but expands her pictorial mode to move backward to embrace classical techniques and forward to experiment with art movements emerging in the late twentieth century. I will discuss the way O'Connor transfers a selection of the techniques she employed in the single-panel cartoon to the novel. The influence of Nathanael West, a cartoonist turned novelist, fifteenth-century still life, and film montage are the focus of this chapter. West's *Miss Lonelyhearts* provides inspiration for some of the pictorial pauses featuring Hazel Motes. However, O'Connor goes way beyond West's cartoonish renderings, looks to Eliot's "The Waste Land," and establishes her pictorial technique in a unique, particular way. She places Hazel Motes *mise en scene* into a stylized version of a fifteenth-century *vanitas* still life, using his head in place of the requisite skull, and, influenced by the style of Eliot and West, she substitutes detritus culled from the city streets in place of the familiar objects that normally compose a *vanitas* painting. These objects, chosen by the artist, whether they are fifteenth century or twentieth century, are assembled to illustrate the same message. Life is transitory.

Enoch Emory's cartoonish behavior suggests that of the animated characters that O'Connor, the student, might have viewed before a movie in the theater located within walking distance of the campus of Georgia College for Women. Each week films were advertised in *The Colonnade* on the page directly opposite her weekly cartoon. The movies play a significant role in Enoch's obedience to his wise blood, and part of his story in the book is told by adapting the conventions of montage. In Enoch's part of chapter 2, I will consider the influence of twentieth-century assemblage and montage techniques and the direct influence of the movies on Enoch's behavior. Chapter 3 is the chapter that relies most heavily on the *Wise Blood* manuscript for verification. When I first began to read O'Connor's manuscripts

[16] O'Connor, *The Habit of Being*, 536.

in 2009, beginning with *Wise Blood*, I was fascinated with the ensemble of female characters that exist in the manuscript but that are either greatly altered or do not exist at all in the published version of the novel. At first I looked at these women as muted texts, but once I began to analyze the effect of the pictorial frameworks in which they appear, I began to see how O'Connor supplies through them a sort of "sign language," a visual text concerning the place of women, that was acceptable in the gendered context of 1952. I use the manuscript as a way to document O'Connor's ideas while creating these women and as a validation of my interpretation.

The pictorial pauses that feature Leora, Sabbath, and Ruby take the forms of recognizable *tableaux vivants* that suggest the work of both classical and contemporary artists. As she did with the Hazel Motes *vanitas*, O'Connor uses the detritus of the twentieth century to design her compositions. These women are not muted but they speak in signs, not words, necessarily. Any reference to a mid-twentieth-century woman is, today, often accompanied by a multitude of stereotypical implications. By creating Ruby, Leora, and Sabbath Lily, O'Connor has given her readers a view of the woman on the outside of that picket fence that so effectively encloses the 1950s housewife.

Chapter 4 marks a distinct difference in the way that O'Connor exhibits her pictorial technique. The pictorial moments in *The Violent Bear It Away* feature mode rather than tableaux. In this novel, it becomes necessary for O'Connor to feature flashes of Divine reality as it coexists with the reality we know. She does this by using the properties of the snapshot. Roland Barthes provides the terminology while Gregory Jackson provides the precedent in American literature called upon for analysis of the snapshot moment. Windows and doorways frame these snapshots, which enclose discarded, abject, and broken humans as well as objects. As it is in *Wise Blood*, there is not one person in this novel who emerges whole or unblemished. However, with the assistance of photographic realism, there is not one person in *The Violent Bear It Away* who does not come in contact with terrible violence.

In chapter 5, I look at "Parker's Back," O'Connor's last story. The frame that has encased the pictorial text up to this point disappears, and Christ's image is tattooed right onto the human body of O. E. Parker. The ink mixes with Parker's wise blood. The eyes of the Christ follow Parker wherever he goes, whatever he does. He cannot escape. Parker becomes an image-bearer in a way that none of the other characters have been before.

Strangely, the only one who comes close is Enoch Emory, who, while following the promptings of his wise blood, bears the visage of the "new jesus." These two bookend O'Connor's writing career. In her first novel, Enoch builds a receptacle for the "new jesus" out of a washstand, and in her last story, Parker, himself, becomes a receptacle for the "old jesus," the only Jesus, as far as O'Connor is concerned. "Parker's Back" is also concerned with the community of believers in a way that is distinctively different from the two novels. I will use this story as a final examination of the pictorial threads that run through the other chapters.

O'CONNOR AND HAWTHORNE

I cannot fail to mention that alongside and above the other influences on O'Connor's pictorial art, there stands Nathaniel Hawthorne. So many of her pictorial techniques can be tied directly back to a similar moment in a Hawthorne novel or tale. In *Blythedale Romance*, he features a character as part of the composition of a still life. O'Connor does the same with Hazel Motes in *Wise Blood.* In *The House of the Seven Gables*, he uses the daguerreotype to lift the veil between the natural and the supernatural in the same way that O'Connor uses the snapshot moment in *The Violent Bear It Away*. In *The Scarlet Letter*, he fashions, if not a marriage, a relationship that produces a child between the image-bearer, Hester Prynne, and Arthur Dimsdale, the bearer of liturgical law. In "Parker's Back," O'Connor fashions a marriage between Parker, who wears the image, and Sarah Ruth, who tells him, "God don't look like that! He don't *look.* He's a spirit. No man shall see his face."[17] This marriage, too, will soon produce a child. Wendy Steiner writes that such oppositions "deeply embedded in the structure of pictorial art [are] destined to play an important role in the symbolism of literary romance."[18] Writing literary romance was Flannery O'Connor's intention. She wrote to John Hawkes in November of 1961, "I think I would admit to writing what Hawthorne called 'romances,' but I don't think that has anything to do with the romantic mentality. Hawthorne interests me considerably. I feel more of a kinship with him than with any

[17] Flannery O'Connor, *Collected Works* (New York: Library of America, 1988) 674.

[18] Steiner, *Pictures of Romance: Form against Context in Painting and Literature* (Chicago: University of Chicago Press, 1991) 43.

other American."[19] Wendy Piper establishes O'Connor's connection to Hawthorne's particular style of American romance—that which is concerned not with "social verisimilitude" but with the "truth of the human heart," with the genre that "embraces mystery rather than factuality," and "characters are brought to a recognition of their own finitude."[20] Like Hawthorne, O'Connor is interested in creating "characters who are forced out to meet evil and grace and who act on a trust beyond themselves—whether they know very clearly what it is they act upon or not."[21] O'Connor's Hazel Motes, thrusting "forward," sitting on a train, rushing from a place that no longer exists to the modern city, is one of these knights errant—albeit a comical one. Sir Walter Scott, in the definitive "Essay on Romance," addresses the idea of romantic satire, O'Connor's as well as Hawthorne's oeuvre, as he writes:

> but the proper Comic Romance was that in which the high terms and the knightly adventures of chivalry were burlesqued, by ascribing them to clowns, or others of a low and mean degree. Such compositions formed, as it were, a parody on the Serious Romance, to which they bore the same proportion as the anti-masque, studiously filled with grotesque absurd, and extravagant characters, "entering," the stage direction usually informs us, "to a confused music," bore to the masque itself, where all was dignified, noble, stately, and harmonious.[22]

The adventures of *Wise Blood*'s Hazel Motes, Enoch Emory, and Sabbath Lily Hawkes quite roundly fit this "Quixotic" description as do the short story adventures of Manly Pointer and O. E. Parker.

Hazel's train journey is not unlike the one that Hawthorne's Clifford and Hepzibah make in *The House of the Seven Gables,* rushing from a perceived reality in the city that no longer suffices to the "safety" of the pastoral countryside. Both authors have written tales that adhere to Sir Walter Scott's seminal definition of Romance. The stories seem "to be a narrative

[19] O'Connor, *The Habit of Being*, 457.

[20] Wendy Piper, *Misfits and Marble Fauns: Religion and Romance in Hawthorne and O'Connor* (Macon, GA: Mercer University Press, 2011) 75 and 105.

[21] O'Connor, *Mystery and Manners*, 42.

[22] Walter Scott, *Essays on Chivalry, Romance, and the Drama* (London: Frederick Warne & Co., 1887) 143.

of real facts, and [are], indeed nearly allied to such history as an early state of society affords." In the case of Hazel, it is about *his* history, represented by an empty, crumbling house at the heart of which is an empty chifforobe that formerly housed his mother's belongings. Hepzibah and Clifford, also represented by a house, are the last of the damaged Pynchon dynasty still governed by the image of the patriarch which hangs ominously over the dining room table. This image is replayed again in *The Violent Bear It Away* when the patriarch, Old Tarwater, actually dies at the breakfast table. These family histories are "exaggerated by the prejudices and partialities of the [American] tribe to which [they] belong, as well as deeply marked by...idolatry and superstition." Scott writes further:

> Thus it becomes the trade of romancers still more to exaggerate, until the thread of truth can scarce be discerned in the web of fable which involve it; and we are compelled to renounce all hope of deriving serious or authentic information from materials upon which the compounders of fiction have been so long at work, from one generation to another, that they have at length obliterated the very shadow of reality or even probability.[23]

By constructing a performance plane—a stage, "a neutral territory, somewhere between the real world and fairy-land, where the Actual and the Imaginary may meet...a semblance of the world,"[24] the romancers, Hawthorne and O'Connor, seek to expose a "web of fable" in a neutral territory that will provoke the appearance of truth—"the truth of the human heart."[25] In this way, the truth of a time, at least the truth perceived by these romantic authors, can be ascertained and amplified by future generations.

The picture—the image—has long been elemental in the romance. Writers preoccupied with "identity, time, and repetition" and "concerned with love, metamorphosis, action" are

[23] Ibid., 139.

[24] Nathaniel Hawthorne, "The Custom House," *The Scarlet Letter and Other Writings*, ed. Leland S. Person, Norton Critical Editions (New York: W. W. Norton & Co., 2005) 29.

[25] Nathaniel Hawthorne, "Preface," *The House of the Seven Gables*, ed. Robert S. Levine, Norton Critical Editions (New York: W. W. Norton & Co., 2006) 3.

> inevitably drawn to the picture, the mirror, the statue as images of love gone wrong, metamorphosis, thwarted, action frozen. At the same time, as art, the romance shares the ideality of the visual arts, escaping the temporal finitude of the mortal that creates it. As both a narrative of events and a self-conscious artifice, the romance is repelled and fascinated by the visual artwork and the unchanging identity that it represents.[26]

Throughout this study of Flannery O'Connor's pictorial text, it behooves us to examine the precedent set by Nathaniel Hawthorne. Failure to do this would be to ignore O'Connor's strongest pictorial influence.

[26] Steiner, *The Colors of Rhetoric*, 51.

Chapter 1

"Oh, well, I can always be a PhD."

I don't dance. I have never danced.
—Bette Davis, *The Old Maid*, 1939[1]

But Flannery did talk some on that train trip. She said that while she was an undergraduate student at GSCW in Milledgeville, she'd always thought of herself as a cartoonist.[2]

Flannery O'Connor's distinctive pictorial way of writing addresses her readers in a manner that, like Hazel Motes, moves "backward and forward"[3] at the same time. In a fashion that resembles Hawthorne, she experiments with opaque, veiled surfaces, employing techniques like the creating of pictorial moments or pauses in her narrative with a classic painterly style or by creating verbal "combines," constructed in the manner of those by her contemporary, Robert Rauschenberg. Like Rauschenberg, O'Connor uses objects extracted from urban trash to experiment with her readers' sensibility and perception. She attempts this juxtaposition of common street objects to startle her readers into a deeper exploration of a character's words and interactions. O'Connor's use of pictorial text references the classical, yet she thrusts the technique forward into the twentieth century by applying the genre to photographs and to cartoon-inspired pictures, resulting in "artistic arrangements of images which [are] pictures in themselves" and which are constructed using "methods generally associated with the plastic arts."[4] Ap-

[1] Casey Robinson, *The Old Maid,* directed by Edmund Goulding (Burbank, CA: Warner Bros., 1939).

[2] Jean Wylder, "Flannery O'Connor: A Reminiscence on Some Letters," *The North American Review* 255/1 (Spring 1970).

[3] *Collected Works*, 23.

[4] Emily Stipes Watts, *Ernest Hemingway and the* Arts (Urbana: University of Illinois Press, 1971) 11. Watts explains the influence of the Dadaists, surrealists, Cezanne, and the Cubists on modern writers. This influenced served to create "a new interest in a total sensual involvement in the arts." She writes: "Moreover these orders also represented a shattering or splintering of man's own creative, as well as sensual expressions. There could be no freedom for 'LIFE' when only the visual or

plication of this stylistic technique culminates in a distinctive writing style that is representatively American and that embodies the past and, at the same time, embraces the Cold War present, while paving the pathway to the future, and causes indelible images to formulate in the minds of her readers.

Examination of the chronological development and refinement of this pictorial technique will open a new perspective in interpreting Flannery O'Connor's novels. The pictorial pauses in her narrative text enable readers to "see" the mid-century historical milieu that surrounds her. She writes,

> The longer you look at one object, the more of the world you see in it; and it's well to remember that the serious fiction writer always writes about the whole world, no matter how limited his particular scene. For him, the bomb that was dropped on Hiroshima affects life on the Oconee River, and there's not anything he can do about it. People are always complaining that the modern novelist has no hope and that the *picture he paints* of the world is unbearable.[5] (emphasis mine)

"People without hope do not write novels" nor do they read them is the way she answers the complainers. O'Connor also uses pictorial pauses to raise the veil and to briefly allow a glimpse of the Divine, having a "sense of mystery deepened by a contact with reality,"[6] in essence, to view the invisible world in tandem with the real world. Finally, O'Connor uses the pictorial pauses to illustrate a marriage between the literal and the visual.

Early manifestation of the pictorial technique is evident in O'Connor's college cartoons. She excelled at "capturing a representative moment in pictorial form and a rare facility for creating caricature for the purpose of social

audible or tactile sense could be exercised in any artistic creation or in any response. This is not to say that painters did not use paint, writers words, and composers music. They did employ the traditional modes of expression. Painters, however, also used words; writers used methods generally associated with plastic arts, such as artistic arrangement of type or images which were pictures in themselves; composers attempted to juxtapose painting and poetry with their music. In short, boundaries were crossed and modes mixed."

[5] O'Connor, *Mystery and Manners*, 77.

[6] Ibid., 79.

and political commentary."[7] In her writing, which Jill P. Baumgaertner argues is emblematic, O'Connor "often paints stark pictures which draw attention to themselves both pictorially, as still moments caught in time, and emblematically, as exaggerated representations of deeper spiritual truths."[8] This is obvious in both her cartoons and in her later writing. In 1963, the year before her death, O'Connor wrote to her friend Janet McKane, reminiscing about her youthful dream of becoming a cartoonist. "I like cartoons," she wrote. "I used to try to do them myself, sent a batch every week to the *New Yorker*, all rejected of course. I just couldn't draw very well."[9] While her cartoons were happily accepted by her audience at Georgia College for Women in Milledgeville in the mid-1940s, the young Mary Flannery was frustrated by the fact that her captioned images did not speak to the larger audience of *New Yorker* readers.

John Updike, himself a cartoonist, notes in his essay "Writers and Artists" that we should not be surprised that Flannery O'Connor began as a cartoonist "when we think of her vivid outrageousness, the definiteness of her every stroke"[10] evidenced in her finely crafted novels and short stories. "Alphabets begin in pictographs," Updike writes, "and though words are spoken things, to write and read we must *see*."[11] Interestingly, Updike situates the art of the cartoon alongside that of the Cubists and Abstract Expressionists. "Most paintings 'tell a story,'" he writes, "and even departures from representation carry a literary residue; e.g., the labels and bits of newspaper worked into Cubist collages, and the effect of a monumental calligraphy in the canvases of Pollock and Kline. The art of the comic strip exists as if to show how small the bridge need be between two forms of showing, of telling."[12] Will Eisner, a comic artist, graphic novelist, and instructor at New York City's School of the Visual Arts, writes about how the abstract nature of the cartoon assists in the reading of the language of the visual text:

[7] Jill P. Baumgaertner, *Flannery O'Connor A Proper Scarring* (Wheaton, IL: Harold Shaw Publisher, 1988) 20.

[8] Ibid., 22.

[9] O'Connor, *The Habit of Being*, 536.

[10] John Updike, "Writers and Artists," *The Writer's Brush: Paintings, Drawings, and Sculpture by Writers*, ed. Donald Friedman, (Minneapolis, MN: Mid-List Press, 2007) 429.

[11] Ibid.

[12] Ibid.

> The reading process in comics is an extension of text. In text alone the process of reading involves word-to-image conversion. Comics accelerate that by providing the image. When properly executed, it goes beyond conversion and speed and becomes a seamless whole. In every sense, this misnamed form of reading is entitled to be regarded as literature because the images are employed as a language. There is a recognizable relationship to the iconography and pictographs of logographic (or character-based) writing systems, like Chinese *hanzi* or Japanese *kanji.*[13]

As is evident in a number of studies like Friedman's *The Writer's Brush,* writers, themselves, often create some form of visual text, because, as Updike contends, "The subtleties of form and color, the perspective and composition—all these are good for a future writer to explore and will help him to visualize his scenes, even to construct his personalities and to shape the invisible contentions and branchings of plot."[14] Cartoons, in particular, like the novel, arrange "stylized versions of people within a certain space; the graphic artist learns to organize and emphasize, and this knowledge serves the writer."[15] Stylized characters and distorted stereotypes arranged in narrative tableaux in Flannery O'Connor's novels and short stories are the inheritors of her early cartoon making. She argues in "The Nature and Aim of Fiction" that if a writer is selective in the details, "certain of the details will tend to accumulate meaning from the story itself, and when this happens, they become symbolic to their action."[16] The selection of those details and their arrangement in the single-cartoon panel along with one line of narrative tell the story and imbue it with symbolism.

In the summer of 2012, I sat in Special Collections at Georgia State College and paged through the archived copies of *The Colonnade,* 1942 to 1945, looking at the context in which Mary Flannery's undergraduate cartoons appeared. Sarah Gordon's words—"shared sisterhood"—kept coming back to me as I thought about the variety of young women as well as faculty

[13] Will Eisner, *Graphic Storytelling and Visual Narrative* (New York: Norton & Co., 1996) xvii.

[14] Updike, "Writers and Artists," 430.

[15] Ibid.

[16] O'Connor, *Mystery and Manners,* 70.

that composed O'Connor's audience.[17] Even though the assortment of young women in O'Connor's cartoons represent the coed culture of the mid 1940s, in many ways, they are not different from the assortment of female eighteen- to twenty-five-year-olds that appear in fiction and on television and in movies today. Quite often, in order to make the caption or punch line "work," the single-panel cartoon demands that the viewer make immediate character assessments about figures *mise en scene*. Critics have labeled O'Connor's finely honed characters as distorted, satiric, and stereotypical. A study of the cartoon figures drawn during her college years offers an examination of the roots of the unique character creations that populate her short stories and novels. The single-paneled cartoons that appeared weekly in the college newspaper had to be immediately appealing to the young women attending Georgia State College for Women. Naturally, this demographic would be adept at reading clothing as secondary text. Consequently, in the cartoons she creates for *The Colonnade*, the young O'Connor uses a minimalistic assortment of clothing pieces to create iconological compositions which would be easily interpreted by the shared culture of a small campus. "Girlie-girls" wear puffy sleeves and pinafores; "smart" girls wear glasses, sensible clothing, and saddle shoes; and WAVES (the woman's section of the US Naval Reserve stationed on the campus of Georgia State College for Women) are "far-sighted," serious, and detached from the coed scene that surrounds them. Because O'Connor was submitting her cartoons to the *New Yorker* at this time, a study of *New Yorker* cartoons that appeared in the magazine between the years 1942 and 1945 offers for analysis what O'Connor would have considered as desirable models for her work and can provide a template for what was considered humorous by readers at the time. Even though "the typical New Yorker cartoon is as difficult to define as is the magazine's typical prose," there are some familiar

[17] Essentially, however, the cartoons display myriad images of young women, who, according to Sarah Gordon, "draw the viewer into recognition and common laughter at life in a woman's college. This is 'inside humor,' these are 'inside jokes': they rely for their interpretation and enjoyment, on a kind of shared sisterhood." (5). O'Connor's "delight in her time and place" is conveyed by the activities of the mostly unsmiling young women who are enclosed *mise en scene* in the frames of the cartoons, revealing "the wry vantage point from which O'Connor approaches the world" (5). (Sarah Gordon, *Flannery O'Connor: The Obedient Imagination* [Athens: University of Georgia Press, 2000].)

and recognizable characteristics. The cartoons "are witty, frequently subtle, often rely on sophisticated use of language, and depend on an educated, informed, and intelligent audience" and "there is usually a social element involved."[18] Measuring herself against the criteria displayed by the illustrious *New Yorker* cartoons started early on in O'Connor's development as a cartoonist. While still in high school, the young Mary Flannery was called "a female Ogden Nash"[19] in a local newspaper article, and the connection between O'Connor and the *New Yorker* is documented by both Brad Gooch and Kelly Gerald.[20] Gerald goes so far as to postulate that the simple lines drawn to depict the facial features of her cartoon characters, using "as few strokes as necessary to give [the] creations substance...read like a [James] Thurber study."[21]

THURBER AND THE MELANCHOLY OF SEX

If, in fact, O'Connor did study Thurber, the leading cartoonist of her day, (and there is no reason to think that she would not use him as a model), looking back, we would be able to determine Thurber's influence in her work. E. B. White identified Thurber's "themes as the 'melancholy of sex' and the 'implausibility of animals.'"[22] Thurber's *New Yorker* cartoons dur-

[18] Steven H. Gale, "Seventy-Five Years of *The New Yorker* Cartoons: A History," *American Periodicals* 11 (2001): 95–130, 105–106.

[19] Brad Gooch, *Flannery: A Life of Flannery O'Connor* (New York: Back Bay Books, 2009) 73.

[20] Ibid., 110 and 114.

[21] Kelly Gerald, "The Habit of Art," *Flannery O'Connor: The Cartoons*, ed. Kelly Gerald (Seattle, WA: Fantagraphics Books, 2012) 114. "Like his, O'Connor's faces were a simple circle or oval. Most frequently, she used only dots for the eyes. The shape and position of the eyebrows, made of single line slashes or arches, were the primary cues for attention and emotion. The triangular noses jutting out from the faces at varying lengths—sometimes a beak, sometimes elongated like a carrot—also comparable. For both cartoonists, the one-line stroke that was used for the mouth became a semicircle or wedge, cutting into the face when a character spoke, like a section extracted from a pie. O'Connor's characters in conversation also duplicate a mainstay of Thurber's style, with one character speaking while a companion looks on with an irritated dissatisfied or indifferent expression. This monologue-reaction scenario was a basic set up for both of them."

[22] Gale, "*New Yorker* Cartoons," 100.

ing the time that O'Connor was sending in submissions featured "a state of war between the sexes" that provided him "with what every artist prays for: perfect subject matter that he didn't even have to leave the house for."[23] The Thurber "Little Man cannot understand women's logic [or] her relationship to the universe or her emotions and sensitivity."[24] Wives and attractive, young temptations rounded out the depictions of women seen through the male gaze and drawn by James Thurber. Thurber's men are often slumped and put upon as the women carry on skirmishes in the legendary "battle," the purpose of which is unfathomable to these men. In her preface to Thurber's *Men, Women, and Dogs,* Dorothy Parker describes one of his cartoons that epitomizes, for her, the "war between the sexes." The cartoon features

> a man, his wife, and a male guest. They are standing in a something less than gracious enclosure, furnished mainly with a bookcase apparently ordered by mail from the company that did such notable work in Pisa. And on top of the bookcase is a woman on all fours. So help me God, there is a woman on all fours on top of the bookcase. And the host is saying, "That's my first wife up there, and this is the *present* Mrs. Harris."[25]

In the next paragraph, Parker guides her readers through an analytical set of questions designed to determine the meaning of the particular cartoon. She describes the first wife as "limp," "resigned," a "trifle bewildered," and as having the "look of having been where she is for a long time." It would seem that, as Parker would have it, "the new spouse is no more sweetly shaped, no more elegantly clothed, no more carefully coiffed than the old one. They look equally terrible."[26] Clearly, this is Thurber's conundrum. What does the "first wife" represent in the battle of the sexes? Why would the man marry the replica of the first wife who he presumably had disposed of? Why does the "first wife" not go away? Parker summarizes all

[23] Wilfrid Sheed, "The Tragedy of James Thurber," *Slate* (September 18, 2003).

[24] Gale, "*New Yorker* Cartoons," 101.

[25] Dorothy Parker, "Preface," *Men, Women, and Dogs,* ed. James Thurber (New York: Harcourt, Brace, & Co., 1943) viii.

[26] Ibid.

of this when she writes, "You understand what I mean when I say that eternity will not be long enough for my figuring?"[27]

The Thurber themes described by White are present in O'Connor's coed cartoons but altered to fit the strictures of a Southern women's college. Looking at the cartoons en masse clearly reveals that the young O'Connor had an agenda for the shape of the satire and the gentle "ribbing" of her "speaking pictures." One of her prevailing themes was the priority placed on academic study in the small Southern school. It is apparent that the young cartoonist took academic study seriously, but as in all human endeavors, oftentimes, "the spirit is willing, but the flesh is weak." "Aw, don't worry about not getting on the Dean's List," one of O'Connor's happy little coeds tells her taller, bespectacled, disapproving companion (an O'Connor lookalike). "It's no fun going to the picture show at night anyway."[28] This particular cartoon appeared in the Dean's List issue of *The Colonnade* on January 9, 1943. Usually, the cartoons were placed either on the same page or across from the movie ads, and it would seem that O'Connor, the art editor, probably considered this point of layout when designing this particular cartoon. Ironically, the movies would seem all the more enticing if one had to stay in on the weekend and study.

O'Connor does not shy away from depicting the "melancholy of sex." She addresses the issue in her cartoons as well as in cartoonish images in her later fiction, quite often through a decidedly female gaze. In *The Colonnade* on March 7, 1944, an O'Connor cartoon appears that uncharacteristically features boys. The presence of these boys brings to mind the conversation between Mrs. Prichard and Mrs. Cope while discussing the adolescents that have invaded Mrs. Cope's farm in "A Circle in the Fire": "You take a boy thirteen years old is equal in meanness to a man twict his age. It's no telling what he'll think up to do. You never know where he'll strike next."[29] In the cartoon, two prepubescent floppy-haired lads are strolling past GSCW and one says, "I hope the rules of that place slacken up before we start going out with girls."[30] Of course, the caption of the cartoon is addressing the issue of the strict rules regarding the conduct of the female students. However, the

[27] Ibid.

[28] *The Cartoons of Flannery O'Connor at Georgia College* (Milledgeville: Georgia College) 39.

[29] O'Connor, *Collected Works,* 243.

[30] *The Cartoons of Flannery O'Connor,* 67.

visual text addresses the issue from a different light. The two boys are very obviously adolescents, paunchy and frumpy, yet completely confident that they will soon be dating the college girls. This is the reality for these young women who have chosen to pursue higher education. Could the only young men that are awaiting them outside of the protective academy be versions of these two juveniles? Have the coeds sealed their fates by taking time off from pursuing a mate and by attending college, or will a college degree secure for them a higher-level husband than the adolescent residents of Milledgeville?

Attracting the husband of one's dreams is addressed in "The Crop," written by O'Connor for her master's thesis at Iowa and later published in *Mademoiselle* magazine. This story marks an interesting transition between the coed cartoons and the published writing. In it, O'Connor examines the iconic fixtures of the traditional romantic melodrama as seen through the eyes of middle-aged Willie Willerton, a would-be writer. Frederick Asals describes the tension in this story as that "between 'art' and 'life,' [but it] is handled in a thoroughly conventional way. With her use of literature as fantasy gratification and the inevitably awkward and absurd figure she cuts in everyday life, Miss Willerton is no more than a stock character."[31] Of course, a simply drawn "stock character" is exactly the type of character that would suffice for a cartoonist. Miss Willerton is "drawn" with levels of complexity, however. There are two Miss Willertons: one is the writer who exists in a dreary reality, positioned like Thurber's "first wife" at her dining room table, and the one who is the fantasy character created as a mate for another stock character, the romantic male in the story, Lot Motun, a sharecropper who is "tall, stooped, and shaggy but with sad eyes that made him look like a gentleman in spite of his red neck and big fumbling hands. He'd have straight teeth and, to indicate that he had some spirit, red hair."[32] Lot bears a cartoonish resemblance to Al Capp's "Li'l Abner." Marital bliss between the caricatured Lot Motun and Willie Willerton reads this way: "Even with as little as they'd had, it had been a good year. Willie had cleaned the shack, and Lot had fixed the chimney. There was a profusion of petunias by the doorstep and a colony of snap-dragons under the window.

[31] Frederick Asals, *Flannery O'Connor: The Imagination of Extremity* (Athens: University of Georgia Press, 1982) 16.

[32] O'Connor, *Collected Works,* 736.

It had been a peaceful year."[33] Framed by flowers, this picture of stock domestic bliss is all a young woman could ask for. It almost has a commercial aspect, like an ad in a magazine. Lot Motun, the rugged dream hero, falls in line with cartoonish counterpart, Li'l Abner. In fact, in his essay entitled "Li'l Abner," Marshall McLuhan writes of Al Capp's leading males: "It is Pappy and his son who live in a world of trashy delusions. The senile and the querulous malice of the elder Yokum is precisely the old age reserved for the hensure types who squander their best energies in maintaining the sentimental illusions of commercially imposed social ideals."[34] The "fictional" Willie's romance follows the traditional pathway of the aforementioned "sentimental illusions," but when the "real" Willie is jolted out of her pleasant dream and reminded that she has promised to do shopping for lunch, the creator of Lot and his fictional Willie visits the grocery store, and a feeling of melancholy overcomes her: "Silly that a grocery should depress one—nothing in it but trifling domestic doings—women buying beans—riding children in those grocery go-carts—higgling about an eighth of a pound more or less of squash—what did they get out of it? Miss Willerton wondered. Where was there any chance for self-expression, for creation, for art?"[35]

In the grocery store world, Willie, alongside real wives and real children, is surrounded by the commodities that define her existence. This juxtaposing the physical bodies of women with groceries is a theme in O'Connor's early writing. Prior to the writing of "The Crop," an O'Connor drawing of a coed struggling to grasp an armload of groceries is featured in the 1945 *Spectrum*, the yearbook of the Georgia State College for Women. In the drawing, captioned by the words "Where our pennies go," a wreath of grocery products surrounds the young woman's face making it seem like the bananas, canned goods, and the head are interchangeable. O'Connor features these framing groceries again, in Warhol fashion, when she has Ruby's face juxtaposed with a can of beans atop a grocery sack in "A Stroke of Good Fortune." The collard green adhered to Ruby's face marks and defines her in a way that no amount of description could do. The lives of these

[33] Ibid., 737.

[34] Marshall McLuhan, *The Mechanical Bride: Folklore of Industrial Man* (Boston: Beacon Press, 1951) 64.

[35] O'Connor, *Collected Works,* 739.

women are defined by the products advertised daily on television and in women's magazines.

After leaving the grocery store, Willie encounters a couple of real-life "soulmates." Could these two be the realistic counterparts of her fictional characters?

> The woman was plump with yellow hair and fat ankles and muddy-colored eyes. She had on high heeled pumps and blue anklets, a too-short cotton dress, and a plaid jacket. Her skin was mottled and her neck thrust forward as if she was sticking it out to smell something that was always being drawn away. Her face was set in an inane grin. The man was long and wasted and shaggy. His shoulders were stooped and there were yellow knots along the side of his large red neck. His hands fumbled stupidly as they slumped along.[36]

This couple unfortunately resembles the lurking adolescents of the cartoon rather than the romantic Lot and fictional Willie. Love and marriage in reality is not quite as attractive as it is in fiction. Asals writes,

> The story casts an oblique light on O'Connor's dilemma at this early stage of her career: How to realize that "delicate adjustment of the outer and inner worlds,"[37] that interaction between reality and imagination, that would result in convincing and original fiction. Miss Willerton's pseudo solution—the arbitrary selection of fashionable "subjects," elaborated by free-floating fantasy—is of course held up to laughter, but the implied alternative—immersion in the banalities of everyday life, the sights of the supermarket, runny-nosed children, vulgar lovers—was already proving an inadequate medium for Flannery O'Connor.[38]

I contend that O'Connor never abandons these women and that, in fact, she continues to depict their melancholy lives, as well as their attempts at capturing for a moment some of the idyllic romance represented by Lot and Willie's flower-framed cottage. She could not have characterized any

[36] Ibid., 740.
[37] O'Connor, *Mystery and Manners*, 34.
[38] Asals, *The Imagination of Extremity*, 16–17.

situation in a more somber and wistful fashion than in the narrative of Sabbath Lily's seduction of Hazel Motes, or in Joy-Hulga's seduction of Manly Pointer. When we do get a glimpse inside a marriage in O'Connor, she usually casts a wry eye on the institution—i.e., Ruby and Claude in "Revelation," Mrs. Shortly and Chauncey in "The Displaced Person," and O. E. and Sarah Ruth in "Parker's Back." All of these marriages are comedic renditions, but they are presented with moments of warmth, interaction, and companionship as well as satire, a mixture that may well constitute O'Connor's recipe for a realistic marriage.

HELEN E. HOKINSON, THE "SOCIETY" WOMAN, AND THE SALES CLERK

Helen E. Hokinson was the one female cartoonist whose drawings appeared consistently in the *New Yorker* during O'Connor's college years. These cartoons featured middle-aged, overweight "society" women who floated through life occupying a space on the margins of reality, oftentimes, particularly during wartime, depicted performing the illusionary rituals in honor of a time that has passed or that never really existed. Julian's mother in "Everything That Rises Must Converge" would serve as a perfect example of this kind of woman. In fact, Hokinson more often than not adorns these women with an interesting, if not ridiculous, hat. Many of these cartoons feature supporting players: women who maintain positions in real life—hairdressers, hat saleswomen, librarians, sales clerks, etc. The faces of this ensemble cast of supporting characters serve as texts bearing witness to the complete obliviousness of her society matrons. In this way, Hokinson creates the visual cliché, that of the empty-headed rich woman that will prove humorous to part of her audience. However, including the reactionary cast of characters offers an ironic complexity to the cartoon. It, in a way, upends the cliché. It reveals the stereotype as just that—a creation, an illusion fabricated by admen and Hollywood. This upending of clichés, particularly about women, is one of the messages that I think reached the young Flannery O'Connor, a reader of the *New Yorker*.

In the coed cartoons, WAVES often serve as a counterpoint to the youthful version of Hokinson's "society woman"—the "silly girl." O'Connor often uses clothing to visually signify the vast gap between campus life and the war. In the April 10, 1943, edition of *The Colonnade,* a cartoon appears that features an extravagantly ruffled and coiffed coed viewed from the back and wearing sandals blocking the path of two uniformed WAVES. The caption is, "I think it's perfectly idiotic of the Navy not to let you WAVES dress sensibly like us college girls."[39] Another cartoon, published on January 23, 1943, spotlights two coeds standing on the sidewalk commenting on the approach of two WAVES. One "silly" girl says to the other, "Officer or no officer, I'm going to ask her to let me try that hat."[40] The war is always present in the issues of *The Colonnade*. In every issue, there is a weekly syndicated column that summarized the week's straight war news, ads recruiting young women into the armed services, and pictures of the WAVES themselves cutting a large swath as they march across the GSCW campus. Appearing on the inside of the front and back cover of the 1945 edition of *The Spectrum* is an O'Connor drawing of a seemingly endless stream of WAVES marching in a zigzag fashion across the college grounds. The WAVES take up the entire sidewalk, and umbrella-carrying coeds have to walk around them in the rain on muddy ground that is pockmarked by potholes, remnants of construction. Girls are stepping on planks in order to get their footing, falling in holes presumably dug by construction workers, and one girl is even climbing a tree to get out of the way of the passing WAVES. Even in the protected environment of this Southern women's college, always in the process of perpetuating the complexity of Southern womanhood, there is no refuge from the cultural deconstruction and the inevitability of the war. The WAVES are an ever-present incredulous audience to the "silly girl" antics of the coeds, responding in the same way as the sales clerks in a Hokinson cartoon.

In her later fiction, O'Connor could have been thinking of Hokinson and of the carefully constructed illusions of womanhood—particularly Southern womanhood—when, in "Everything That Rises Must Converge, she has Julian's mother describe her conversation with the woman who sold her the "hideous hat."[41] Julian's mother recounts the hat-buying experience in this way: "This hat looked better on me than any of the others, though when she brought it out I said, 'Take that thing back. I wouldn't have it on my head,' and she said, 'We-ull,' and she said, 'If you ask me, that hat does

[39] *The Cartoons of Flannery O'Connor,* 51.

[40] Ibid., 41.

[41] O'Connor, *Collected Works,* 485.

something for you and you do something for the hat, and besides,' she said, 'with that hat you won't meet yourself coming and going.'"[42]

Discovering a *New Yorker* cartoon drawn by Hokinson and depicting a middle-aged matron in a hat shop accompanied by a sales woman occasions a moment of déjà vu for an O'Connor reader. O'Connor builds her story around a cartoonish hat and around the cartoonish situation that occurs when an aging woman tries to maintain the structures and rituals of a past—a perceived past that, in the case of Julian's mother, never was a reality, always was an illusion. The story begins with humor and ends with the horror Julian experiences as he holds the body of his dead mother in his arms. It is then that he realizes that the illusions which shaped his own life have died along with her, there on the gritty sidewalk. Again, in this story, as in the coed cartoons, the chasm that exists between the world of illusion and the world of reality is bridged by a piece of clothing—a hat.

GEORGE PRICE AND ANIMAL OBSERVERS

In his introduction to *Everything That Rises Must Converge*, Robert Fitzgerald compares Mary Flannery's cartoons to those of another *New Yorker* cartoonist, George Price.[43] Alstair Cooke, in his introduction to the *The World of George Price: A 55-Year Retrospective*, writes of Price as "a born anarchist" whose "upbringing had...thrown him in with a cast of characters whose comicality impressed him more than their social plight."[44] Many of Price's cartoons feature bodies splayed in outrageous positions. One on-going joke that appeared in more than one *New Yorker* cartoon drawn by Price presents the body of a man suspended in repose three or four feet above his bed. His wife is sweeping the floor and commenting to a female visitor,

[42] Ibid., 486.

[43] Kelley Gerald, in her essay "The Habit of Art," contends that Fitzgerald was mistaken in making this comparison and writes that it "seems more likely that Fitzgerald had in mind someone like John Held, Jr." That contention might be true except that one must consider when Fitzgerald wrote the introduction. He wrote it at the end of Flannery O'Connor's career, after her death. He wrote it after having read all of O'Connor's short stories and her two novels and while familiar with her cartoonish characters (Gerald, "The Habit of Art," 114).

[44] Alistair Cook, "George Price on Marriage and Other Disasters," *The World of George Price* (New York: Beaufort Books, 1988) 2.

"He's been up a week now, and there's nothin' we can do about it."[45] This man and woman appear in later "episodes" of this cartoon (the man is eating, twirling a lasso, looking through a telescope, etc.) until she finally shoots him down, telling the police, "He never knew what hit him."[46] At first the situation between the woman and her husband is unexpected and humorous, but the eventual shooting presents these cartoons in a different light. Price may not have originally planned the violent ending to the sequence, but having the last cartoon spotlight the husband's dead body with cross-hatching on his chest that can only indicate blood cannot help but elicit more commentary on "the battle of the sexes."

Bodies in outrageous positions materialize in O'Connor's cartoons, as they do in her later fiction. Coeds upside down in potholes while WAVES march across the campus were mentioned previously. Page 4 of the January 2, 1943, *Colonnade*, shows an O'Connor cartoon of a crowd of coeds in a near riot outside of the college bookstore. The crowd fills the entire frame of the cartoon except for a small bookstore sign in the upper left corner. Angry slashes portray eyes and mouths. Disembodied limbs are sticking out of the crowd at all angles. The caption reads, "Business as usual."[47] A similar pile of bodies appears in the April 4, 1944, *Colonnade*, only this time eyes are replaced by "Xs" and one young woman stands and speaks directly to the reader, saying, "Madam Chairman, the committee has reached a decision."[48] Even at this early stage, O'Connor exhibits her concern as a "storyteller" for "what is," and, as she points out in "The Fiction Writer and His Country," if "what is can be determined by survey, then the disciples of Dr. Kinsey and Dr. Gallop are sufficient for the day thereof." The writer as storyteller "may well be forced to take ever more violent means to get his vision across to his hostile audience."[49] In O'Connor's vision, "what is" is often a bitter pill to swallow—conflict resulting in a violent eruption.

Complexity of habitus is another staple in Price's cartoons. His single panels often feature rooms that are cracked and falling apart, while the people who inhabit them carry on and comment amidst the ruin. Many of

[45] George Price, *The World of George Price* (New York: Beaufort Books, 1998) 13.

[46] Ibid., 29.

[47] *The Cartoons of Flannery O'Connor,* 38.

[48] Ibid., 68.

[49] O'Connor, *Mystery and Manners*, 31–34.

these rooms have pictures hung or taped on the walls that exhibit visual commentary on the action in the cartoon. Reminiscent of E. B. White's Thurber observation about the "implausibility of animals," many of these pictures are of animals looking in on the doings of people. They are like cartoons within the cartoon and not unlike the pictures that hang on the walls in Enoch Emory's room in *Wise Blood,* which, in fact, could have been inspired by a George Price cartoon. An examination of Enoch's environment is a study of habitation amidst the ruin and decay of loneliness, neglect, and poverty. Hanging on one wall is a "brown portrait of a moose standing in a small lake" that belonged to his landlady:

> The look of superiority on this animal's face was so insufferable to Enoch that, if he hadn't been afraid of him, he would have done something about it a long time ago. As it was, he couldn't do anything in his room but what the smug face was watching, not shocked because nothing better could be expected and not amused because nothing was funny. If he had looked all over for one, he couldn't have found a roommate that irritated him more.[50]

Enoch finds that taking off the frame denudes the moose and makes him less fearsome. The infringement of the animal on the human realm, the idea of an animal wearing clothes, is insufferable to Enoch, who has a hard enough time distinguishing himself among humans. He has no patience with animal usurpers over whom he, even though afraid, must reign. "Taking off the animal's clothes"[51] gave Enoch power over his fears. This is a foreshadowing of Enoch's obsession with the gorilla suit. In fact, many of George Price's cartoons present monkeys—sometimes center stage, sometimes just sitting in the picture, sometimes in a zoo watching the people watching them—reminiscent again of Enoch Emory. The demeanor of the ape drives Enoch over the brink as he stops at the last of the monkey cages during one of his ritualistic visits to the animals in the zoo in the center of the city. "'Look at that ape,' he said glaring. The animal had its back to him, gray except for a small pink seat. 'If I had a ass like that,' he said prud-

[50] O'Connor, *Collected Works,* 75.

[51] Ibid.

ishly, 'I'd sit on it. I wouldn't be exposing it to all these people come to this park.'"[52]

The donning of gorilla suits was everywhere in the popular culture when O'Connor was drawing her cartoons. There are myriad examples in *New Yorker* magazines when animal costumes are employed as visual humor delivering two messages: either humans are so far advanced from animal behavior that it is funny to see them imitate animals ("the implausibility of animals")[53] or maybe that human behavior is not that far removed from that of the animal kingdom. Jon Lance Bacon posits that Enoch's donning of the gorilla suit is his attempt to ameliorate his feelings of inferiority to the animals—particularly to the apes in the zoo. Adopting Gonga as a role model suggests "that Enoch's own identity, grounded in his own experience, is unimportant."[54] Enoch's gorilla suit is again an example of O'Connor providing a visual cliché and then upending it:[55] "The gorilla stood as though surprised and presently its arm fell to its side. It sat down on the rock where they had been sitting and stared over the valley at the uneven skyline of the city."[56] At the end of the episode, the suit is no longer a source of humor. The suit is no longer a suit. Enoch has become the gorilla. He has succumbed to his fears by taking on the very characteristics that he previously despised.

THE PHD CARTOON

The examination and analysis of one of O'Connor's single-panel cartoons, one that seems to attract notice of biographers and critics alike, both demonstrates the *New Yorker* influence and sheds a light on the connection between O'Connor's actual drawings and the textual cartoons that she sketches in her narratives. The cartoon from the April 3, 1943, issue of *The Colonnade* features a young woman, wearing glasses, her long hair tied back, sitting sideways on a chair at a dance. Her head is turned away from the

[52] Ibid., 53.

[53] E. B. White in Gale, "*New Yorker* Cartoons," 100.

[54] John Lance Bacon, "A Fondness for Supermarkets," *Wise Blood and Consumer Culture: New Essays on Wise Blood,* ed. Michael Kreyling (Cambridge, UK: Cambridge University Press, 1995) 25–49, 31.

[55] This will be discussed further in the Enoch section of chapter 2.

[56] O'Connor, *Collected Works,* 112.

dancing couples in the background, and she is looking out of the frame of the picture squarely into the eyes of the reader. Her eyes are black beads, her nose a dot, and her mouth is a curved line turned up into a grin. She has wrapped her right arm around the back of the chair, in exactly the same manner that two of the women dancing behind her have placed their right arms on those of their male partners. Instead of placing her hand around a dancing partner's neck, the featured young woman holds her hand up beside her mouth in a gesture that indicates she is communicating an "aside" to her listener, who can only be the reader, located outside the frame, and with whom she shares a steady gaze. The caption to this picture is "Oh, well, I can always be a Ph.D."

This cartoon is sometimes referred to as the "wallflower cartoon" and the young woman's unflinching gaze has attracted the commentary of several scholars. Claire Kahane, a "feminist-psychoanalytic critic," sees the PhD cartoon as a "self-deprecating cartoon of [O'Connor] herself at a school prom." Kahane writes:

> O'Connor...portrayed herself as a wallflower watching from the sidelines while couples swirl around on the dance floor. Why is this funny? In answer to that question lies the dilemma of a generation of women who came to maturity in that pre-feminist moment of the early sixties, when women were being released from domestic strictures that had been placed on them in postwar America, and could imagine finding a vocation in work. Love and work: how to apportion the commitment without sacrificing or demeaning either. That dilemma informed my experience and, I imagine, O'Connor's as well, though clearly to different ends. To "be" a Ph.D. in O'Connor's cartoon signifies a secondary compensation for being excluded from the pleasures of the dance.[57]

In this single panel Kahane reads the anger of a generation of intelligent women who seem doomed to sit without a partner on the sidelines, observers of the dance of love, rather than participants. Kahane refers to herself as a member of a later generation to whom choosing to become a

[57] Claire Kahane, "The Revisions of Rage: Flannery O'Connor and Me," *The Massachusetts Review* 46/3 (Fall 2005): 439–461, 457.

PhD would not represent compensation (as she contends it does for O'Connor) for not being asked to dance, but *for her* it would be a desirable life choice. By characterizing the "situation" of the cartoon as a "dilemma," Kahane indicates that the young woman's choice, like that of her own, is a binary one—either to commit oneself to the life of a scholar and earn a PhD, or to commit oneself to finding love and/or to having and raising children. Earlier in her article, Kahane elucidates this dilemma by framing it with her own experience at the time she was writing her dissertation on O'Connor: "Months passed; I stared at the blank page, smoked incessantly...read and reread the stories and obsessively worried about my biological clock running down. Shouldn't I be having a child before it was too late instead of sitting alone in my attic apartment trying to produce a dissertation?"[58]

Using caricature, according to Kahane, O'Connor designed a graphic that "expresses aggression through the reduction of a complex figure [the young woman] to a flat line that tells a negative truth."[59] By offering the comment, "Oh, well, I can always be a Ph.D," the young woman in the "PhD" cartoon is expressing rage at being imprisoned in her gender, in the expectations of her family, in her ambition, and in her diminutive, immature, bespectacled looks themselves. It would seem that to Kahane, the cartoon is a less-than-humorous visual depiction of Dorothy Parker's statement, "Men seldom make passes at girls who wear glasses."[60]

[58] Ibid., 442.

[59] Ibid., 448.

[60] The idea that this cartoon is autobiographical, however, is not limited to Kahane's surmises, as there exists a great deal of curiosity among O'Connor readers about Mary Flannery's love life. Biographer Brad Gooch also refers to the young woman featured in the cartoon as a representation of Flannery O'Connor herself and goes on to cite a short romantic involvement between Mary Flannery and a young Marine sergeant, John Sullivan, who discovered, when he escorted her to a college dance "that she was truly a bad dancer—she later claimed to have a 'tin leg'" (Gooch, 100). The two young people exchanged letters until the end of the war when Sullivan entered seminary and began studying for the priesthood. Gooch posits that what remained of this relationship for O'Connor was the "PhD thought balloon that she floated during their time together" (101). The "PhD thought balloon" is evidence of a young woman writing the script of her own dramatic sequence and "hatching a plan for a life away from Milledgeville" (101). It would seem that Gooch sees the single panel PhD cartoon not as the story of a bespecta-

Commenting on how O'Connor recycles well-worn jokes or clichés, Kelly Gerald contends that the PhD cartoon "is an interesting one, not simply because O'Connor recycles the butt of the joke (the sexual desirability of the lady intellectual) in the character Joy-Hulga in 'Good Country People,' but because O'Connor's joke extends beyond the frame of the cartoon in this case." Gerald goes on to describe an article that appears "directly above the cartoon in the same column of the [college] paper" about the "opening of the gym on Sunday so that the students [could] entertain male visitors." The article "asserts that 'students who get dates deserve help in entertaining them.' So much for the unlucky girls who do not get dates. Oh well. [Gerald comments] They can always be Ph.D.s."[61] The cliché concerning the lack of sexual desirability of an intelligent woman does extend beyond the frame of the cartoon panel, but it extends far beyond the preceding column in the April 3, 1943, issue of the *Colonnade*. Interestingly, parsing this assertion will require reference to another cartoon drawing that appeared in the January 17, 1942, *New Yorker* magazine.

At the bottom of the "On the Town" section of the 1942 edition of the *New Yorker* is an unframed (as is the custom with these column-filling drawings) cartoon drawing of a young woman at a dance. Her hair is pulled back from her face and she has detailed, expressive eyes that dominate her countenance and that reflect sadness. Unlike the dot eyes of O'Connor's cartoon, these eyes are fully drawn with lids, pupils, and long lashes. Her head droops to the right and her right arm cups her chin presenting an air of dejection. Her left arm lies across her lap, her hand dangles listlessly. Her hair is pulled back in the same manner as O'Connor's young woman, but the *New Yorker* girl has a flower perched over one ear and does not wear glasses. Her strapless dress seems to be animated and living a life of its own, as it expectantly bells out and virtually preens on the human body it adorns. The young woman's form slumps on a rather ornate bench in the left foreground of the picture. Behind the young woman and *mise en scene* are the dancing couples. The faces of these couples are much more defined than O'Connor's dancing couples. The attractive first couple is captured serious-

cled wallflower, but as a graphic depiction which "can be likened to a freeze frame from a film of some dramatic sequence"(Gerberg, 42). Gooch, *A Life of Flannery O'Connor*, 100–101. Mort Gerberg, *Cartooning: The Art and the Business* (New York: William Morrow & Co., 1989) 42.

[61] Gerald, "World," 34.

ly staring into each other's eyes—her gown is striped and he is wearing tails. The second couple is dancing cheek to cheek, while only the girl's face of the third couple is visible over the male's shoulder—her eyes closed, her hand around her partner's neck. The last pair of dancers is holding a dip pose and, again, the girl's eyes are closed. For whatever reason, the young woman in the *New Yorker* drawing has not been chosen by any man present to dance the dance of love. There seems to be no discernible reason for her condition as a wallflower. The *New Yorker* drawing, according to the formula set down by Mort Gerberg in *Cartooning: The Art and the Business*, exists somewhere in the zone between a single-panel cartoon and illustration[62]. It obviously inspired the young O'Connor to create what seems, upon first glance, to be her own version of a visual cliché, but in typical O'Connor fashion, she satirically turns that cliché upside down. This would be, according to Gerberg, the purpose of the use of cliché by a cartoonist—not to perpetuate it, but to upend it. To think that the PhD cartoon spoke to the context of the college paper only would be limiting the depth and perception of the young O'Connor, who even in high school unabashedly made public her ambition to publish her writings and cartoons in a much larger venue. O'Connor's single-panel cartoon featuring the grinning young woman in the foreground, to the left of the dancing frenzy taking place *mise en scene*, exists as evidence of a rudimentary philosophy concerning a woman's position in America in the middle of the twentieth century—a philosophy that plays out in the manuscripts, the novels, and the short stories. It is by examining what O'Connor does with the basic structure of her illustration, how she essentially inverts the message of the *New Yorker* illustration/cartoon, that we are able to discern meaning and that we are able to begin at this seminal point to analyze the process of and purpose for the pictorial text that would become her signature style and that would influence the writers who followed her.

Since it is necessary for a cartoon to communicate immediately, the composition of the drawing should be of the first concern. "Indeed," Barry Moser writes,

[62] "Familiar elements commonly associated with art and drama" are often found in the single-panel cartoon. These include the "cast" of characters, the captioned "dialogue," body language expressed by "gesture," and "setting," which includes costumes and props (Gerberg, *Cartooning: The Art and the Business*, 38).

> it is all a matter of gesture. O'Connor also had a strong natural sense of composition that becomes evident after studying the prints. The overall pattern of "Oh, well, I can always be a Ph.D.," is a good example. She divides the rectangle into many near repetitive black shapes, contrasts them with smaller, similar shapes in white, and then throws in a series of circle-like shapes and bold angular stripes—all in all it reminds me, distantly, of Pablo Picasso's *Girl Before a Mirror* (1932). [63]

Regardless of the fact that the O'Connor cartoon employs gestural similarities to the Picasso painting and contains the same elements as the *New Yorker* illustration/cartoon, it tells a different story.

The perspective and consequently the message of the *New Yorker* illustration is clearly defined by the artist. The young woman in the left-hand corner is twice the size of the largest pair of dancers located to her right. Each pair of dancers in the illustration is drawn smaller and smaller in proportion to the young woman, finally forming a vanishing point at the top. The reader's eye then is drawn first to the drooping young woman in the foreground, her importance determined by her size. An intriguing part about this illustration is the character of the black dress with white polka dots.[64] This dress, or its polka dot facsimile, seems to signal just by its presence a visual connection to the war, as it did when polka dots were worn by Vivien Leigh in *Waterloo Bridge* or Greer Garson in *Mrs. Miniver*. The dress in this illustration stands by itself, failing to droop and bend with the body

[63] Barry Moser, "Working Backward: A Reflection on the Linoleum cuts of Flannery O'Connor," *Flannery O'Connor: The Cartoons*, ed. Kelly Gerald (Seattle, WA: Fantagraphics Books, 2012) ix.

[64] "The journey exploring the relationship between cinema and the polka dot pattern opens on the note of the famous *Auld Lang Syne* (Old Long Since). It's 1940 when, with this tune in the background, clad in a white dancing gown with contrasting black polka dots, the beautiful Vivien Leigh fell in love with an officer of the British army in the movie *Waterloo Bridge*. In 1942, under the German bombing raids, Greer Garson wore a dark suit with white polka dots in the film by William Wyler that earned her the Best Actress award, *Mrs Miniver*; whereas in the same year, *Woman of the Year* featured Katharine Hepburn clad in a dressing gown made up by pants and blouse with black macro polka dots on a white background, arguing with the recently married husband, Spencer Tracy" ("Polka Dots," Vogue Encyclopedia, http://www.vogue.it/en/encyclo/cinema/p/polka-dots)."

it is wearing. Behind the dress is a bench upon which the young woman is supposed to be sitting. However, even though the young woman's arms and head mimic the posture of a seated person, the dress stands straight up, a costume wearing its actor. It stands at attention as if it is waiting for a young gentleman (again, reminiscent of the aforementioned popular films) to come and sweep it off to join the couples on the dance floor. The purpose of the dress is thwarted just as is the purpose of the pretty girl at a dance.

The message is that the young woman exists on a separate plain from the dancers clearly because she is alone. She has no man. Having no caption to use as a guide, it is up to the reader to mentally create the young woman's story. Why would such a beautiful young woman be sitting alone at a dance without a man? Perhaps she has been stood up. Perhaps her man is a soldier for whom she is pining. Perhaps her soldier has been killed. The location of this particular illustration at the bottom of a column in "The Talk of the Town" section cannot help but cause the reader to pause and ruminate as to the root of the sadness in the young woman's eyes. The tragic figure in the foreground of the drawing starkly contrasts with the whirling frivolity of the dancers in the background. The relationship between the young woman and the other dancers, the way her animated dress seems to be wearing her (she is not in control of her dress, much less of events that surround her), the way the detailed drawing of her eyes expresses sadness, the way her left arm hangs listlessly, and the way her right hand has to prop up her drooping head visually formulates the cliché that is upended: pretty girls always have dance partners. No, they do not—not on January 17, 1942.

Flannery O'Connor's PhD cartoon is composed of the same elements as the *New Yorker* illustration, but she has altered the pictorial perspective of the visual text to tell a different story. The figure ground relationship has been altered. There are only figures—no ground. All of the figures exist on the same plain as if on a flat surface like a collage. The young woman is located in the lower left corner of the frame but she shares the mid-ground with the dancers that surround her. The face of the young woman, her grin, her steady eyes, her hand held up to the side of her mouth as if whispering an aside to someone outside the frame are what engage the reader and determine the speaker of the caption. When compared to the *New Yorker* illustration, O'Connor has stripped down the facial features of her young woman not to eliminate details, but to focus on specific details. According to Scott McCloud, "By stripping down an image to its essential 'meaning,' an artist [cartoonist] can amplify that meaning in a way that realistic art can't."[65]

Essentially, O'Connor is abstracting the cartoon image in order to "focus" her readers on an idea rather than on the individual character. When viewing the more detailed *New Yorker* illustration, the reader is unable to detach herself from the story and asks: "What happened to *her* boyfriend? What has made *her* so sad? What is *her* story?" By eliminating the sad eyes, the eyebrows, the long slender nose, and replacing them with three dots and adding a pair of glasses, O'Connor has increased the universality of the image of a young woman in her cartoon. This paring down of images has been an element of cartooning since Rodolphe Topffer (championed by Goethe)[66] published his comedic picture stories in 1831. Appearing weekly in *The Colonnade*, it was important to Mary Flannery that her cartoons had as wide an appeal as possible to her audience of coeds and faculty. Some of her cartoons did deal with activities specific to the campus, such as the Golden Slipper Contest, but the PhD cartoon addresses an issue that is core to a young woman attending college in 1942, and beyond that, this issue is still relevant to twenty-first century coeds. Clare Kahane clearly vocalizes the gendered dilemma with regard to her own life when she asks, "Shouldn't I be having a child before it [is] too late instead of sitting alone in my attic apartment trying to produce a dissertation?"[67] As I paged through the issues of *The Colonnade* from 1942 to 1945, stored in the archives in Special Collections at Georgia State College, I began to read weekly columns written by contemporaries of Mary Flannery. Quite often, as I was searching for a specific column, I would come upon a notice that the girl for whom I was searching had gotten married and had become a Mrs. and had left school before graduating. I began to think about these women, now the age of my mother, who had had such distinct voices in print. Did they ever regret their choices? Did they ever finish school? Desire, desirability, and

[65] Scott McCloud, *Understanding Comics: The Invisible Art* (New York: William Morrow, 1993) 30.

[66] Goethe said of Topffer, "If for the future he would choose a less frivolous subject and restrict himself a little, he would produce things beyond all conception" (McCloud, *Understanding Comics*, 17).

[67] Kahane, "The Revision of Rage," 442.

childbearing are part of the story of the dance that swirls around the head of O'Connor's cartoon coed and around the heads of all women.

The fact that all of the women in the cartoon appear on the same plane[68] is O'Connor's clear statement that the concerns raised by the caption exist for all of the women at the dance—they are all coeds, in fact. The first couple to the right of the PhD girl seems like they are seriously trying to work together to follow the proper steps of the dance. The next couple is doing a "bunny hop," the girl clinging to the boy's shoulders and following. The last couple seems to be laughing so uproariously that they are no longer able to perform any recognizable dance steps. The PhD girl has wrapped her right arm around a folding chair for support, not around a dance partner. This folding chair appears in the place of the rather more substantial, more permanent bench, the piece of furniture upon which the young woman in the *New Yorker* illustration is sitting. The differentiation between these seats is essential because "just as stereotype employs images of people who can be easily identified in comics or film, objects have their own vocabulary in the visual language of comics."[69] Even early on, O'Connor carefully selects the objects that serve as props to her characters. By its very nature, a folding chair is transient. It can be easily picked up and transported. It is a chair that might be selected by a young woman "hatching a plan for a life away from Milledgeville."[70]

O'Connor uses costume in her cartoon to delineate character. However, she does it in a fashion that has become familiar to the readers of her

[68] Roland Barthes, in his introduction to *S/Z*, describes the type of text that would lend itself to this form of analysis. He calls such a text a *writerly* text because it presents a perpetual present upon which no *consequent* language (which would inevitably make it past) can be superimposed: the writerly text is *ourselves writing* before the infinite play of the world (the world as function) is traversed, intersected, stopped, plasticized by some singular system (ideology, genus criticism) which reduces the plurality of entrances, the opening of networks, the infinity of languages (5). In a writerly text the reader is "no longer a consumer, but a producer of the text" (4). All of the reader's experience is brought to bear in the formulation of meaning. The text is dynamic, and "we gain access to it by several entrances" (6). (Roland Barthes, *S/Z*, trans. Richard Miller (New York: Hill and Wang, 1974) 4–6.

[69] Will Eisner, *Graphic Storytelling and Visual Narrative* (New York: Norton & Co., 1996) 15.

[70] Gooch, *Flannery*, 101.

novels and short stories. Instead of having an array of costume elements for each character, O'Connor is inclined to focus on one or two definitive costume choices. Examples of this abound: Hazel Motes's animated "preacher hat," Mrs. Watts's "pink nightgown that would have better fit a smaller figure," Lucynell's "Panama hat with a bunch of wooden cherries on the brim,"[71] Joy-Hulga Hopewell's "six-year-old skirt and a yellow sweatshirt with a faded cowboy on a horse embossed on it,"[72] and finally, Julian's mother's "hideous hat."[73] Wearing comfortable clothing that fits and that reposes on her body, the PhD girl sports an overlarge pair of glasses reminiscent of those sported by Dr. T. J. Ekleberg, the oculist featured in *The Great Gatsby*. Eyes seeing or seen through glass or cellophane lenses are an important image for O'Connor.[74] Sally Fitzgerald notes that while a student at Peabody High School in 1941, young Flannery had developed "a taste on her own for Poe"[75] and that one of her favorite stories was "The Spectacles," in which a young man vainly refuses to wear the spectacles he dearly needs and ends up marrying his own grandmother as a result. When he finally dons a pair of spectacles after the marriage has taken place, he surveys the countenance of his bride through new eyes: "What, in the name of everything hideous, did this mean? Could I believe my eyes?—*could* I?—that was the question. Was that—was that *rouge*? And were those *wrinkles*, upon the visage of Eugenie Lalander? And oh! Jupiter, and every one of the gods and goddesses, little and big! What—what—what—*what* had become of her teeth?"[76]

Throughout her writing life, O'Connor creates characters whose perceptions of reality—of habitats—are altered either by the putting on or the

[71] O'Connor, *Collected Works*, 180.

[72] Ibid., 268.

[73] Ibid., 485.

[74] Barthes has designed a semiotic schema that examines the mythical speech of the object as it stands alone or the juxtaposition of objects or the arrangements of objects in a scene. In this way, "a photograph will be a kind of speech for us in the same way as a newspaper article; even objects will become speech, if they mean something" (Roland Barthes, *Mythologies*, trans. Annette Lavers [New York: Hill and Wang, 1972] 111).

[75] O'Connor, *Collected Works*, 1239.

[76] Edgar Allen Poe, *Complete Tales and Poems* (New York: Barnes and Noble Books, 1992) 511.

taking off of spectacles. Of course, in *Wise Blood,* there is the mirror image of Hazel Motes peering through his mother's glasses. Asa Hawkes's "seeing" eyes are exposed when his dark glasses are removed. In the manuscript for *The Violent Bear It Away*, O'Connor experiments with glasses on many of the characters, but they remain in the published version as both a hearing and seeing device on Rayber. Rayber's glasses do not, however, relieve his spiritual blindness and deafness.

In her unfinished *Why Do the Heathen Rage?*, O'Connor writes and rewrites a scene that focuses on a pair of wooden spectacles with empty holes where glass should be. The novel begins as Tilman, a well-off landowner, arrives home from the hospital after suffering a stroke. It seems that "only his left eye, twisted inward, seem[s] to harbor his former personality. It burn[s] with rage." His former yardman, Roosevelt, "who from now on would be [his] nurse," peers forward at "what [is] on the stretcher" while "tears glaze and glisten on his black cheeks like sweat."[77] Each of these characters is introduced with a spotlight on his eyes—in Tilman's case, a raging left eye, and in the case of Roosevelt, peering eyes full of tears. In a flashback, O'Connor describes the first meeting of these two men. Thirty years prior, Tilman was managing six Negroes at a sawmill using a very sharp penknife. One day he notices Roosevelt standing just outside of a clearing insolently watching him. Tilman, wearing glasses himself, calls Roosevelt over, and his hands, flashing the penknife, begin whittling a pair of wooden glasses with empty eyeholes. Tilman determines that Roosevelt should put on these glasses and see him as the white man—the man in power—and that Roosevelt should begin to behave accordingly. Roosevelt acquiesces, though the reader is not quite sure as to whether the original insolence is abated. It would seem that it is, based on Roosevelt's emotional reaction at seeing Tilman arrive home on a stretcher.

This scene is finally transferred to and published in "Judgment Day" as a scene between Tanner and Coleman. Tanner is whittling as Coleman approaches:

> He had no idea what he was carving, but when he reached the negro, he had already made two holes the size of half dollars in the piece of bark.

[77] O'Connor, *Collected Works*, 797.

> The negro's gaze fell on his hands and was held. His jaw slackened. His eyes did not move from the knife tearing recklessly around the bark. He watched as if he saw an invisible power working on the wood.
>
> He looked himself then and, astonished, saw the connected rims of a pair of spectacles.[78]

Tanner tells Coleman to put on the glasses, and when he does, Tanner has an "instant's sensation of seeing before him a negative image of himself, as if clownishness and captivity had been their common lot. The vision failed him before he could decipher it."[79] The wooden glasses have produced a vision serving as a reflective surface in the same way that the lawn ornament does for Nelson and Mr. Head: "Mr. Head looked like an ancient child and Nelson like a miniature old man. They stood gazing at the artificial Negro as if they were faced with some great mystery, some monument to another's victory that brought them together in their common defeat. They could both feel it dissolving their differences like an action of mercy."[80] These two objects, "eyeless" wooden glasses and a chipped lawn ornament, have been transfigured in a moment of mystery.

The oversized glasses in the PhD cartoon are transfigurative as well. Just their presence activates an iconic cultural code that visually indicates "smart girl." O'Connor elaborates on a woman's glasses and how they serve as a measure of desirability in "Good Country People." Joy-Hulga's glasses, along with her cowboy sweatshirt, work together to comedically evoke the skewed cowboy and the schoolmarm narrative that accompanies the seduction in the hayloft. "The boy dropped down by her side and put one arm under her and the other over her and began methodically kissing her face making little noises like a fish. He did not remove his hat but it was pushed far enough back not to interfere. When her glasses got in his way, he took them off of her and slipped them into her pocket."[81]

Joy-Hulga, not realizing that Manly Pointer has removed her glasses, looks away from him and begins to see the landscape in a different way,

[78] Ibid., 683.
[79] Ibid.
[80] Ibid., 230.
[81] Ibid., 279.

"She smiled, looking dreamily out on the shifty landscape. She had seduced him without even making up her mind to try."[82] Again, in the same way as in the cases of Rayber and Tanner, the removal of glasses spurs a shift in the known landscape and marks a moment of mystery as Joy-Hulga finds that it is not only Manly Pointer who has been seduced. She, a "smart girl" herself, has been seduced by the very "good country people" narrative that she has been at pains to ridicule to Mrs. Freeman and her mother.

In the light of the cultural narratives that dance around her, both literally and figuratively, it is not surprising that the PhD girl with the glasses is sitting on the sidelines at a dance. It is an expected, stereotypical image to say the least. What is surprising, what rewrites the cultural narrative, is the grin that appears on her face and the way that she exists in the same space as the dancers. She is not separated, as is the young woman in the *New Yorker* illustration. She is part of the life dance that surrounds her just as her successors Joy-Hulga,[83] Mary Grace,[84] and the twelve-year-old girl who is cousin to Temple One and Temple Two[85] will be. Flannery O'Connor has taken this stereotypical, bespectacled young woman from her position on the sidelines (largely created by male authors and admen) and has thrust her into the complex ebb and flow of a woman's life as an intellectual, sexual, and spiritual being.

THE LINOCUT

I would be remiss if I did not at least mention O'Connor's cartoon medium—the linocut. A list of the properties of the linocut could be a list of the properties of Flannery O'Connor's writing process. No other form of printmaking "could be more direct and fundamental."[86] Linocut is a relief printing technique, "a collection of negative techniques where the plate or block is cut using knives, gouges, or chisels to create an image," that offers "endless possibilities for experimentation and creativity. The concept of printing a lino block is quite simple and the result quite immediate, but with a little practice and exploration, some incredibly complex and rich re-

[82] Ibid., 280.
[83] "Good Country People"
[84] "Revelation"
[85] "A Temple of the Holy Ghost"
[86] Moser, "Working Backward," vii.

sults can be produced."[87] In O'Connor's case, it is important to note that "linocuts are drawn and cut backward. This is a categorical fact of all printmaking media, except offset lithography: The image, as cut, engraved, or etched on the plate or block is reversed left and right when it is printed."[88] From the inception, the dialectic—the tension that occurs between the backward and forward movement—takes on a materiality in the very selection of the printmaking medium. "Art, first of all," Maritain writes, "is of the intellectual order, its action consists in imprinting an idea in some matter" [89] and the iconology, the symbolism of the imprint attends O'Connor throughout her writing life. In "Temple of the Holy Ghost," the young girl virtually has the God symbol imprinted on her face: "As they were leaving the convent door, the big nun swooped down on her mischievously and nearly smothered her in the black habit, mashing the side of her face into the crucifix hitched onto her belt and then holding her off and looking at her with little periwinkle eyes."[90]

And in another story, "Circle in the Fire," the pastoral landscape imprints itself again on the face of a prepubescent girl, literally, in Louise Westling's interpretation, marking "her humiliated femininity just as it carries the imprint of the tree that identifies her with the ravaged wood"[91]: "The child stood partly hidden behind a pine trunk, the side of her face pressed into the bark. Then without any more discussion, Powell picked up the suitcase and they got up and moved past the child and entered the woods not ten feet from where she was standing, slightly away from the tree now, with the imprint of the bark embossed red and white on the side of her face."[92]

Everything, from the earliest drawings of Gertrude the goose that she made for the enjoyment of her family to the Christ embossed on "Parker's Back," was imprinted with Flannery O'Connor's "habit of art." Examina-

[87] Susan Yeates, *Learning Linocut: A Comprehensive Guide to the Art of Relief Painting through Linocut* (Bedfordshire, UK: Authors Online Ltd., 2011) 8.

[88] Moser, in Gerald, *Flannery O'Connor: The Cartoons*, vii.

[89] Maritain, *Art and Scholasticism*, 13.

[90] O'Connor, *Collected Works*, 209.

[91] Louise Westling, *Sacred Groves and Ravaged Gardens: The Fiction of Eudora Welty, Carson McCullers, and Flannery O'Connor* (Athens: University of Georgia Press, 1985) 105.

[92] O'Connor, *Collected Works*, 249–50.

tion of the development of this pictorial process will signify the reality of Flannery as maker and of her voice or presence in her work.[93]

[93] Steiner, *The Color of Rhetoric*, 5.

Chapter 2

Hazel Motes and Enoch Emory: Dead Men Walking

The cultural business of the artist is to help us assimilate our generation's catastrophes—the Bomb and the Holocaust—by asking questions that help us reimagine and rediscover "what gods we might worship."[1]

As a cartoonist, short story writer, and a novelist, living in mid-twentieth century America, Flannery O'Connor was well aware of the writer's "cultural business." The business of exaggerating cultural atrocities has always been the business of cartoonists. When that cartoonist becomes a novelist, that tendency for exaggeration is evident in his or her pictorial renditions of characters and situations, as is the case with former cartoonists William Faulkner, John Updike, Nathaniel West, Jay Cantor, and Flannery O'Connor herself. O'Connor does not abandon the power of the pictorial in delivering a message. Instead, she embraces it and envelops it in narrative. In this chapter, we will scrutinize the molding and shaping of Hazel Motes and Enoch Emory. Both characters are composed of a collage of cultural images, superstitions, and beliefs. In creating Hazel, in particular, O'Connor was greatly influenced by Nathanael West (*Miss Lonelyhearts*, *Day of the Locust*), T. S. Eliot ("The Wasteland"), and the vanitas still lifes painted by Bruyn the Elder in the sixteenth century. The images that feed the composite that is Enoch Emory come directly from a strange mixture of the movies he watches and a truncated Catholic education. By the end of the chapter, this goofy, gorilla-suited simpleton becomes one of the walking dead, the bearer of the dead Jesus.

[1] Interview with Jay Cantor. In 1987, Jay Cantor attempted such an amalgamation between the popular visual text and the literary narrative when he published *Krazy Kat: A Novel in Five Panels*, which is a novel established on characters taken from George Herriman's popular cartoon strip. Each chapter is preceded with a single-panel cartoon based on a Herriman drawing. The narrative of each chapter is embodied in the accompanying cartoon panel.

THE INFLUENCE OF NATHANAEL WEST

It is evident why West's writing style would appeal to young cartoonist Flannery O'Connor. In 1949, O'Connor writes about West to her friend Betty Boyd.

> Well, I can't equal you in the matter of clippings, but I enclose a token as I thought you might like to look at An Honest Smiling Face and read some Real Art.* I am obliged for the accounts. They fit in fine with what I can imagine and with a novel I read by Nathanael West called *The Day of the Locust* (which you would like); I also thought of the character in *Sanctuary* who 'had the depthless quality of stamped tin.' I can't believe New York where the culture fog is thicker is much better, but then I am of the school that wants rotgut labeled whether it's in a rosewater bottle or not and that believes fornication is the same thing in New York as Las [*sic*] Angeles.
>
> **A laundry ad in the Ridgefield weekly paper, featuring a smiling picture of the laundryman and a poem he had chosen to quote.*[2]

This short paragraph offers insight into O'Connor's influences and thought processes as she grapples with her first novel, *Wise Blood.* O'Connor's construction of the particular pictorial text that appears in the body of *Wise Blood* is strongly influenced by both *Miss Lonleyhearts* and *The Day of the Locust.* Combine this with the influence of the *New Yorker* cartoons and O'Connor's fine-art experience as a painter and it results in a pictorial text that gives the reader the feeling that she is standing in a gallery surrounded by framed depictions of the spiritual desolation that is the modern world structured in the manner of a graphic novel. This urban wilderness is inhabited by O'Connor's grotesque and twisted characters, unaware pilgrims already spiritually dead rattling around in "rat's alley."[3]

Sarah Gordon, in *The Obedient Imagination,* makes a comparison between the novel *Miss Lonelyhearts,* a novel "concerned with a spiritual quest, [and] is a curious narrative, filled with the grotesque and the bizarre in a

[2] O'Connor, *The Habit of Being,* 15–16.

[3] T. S. Eliot, *The Waste Land,* ed. Michael North, Norton Critical Editions (New York: W. W. Norton & Co., 2001).

modern waste land in which individuals search for the meaning of their suffering,"[4] and *Wise Blood*, which could be described in the same way. The payment for "sins of the flesh," sexuality, and the presentation of the "figure woman" are Gordon's points of comparison between the two novels. It would seem that it is necessary at this point to reflect on the fact that *Miss Lonelyhearts* and *Wise Blood* are both rooted in the conceptual composition of the single-panel cartoon. In chapter 1, I took note of the clear influence of the single-panel cartoon on O'Connor's early stories, and as she grew as a writer, that panel grew and expanded. In the pictorial text of *Wise Blood*, the borders between the inside and outside of her cartoon panels begins to resemble picture frames, and the composition of the material inside the frame begins to resemble the fine art of oil paintings. As a painter herself, Flannery O'Connor was aware of both classical and modern trends, styles, and techniques, and her first novel, *Wise Blood*, is a virtual gallery of painterly pictorial texts featuring an eclectic verbal array of framed art pieces giving center stage to still lifes, Cubist studies, collages, and assemblages, all placed strategically to arrest the forward motion of the viewer and to create a space for meaning. I contend that her study of West was highly influential in the developmental process that took place between the expression of the pictorial in the undergraduate cartoons and early stories and the pictorial array in *Wise Blood*. Both *Miss Lonelyhearts* and *The Day of the Locust* offered the young writer templates for accommodating the pictorial in her own narrative text. As it was, O'Connor took note of West's work and then went on to develop a pictorial technique relevant in 1952 that remains relevant in 2019, and is ever changing because of its ability to absorb the cultural miasma that surrounds it. In creating these pictorial moments, she is influenced by fine art, but the cartoon influences her as well. Like West, her *mise en scene* is composed of detritus and the abject. In O'Connor's case, however, this composition of urban decay is arranged and easily recognizable in the iconic styles of both the old masters as well as in the styles of the artists who are her contemporaries. To begin this chapter on *Wise Blood*, it is beneficial to look at West's two novels as starting points for the young O'Connor. O'Connor's singular pictorial style, however, though rooted in West, deviated greatly from his as she worked and reworked her first novel.

[4] Gordon, 126.

Nathaniel West conceived of *Miss Lonelyhearts* as "a novel in the form of a comic strip," the chapters to be "squares in which many things happen through one action."[5] In his 2009 introduction to the novel, Jonathan Lethem notes that this manner of construction results in "short, sardonically titled chapters [which] persistently end in morbid slapstick and cumulatively take on a slanted, compacted quality, like crashed cars exhibited bumper to bumper."[6] The "car crash" compaction is only one of the motifs employed by O'Connor as she maneuvers the cartoonish Hazel Motes and Enoch Emory through the streets of Taulkinham. Most importantly, however, it is those city streets that form the urban maze in which these "Fisher Kings"—Hazel Motes and Miss Lonelyhearts—are wandering. Both West and O'Connor are largely influenced by Eliot's "The Waste Land"—the "Unreal City" in their own creations of the urban landscape—New York in the case of West, Taulkinham/Atlanta in O'Connor's novel. The pictorial pauses in Eliot's poem were particularly appealing to both novelists because they exhibited a way to insert the single-panel cartoon structure into the narrative, opening a window to the urban landscape. Set in the modern city, the grotesquely illustrated, pictorial coming together of violence and Christianity in *Miss Lonelyhearts* and *Wise Blood* offers a basis for comparison and analysis that elucidates the transitional space between O'Connor's undergraduate cartoons and the pictorial technique employed in *Wise Blood.*

I do not want to move on from these points of comparison without mentioning Eliot's influence on the women in both novels, even though I plan to evaluate the women of *Wise Blood* in chapter 3. Women's voices are part of the *heteroglossia* in "The Waste Land." The bored aristocratic woman, the women in the bar, and the typist play a necessary role in portraying the sexual dysfunction, the sterility, the barrenness, and the lack of any kind of spiritual center in the modern city or in the postwar modern life. Women's stories like these are acknowledged in *Miss Lonelyhearts* in the letters,[7]

[5] Nathaniel West in Miles Orvell, "Writing Posthistorically: Krazy Kat, Mausm and the Contemporary Fiction Cartoon," *American Literary History* 4/1 (Spring 1992): 110–128, 110–111.

[6] Nathaniel West, *Miss Lonelyhearts & The Day of the Locust* (New York: New Directions, 2009) ix.

[7] The letters that Miss Lonelyhearts receives are written mostly by women. The lives of these women are filled with degradation and despair. West uses them to stand as witnesses to the collapse of modern social values. His women tell stories

pleas for help which are sent to the advice columnist daily. Miss Lonelyheart's inability to resolve any of the situations, both literally and figuratively, leads to the death of his Christ complex and eventually to his physical death. O'Connor uses pictorial pauses in her narrative to tell the woman's story in ways that visually frame the abject and lack in each existence. It is also interesting how both O'Connor and West pay homage to Tiresias, Eliot's hermaphroditic central figure. Miss Lonelyhearts is a man posing as a woman and Hazel Motes bears a gender unspecific name. Eliot's influence is strongly felt in both novels, and how it shapes O'Connor's women will be discussed in chapter 3.

Just as she did in the case of the "PhD cartoon" and the *New Yorker* drawing, O'Connor has built on a number of the characteristic elements of West's novel. Both of the novelists use the evocative cadence of poetry to establish the primary perspective of each of their pieces. West opens *Miss Lonelyhearts* with a "prayer" propped on Miss Lonelyheart's desk and printed on a piece of white cardboard. The prayer was penned by Shrike, the feature editor and Miss L's boss.

> Soul of Miss L, glorify me.
> Body of Miss L, nourish me.
> Blood of Miss L, intoxicate me.
> Tears of Miss L, wash me.
> Oh good Miss L, excuse my plea, and hide me in your heart,
> And defend me from mine enemies.
> Help me, Miss L, help me, help me.
> In saecuala saeculorum Amen.[8]

Christ is mockingly evoked. Shrike has taken the elements of the Divine Christ celebrated in the sacraments and has twisted them into an anthem of praise for the "advice" columnist, Miss L. The Divine aspects of

that are representative of a world in which the only surety is urban decay. They slog through emotional and material detritus in a way that is very similar to Eliot's women in "The Wasteland." Like the typist, and Lil, and Madam Sosostris, they are dulled to sensation and experience in a way that is hopeless and exempt to any kind of redemption. O'Connor uses women as witness in the same way, and just how she accomplishes this will be the subject of chapter 3.

[8] West, *Miss Lonelyhearts*, 1.

Christianity—the salvation of the soul, the sharing of Christ's body and blood during the Communion of Believers, the tears shed in Gethsemane, and the forgiveness of sins—have been turned into a sacrilegious ditty and have been directed at Miss Lonelyhearts, an imposter—a man posing as a woman, a man with "a Christ complex."[9] He is "like a dead man, only friction could make him warm or violence make him mobile."[10] West has placed a dead man at the religious center of this book. Instead of being spirit-filled, Miss Lonelyhearts "felt like an empty bottle that is being slowly filled with warm dirty water."[11] Chance brings him in contact with a cripple who seems to have been sent by God so that Miss L. could "perform a miracle and be certain of his conversion. It was a sign. He would embrace the cripple and the cripple would be made whole again, even as he, a spiritual cripple, had been made whole."[12] As Miss L. reaches out to "succor" the cripple with love, the cripple shoots him and they both fall down the stairs together—no sign—no miracle—just death. The dead Christ with no hope of resurrection is the only kind of Christ that can exist in West's urban jungle.

Hazel Motes, whose nose is like "a shrike's bill," is a man with a complex about Christ.[13] When we meet him, he is trying to escape a Jesus who moves "from tree to tree in the back of his mind, a wild ragged figure motioning him to turn around and come off into the dark where he might be walking on the water and not know it and then suddenly know it and drown."[14] Instead of the cadence of poetry per se, O'Connor employs the cadence of Southern evangelistic preaching, complete with responses from the audience. This sermon is similar to Shrike's prayer in that the only Christ that can exist in this milieu is the dead Christ. Preaching from his stance on the hood of his car, which is parked outside of a movie theater, like Shrike, Hazel Motes ridicules the basic tenets of Christianity.

> "Well, I preach the Church Without Christ. I'm member and preacher to that church where the blind don't see and the lame

[9] Ibid., 13.
[10] Ibid., 19.
[11] Ibid., 50.
[12] Ibid., 57.
[13] O'Connor, *Collected Works,* 6.
[14] Ibid., 11.

> don't walk and what's dead stay that way. Ask me about the church that the blood of Jesus don't foul with redemption."
>
> "He's a preacher," one of the women said. "Let's go."
>
> "Listen you people, I'm going to take the truth with me wherever I go," Hazel called. "I'm going to preach it to whoever'll listen at whatever place. I'm going to preach there was no Fall and no Judgement because there wasn't the first two. Nothing matters but that Jesus was a liar."[15]

O'Connor has addressed the very same Christian symbols as did West: the blood, the soul, salvation. She has Hazel create a church around a dead man who has not risen, who does not exist in the modern world. However, Hazel is not representative of the dead Christ in the way Miss Lonelyhearts is. O'Connor depicts Hazel as an animated "dead" man—a marionette—at the center of *Wise Blood.* Early on she establishes this image of Hazel, as the narrator describes him, as looking "as if he were held by a rope caught in the middle of his back and attached to the train ceiling."[16] Later, he looks to Enoch as if he is "being held there by an invisible hand, as if, if the hand lifted up the figure would spring across the pool in one leap without the expression on his face changing once."[17] Clearly, O'Connor wants us to visualize Hazel as a kind of puppet manipulated by the hand of God. Where Miss L is urgently trying to achieve salvation in a Godless universe, Hazel is trying to avoid it by avoiding the invisible force that is controlling him. West's novel is empty and void at the center and remains that way throughout. There is no redemption. There is no miracle. The Christ figure is truly a liar and imposter. By not posing Hazel Motes as a Christ figure and by indicating that unseen forces control him, O'Connor has managed to place the hand of God in the center of the modern urban maze navigated by her characters. She does portray Hazel Motes as a "dead" man, but he is just that; a man headed along the "path to dusty death." He is not lost, however. There is someone or something else in control. West's characters are left to slog around in the "Dismal Swamp" with no purpose and trying to rub up against each other for warmth. Miss L is a Christ figure without the power

[15] Ibid., 59.
[16] Ibid., 5.
[17] Ibid., 47.

of salvation. His veins are filled with "dirty water." To drink his blood would be to drink of the polluted world from which there is no transcendence.

West holds true to the single-panel cartoon format throughout *Miss Lonelyhearts*. O'Connor, in *Wise Blood* does draw cartoonish characters, but expands on this format and expands in a way that is influenced in part by West's next novel, *The Day of the Locust*. Tod Hackett, West's protagonist, is essentially a painter. Even though he is at present painting sets in Hollywood, readers are informed that "despite his appearance, he was really a very complicated young man with a whole set of personalities, one inside the other, like a nest of Chinese boxes." And "The Burning of Los Angeles," a picture he was soon to paint, definitely proved he had talent. As we move through the book we continue to encounter this picture and Tod's progress in its completion. We find that the characters that populate Tod's life are captured in Tod's artistic work.

> Abe was an important figure in a set of lithographs called "the Dancers" on which Tod was working. He was one of the dancers. Faye Greener was another and her father, Harry, still another. They changed with each plate, but the group of uneasy people who formed their audience remained the same. They stood staring at the performers in just the way they stared at the masqueraders on Vine Street. It was their stare that drove Abe and the others to spin crazily and leap into the air with twisted backs like hooked trout.[18]

Work on "The Burning of Los Angeles" exists alongside the forward progress of the novel. That work is preparatory and never results in the application of paint to canvas, but exists in a variety of other mediums: lithograph, cartoons, pad and pencil, and finally in charcoal applied directly to the canvas. A great deal of the work on the painting is time spent in contemplation of "earlier and earlier American and European artists, with the aim, not of recreating their vision, but of wrenching his [Tod's] insight free of the past."[19] In fact, the "possibility of meaningful progress [in this novel] depends on the virtual necessity of regress. Artistic growth occurs only after

[18] West, *Miss Lonelyhearts*, 62.

[19] Steven Weisenburger, "Williams, West, and the Art of Regression," *South Atlantic Review* 47/4 (November 1982): 1–16, 2.

one completes imaginatively composed 'backwards motion' in history and eastward across the Atlantic to Europe again."[20] O'Connor and West employ the idea that their books can be read as a "prologue to any true beginning."[21] Artwise, there is continuous backward and forward movement in *Wise Blood*, as well.

THE *VANITAS* STILL LIFE FORM IN O'CONNOR'S PICTORIAL TEXT

O'Connor, too, uses the medium of paint on canvas to express this movement—to pause the linear motion of the novel by constructing framed pictorial moments in her narrative that are constructed in the recognizable styles of iconic art pieces. She composes her visual texts by using people and objects from the modern world—the world that surrounds her. Because of this combination of iconic artistic style and modern world detritus, time is collapsed—as it is in fine art paintings. Bakhtin gives the name "*chronotope* (literally, 'time-space') to the intrinsic connectedness of temporal and spatial relationships that are artistically expressed in literature."[22] He writes, "In the literary artistic chronotope, spatial and temporal are fused into one carefully thought out, concrete whole. Time, as it were thickens, takes on flesh, becomes artistically visible; likewise, space becomes charged and responsive to the movements of time, plot and history. This intersection of axes and fusion of indicators characterizes the artistic chronotope."[23]

This graphic rendering, this "giving flesh" to time-space is reminiscent of the work of a still life painter, and O'Connor on several occasions reaches backward to the fifteenth century and calls upon the form of the *vanitas* still life to constitute textural "units of meaning" in *Wise Blood*. One might ask why exactly she would do this in the middle of an American novel which features a country in motion: people always moving on the streets, cars, trains—all indicative of the postwar bustle which characterizes the early 1950s, the time in which the novel was published. Even though it first came into existence in the fifteenth century, the *vanitas* form has never really left

[20] Ibid., 1.

[21] Ibid., 12.

[22] M. M. Bakhtin, *The Dialogic Imagination*, trans. Carl Emerson and Michael Holquist, ed. Michael Holquist (Austin: University of Texas Press, 1981) 84.

[23] Ibid.

the cultural milieu.[24] The fact is, the employment of the still life form, itself, offers an artist a great deal of plasticity in that

> the still life is an evolving system of representation and of meaning, directly related to the transformations of society and artistic discourse. It addresses certain positions a society maintains in relation to its objects: realities, fantasies, and desires. Similarly, it transcribes the manner in which the art deals with these truths or untruths—the way the artist reinvents a visual language specifically keyed to their implementation.[25]

One of the truths that is expressed by the *vanitas* still life, in particular, is the encapsulation of *death-in-life.* O'Connor's employment of the still life tableaux in *Wise Blood* is reminiscent of the way Hawthorne first introduces the "death-in-life" concept in *Blithedale Romance* by referring to and describing the still lifes hanging on a barroom wall.[26] His narrator, Miles Cloverdale, proceeds to describe a drunk in "an obscure corner of the saloon" by verbally painting "a little picture" in which he compares the dead animals of the pictures on the wall to "a ragged, bloated New England toper, stretched out on a bench, in the heavy apoplectic sleep of drunkenness. The death-in-life [says Miles] was too well portrayed."[27] In this one gesture, Hawthorne uses the eyes of Miles to illustrate the drunk as just another dead animal.

Just as the still life form served Hawthorne's purposes, it works very well for O'Connor in her depiction of the modern world in her own effort

[24] See Picasso's series of *vanitas* still lifes or Audrey Flack's 1977 *Marilyn (Vanitas).*

[25] Margit Rowell, *Objects of Desire: The Modern Still Life* (New York: Henry Abrams, 1997) 9.

[26] First he chronicles the paintings as lifelike representations of: one, "a noble sirloin; another, the hind-quarters of a deer, retaining the hoofs and tawny fur; another, the head and shoulders of a salmon; and, still more exquisitely finished, a brace of canvass-back ducks, in which the mottled feathers were depicted with the accuracy of a daguerreotype" (Nathaniel Hawthorne, *The Blithedale Romance,* ed. Seymour Gross and Rosalie Murphy. Norton Critical Editions [New York: W. W. Norton & Co., 1978] 161).

[27] Ibid., 162.

to create an American Romance in the likeness of Hawthorne.[28] O'Connor writes in "Novelist and Believer" that "the novelist will have to do the best he can in travail with the world he has. He may find that in the end that instead of reflecting the image at the heart of things, he has only reflected our broken condition and through it the face of the devil we are possessed by."[29] Just as she did with the cartoons, O'Connor strives for the image that will startle her readers and the image at the heart of things in Taulkinham, "clearly meant to be modern America—that has been morally polluted and is in need of sacrificial redemption."[30] Using the still life as one of her "units of meaning" establishes a gestural text similar to that described by Peter Brooks as encompassing scenes that end in "a terminal wordlessness in the fixed gestures of the tableau. These instances are typical...at moments of climax and crisis where speech is silenced and narrative arrested in order to offer a fixed and visual representation of reactions to peripety."[31] By employing her pictorial technique to construct recognizable *vanitas* still lifes featuring her modern man, Hazel Motes, at crucial moments in *Wise Blood*, O'Connor creates a "text of muteness" which is "central to the representa-

[28] Regarding Hawthorne, Flannery O'Connor wrote to John Hawkes in November of 1961, "I think I would admit to writing what Hawthorne called 'romances,' but I don't think that has anything to do with the romantic mentality. Hawthorne interests me considerably. I feel more of a kinship with him than with any other American" (O'Connor, *The Habit of Being*, 457). Wendy Piper establishes O'Connor's connection to Hawthorne's particular style of American romance—that which is not particularly concerned with "social verisimilitude but with the 'truth of the human heart'" (75). His is a genre that "embraces mystery rather than factuality," and "characters are brought to a recognition of their own finitude" (105). Like Hawthorne, O'Connor is interested in creating "characters who are forced out to meet evil and grace and who act on a trust beyond themselves—whether they know very clearly what it is they act upon or not" (O'Connor, *Mystery and Manners*, 42).

[29] O'Connor, *Mystery and Manners*, 168.

[30] Christina Bieber Lake, *The Incarnational Art of Flannery O'Connor* (Macon, GA: Mercer University Press) 57.

[31] Peter Brooks, *The Melodramatic Imagination: Balzac, Henry James, Melodrama, and the Mode of Excess* (New Haven, CT: Yale University Press, 1976) 61. Brooks writes further, "Occasionally these tableaux will resemble great paintings."

tion of [the novel's] most important meanings."[32] It is a visual text whose story is told in tableau and form.

Her choice of the *vanitas* form limits the type of objects she selects to inhabit the frame. Just as in the cartoons, the composition of these textual pictures is crucial in the "sinking" of the message or theme of the novel. Flannery O'Connor recognizes the importance of the dramatic and systematic placement of resonant objects that become a part of textual arrangements that she spotlights in order to evoke "passion." "The author has for the most part absented himself from direct participation in the work and has left the reader to make his own way amid experiences dramatically rendered and symbolically ordered. The modern novelist merges the reader in the experience; he tends to raise the passions he touches upon."[33]

O'Connor goes about the selecting and the positioning of "symbolically ordered" *vanitas* objects in her still life tableaux in both a traditional and a non-traditional manner. She chooses objects from the modern fallen world with care and with careful attention to the muted "voice" of each particular object. In order for the *vanitas* to speak, the voice evoked must be both traditional and contemporary. Calling on the plasticity of a spatial form offers O'Connor the temporal freedom that she needs to speak with a look backward into the past and forward into the future evoking the impressions from the eidetic memories of her readers.[34] The "dimension of historical depth has vanished from the content.... Past and present are apprehended spatially, locked in a timeless unity that, while it may accentuate surface differences, eliminates any feeling of sequence by the very act of juxtaposition."[35]

By placing Hazel Motes, whose character is already in the novel represented by an assemblage of resonant objects, into the *vanitas* form, O'Connor is able to inform this visual text in two ways. The first is the discourse that results from the "many discourses" and all of the relationships created by the juxtaposition of all of the objects in the character collage that is Motes. This is the nature of collage. The second level of visual infor-

[32] Ibid., 62.

[33] O'Connor, *Mystery and Manners*, 139.

[34] Jack Stewart, *Color, Space, and Creativity: Art and Ontology in Five British Writers* (Madison, NJ: Fairleigh Dickinson University Press, 2008) 20.

[35] Joseph Frank, *The Idea of Spatial Form* (Newark, NJ: Rutgers University Press) 63.

mation is enveloped in the *vanitas* still life form itself. In the Middle Ages, the genre of still life began to emerge as objects became divorced from figures in paintings and began to convey messages, as symbols or emblemata, "not only an everyday meaning (*sensus litteralis*) but also a religious one (*sensus spiritualis*)."[36] These still lifes became known as *memento mori* or as *vanitas* paintings. They contained recognizable, repeated componential objects that conveyed a symbolic message. The "practice of combining a skull and a moralizing motto to form a *memento mori* ('Be mindful of death') has not changed in its essentials since antiquity, even though the repertoire of symbols has been expanded."[37] The snuffed-out candle in Bruyn the Elder's *Vanitas*, of course, symbolizes the "extinction of life." The fly on the skull and the detached jaw remind the viewer how quickly all that is human will decay and be devoured by maggots. These *vanitas* elements continue to appear in still lifes into the present day. Hazel's head, emblematic of the *vanitas* skull, becomes the pictorial literalization of the "motto, epigram, or scriptural passage to provoke a new response to an old and too familiar saying."[38] By painting Hazel into the picture, O'Connor creates a "stark" image that "draws attention" to itself both "pictorially" as a "still" moment "caught in time," and "emblematically, as [an] exaggerated representation of deeper spiritual truths."[39] In *Art and Scholasticism,* the essay upon which, as O'Connor wrote to "A," "she cut her aesthetic teeth,"[40] Jacques Maritain writes that "art in itself, that is to say, on the part of the form, and of the regulation which comes to mind, is not fluctuating like opinion, but is planted in certitude."[41] There is a historical certitude in the *vanitas* form. By employing it, O'Connor can be assured that the *memento mori* message will be transmitted.

The first appearance of the *vanitas* still life in the novel is when Hazel returns to the Motes's family home in Eastrod after his service in the army. Preceding this, the reader has met Hazel on the train hurtling along, as outside of the window, the Southern pastoral flits by. As the novel opens, the

[36] Sybille Ebert-Schifferer, *Still Life: A History* (New York: Harry N. Abrams, 1998) 29.

[37] Ibid., 31.

[38] Baumgaertner, 20.

[39] Ebert-Schifferer, *Still Life*, 21.

[40] O'Connor, *The Habit of Being*, 216.

[41] Maritain, *Art and Scholasticism*, 17.

action is already in progress and the need for a *memento mori* message is heightened by the fact that "from the first sentence of the novel the picture of Hazel Motes that O'Connor presents to the reader is that of a man who is not settled, who does not have a clear direction."[42] Hazel is a man in motion. He is hurtling forward on the train, but his dreams mixed with memories take him backward in time.

At twilight on the train, Hazel retires to his berth and the narrator ushers readers into the world of Gothic Romance that occupies Hazel's dreams. It is a world of half-light, populated with the coffins of family members who have passed. As Hazel sleeps in his berth, the forward movement of the novel is suspended and the narrator presents in montage the highlights of Hazel's war experience and his return home, the first in four years. He is unable to get a ride the whole distance to Eastrod from Melsy, where the train let him off. He walks and arrives at "nine o'clock at night, when it had just got dark,"[43] the time for passage from the world of the actual into the imaginary world of Romance where a fifteenth-century painting can come to life.

> The house was as dark as the night and open to it and though he saw the fence around it had partly fallen and that weeds were growing through the porch floor, he didn't realize all at once that it was only a shell, that there was nothing here but the skeleton of a house. He twisted an envelope and struck a match to it and went through all the empty rooms, upstairs and down. When the envelope burnt out, he lit another one and went through them all again. That night he slept on the floor in the kitchen, and a board fell on his head out of the roof and cut his face.[44]

In this scene we are able to watch Hazel as he moves around inside of a virtual *vanitas* still life framed by the skeletal shell of what used to be his home. The "emblemata" are there. Both Hazel's head and the shell of the house have been described as skeletal or skull-like. In the place of the candle, O'Connor has chosen to use two "twisted" envelopes. It is interesting to contemplate—why envelopes? Where did Hazel get the envelopes? Certainly they were not lying around the empty house. They must have come

[42] Baumgaertner, *A Proper Scarring*, 126.
[43] O'Connor, *Collected Works*, 13.
[44] Ibid.

from his pocket or his duffle bag. The *Wise Blood* manuscript mentions several letters that pass between Hazel and his sister, Ruby, recounting a shared past fraught with pain and poverty. Ruby has been removed from the published version of the novel, however, so the reader must contemplate what is not said and make suppositions about exactly who is writing to Hazel Motes and why it is so easy for him to burn the envelopes.

At the very least, an envelope suggests absence, and we know that the ideas of absence and lack pervade this scene. Hazel has returned home to a vacated town, a shell of a house, and a kitchen in which the only bit of his mother that still exists is her empty chifforobe. Hazel's head, which has been described as skull-like on the first page of the novel, is injured by a falling board—a virtual eruption of the past—a violent reminder that he is in the realm of the Gothic. His home is no longer familiar. It has become *unheimlich*, uncanny.[45] As in a traditional *vanitas*, fire has been snuffed out—twice in this case. The next morning, Hazel, himself, writes a moralizing motto, a *memento mori*, and ties it to his mother's chifforobe in the kitchen where she always slept. He wrote: "THIS SHIFFER-ROBE BELONGS TO HAZEL MOTES. DO NOT STEAL IT OR YOU WILL BE HUNTED DOWN AND KILLED."[46] Readers recognize that his heart's home is here, encased in a coffin-like wooden box and that he is going to leave it protected only by empty words. The reader is returned to the novel's present as Hazel, sleeping on the train to Taulkinham where we left him, dreams of the bat-like figure of his mother escaping from her coffin.

It is important to note here how the empty house, which O'Connor chooses to use as a frame in this still life tableau, functions as Derrida's conceptualization of a parergon. The "parergon comes against, beside, and in addition to the *ergon*, the work done (*fait*), the fact (*le fait*), the work, but it does not fall to one side, it touches and cooperates within the operation, from a certain outside. Neither simply outside nor simply inside."[47]

This definition is offered by Derrida as a critique of Kant's posit that the parergon marks a clear boundary between the inside and outside of the piece of art. He shows how Kant's examples are constituted as parergon

[45] See Sigmund Freud, *The Uncanny*, trans. David McClintock (New York: Penguin Books, 2003).

[46] O'Connor, *Collected Works*, 14.

[47] Jacques Derrida, *The Truth in Painting*, trans. Geoff Bennington and Ian McLeod (Chicago: University of Chicago Press, 1987) 54.

"not simply [because of] their exteriority as a surplus, it is the internal structural link which rivets them to the lack in the interior of the *ergon*."[48] Derrida argues that because the frame is marginal, both inside and out, it produces the lack in the work. Hazel Motes's abandoned family home is the skull-like object that frames the *vanitas* still life that occurs within it. It functions as both inside and outside in that it both *is* and *encases* the past. The fact that the house is empty, abandoned, represents the lack inside of Hazel himself. He cannot go backward into the dissipated past; therefore, he is thrust forward into an unexplored future.

O'Connor uses Hazel's broken down "rat-colored" car to frame her next *vanitas* tableau. By using the car both as a frame for a pictorial tableau in which Hazel Motes sleeps, O'Connor not only emphasizes again the lack of a past—a home, but the lack of the present—a home, a "place to be." The pause in the narrative occurs on the night Hazel "[preaches] outside of four different picture shows."[49] Composing this arrangement outside of a "picture show" creates a similar atmosphere to the first time we view Hazel Motes's skull-like visage as part of a *vanitas* composition. O'Connor has placed her characters at night, in the lighted space outside of a theater, a place of illusion, of constructed reality. Onnie Jay Holy/Hoover Shoats, a self-avowed radio personality, arrives on the scene and tries to cash in on the "new jesus" gospel. Hazel, who has been preaching from a stance on top of his car, is unable to start it and get away. He has to have Shoats's help pushing the car into a parking space for the night. Shoats is almost able to penetrate the *ergon* of the piece by inserting his thumb in the door when Hazel opens it to get in. After releasing the thumb from the door and then slamming it again, "He pulled down the front shades and lay down in the back of the car on the army blanket."[50]

Like the kitchen of Hazel's Eastrod home, the car is a domestic space. He bought it as a "place to be." It has shades and a blanket and, like the home in Eastrod, the car is inhabited only by Hazel himself. Again, dreams precede the *vanitas* tableau. He dreams "he is not dead but only buried. He was not waiting on the Judgment because there was no Judgment, he was waiting on nothing."[51] Merely mentioning the final judgment implants the

[48] Ibid., 59.
[49] O'Connor, *Collected Works*, 83.
[50] Ibid., 91.
[51] Ibid.

idea of the *memento mori*, the warning motto that Hazel is trying to escape. The Essex has taken on the character of a little dwelling place composed of a two-by-four in the area where a back seat would be. It is a still, enclosed space that frames Hazel, who has again entered the world of dreams surrounded by an arrangement of objects reminiscent of those which define a traditional *vanitas* still life, only those objects that surround Hazel are the fragments, the detritus of modern life. He has gathered these items to construct the semblance of a home. O'Connor's tableau features "his pallet," "a pillow and an army blanket...a sterno stove [in place of the snuffed-out candle] and a coffee pot up on the shelf under the black oval window."[52] These objects surround Hazel's skull-like head as the central object. Even though the action of the novel has been stilled O'Connor focuses on the symbolic rendition of Hazel's *mise en scene* death-in-life. He dreams that he is on exhibit and that eyes stare at him through the back oval window that resembles a picture frame or even a TV screen. He has become an object, part of a picture, a representation of reality, a simulacrum. In the context of the dream, Hazel takes the place of the mummified man (like Hawthorne's drunkard), an object of reverence to Enoch's worshipful gaze. Three women come by with grocery sacks and look at him as if he is a commodity—a fish—a dead fish—(again, an item which is central to one of Hawthorne's barroom still lifes) that they are not interested in purchasing. A man in a canvas hat looks in, puts his thumb to his nose and wiggles his fingers at Hazel, making him an object of ridicule. The woman from the zoo offers to climb in and keep him company. To her, Hazel is a sex object. Hazel Motes is having his *It's a Wonderful Life* moment dreaming of a world in which his doctrine of "The Church of Christ without Christ" is in play. He is buried but not dead, a dead man walking through a landscape mired in concrete matter.

The last time we view Hazel's head as the skull in a *vanitas* still life composition, he has burned out his eyes with lime and actually is dead. The reader views him through the eyes of Mrs. Flood, his landlady.

> The outline of a skull was plain under his skin and the deep burned eye sockets seemed to lead into the dark tunnel where he had disappeared.... She shut her eyes and saw the pin point of light but so far away that she could not hold it steady in her

[52] Ibid., 90.

> mind. She felt as if she were blocked at the entrance of something. She sat staring with her eyes shut, into his eyes, and felt she had finally got to the beginning of something she couldn't begin, and she saw him moving farther and farther away, farther and farther into the darkness until he was the pinpoint of light.[53]

In this version of the still life, Hazel is, in actuality, a body in the process of decomposition. Something has changed, however. O'Connor has taken the traditional *vanitas* tableau, and just as she did in her cartoons, she has upended it. There is no frame. The inside and outside of the work have blurred and become one. The light has not been snuffed out, it has transcended and become, in essence, a luminaria. The only way Mrs. Flood can see the light is with her eyes closed, but she sees it nonetheless. In his essay "Wise Women, Wise Blood," Marshall Bruce Gentry makes a comparison of Mrs. Flood to the eyeless statue of a woman that stands outside the museum at the center of the city. He makes a very good case for O'Connor's application of the pictorial technique of "notional ekphrasis."[54]

> There are early hints of Mrs. Flood's connections to ancient wisdom. Although Mrs. Flood is introduced by the narrator as "resembling the mop she carried upside-down,"[55] we have seen another comparison to a mop a few pages earlier: the owl that Hazel takes very seriously at the zoo is also described as looking "like a piece of mop."[56] Beneath the satire here, we may be reminded of classical associations of owls with divine females—the most famous being Athena. Other details possibly worth rethinking are those about Mrs. Flood's head: she has "a nose that has been called Grecian" and "hair clustered like grapes."[57] Perhaps we should recall the stone women of the classical park museum[58] and

[53] Ibid., 131.

[54] Notional ekphrasis as defined by James Heffernan. James Heffernan, *Museum of Words: The Poetics of Ekphrasis from Homer to Ashberry* (Chicago: University of Chicago Press, 1994).

[55] O'Connor, *Collected Works*, 60.

[56] Ibid., 54.

[57] Ibid., 124.

[58] Ibid., 55.

> see in Mrs. Flood a new version of the female who is more impressive than she is blind.[59]

With Gentry's comments in mind, we return to Mrs. Flood at Hazel's bedside and take note of her thoughts that are focused on the Divine. As she "watches," Hazel becomes the pinpoint of light in the darkness. He is now a representation not of death-in-life, but of life-in-death. The *memento mori* appeared earlier in the preceding chapter in the form of a Christmas card. It is not a warning of life's brevity to Hazel, but it is a warning to Mrs. Flood and to us as readers. In this moment, O'Connor has reached beyond the frame of the novel to deliver her cautionary message. "She imagined it was like you were walking in a tunnel and all you could see was a pin point of light. She had to imagine the pin point of light; she couldn't think of it at all without that. She saw it as some kind of star, like the star on Christmas cards. She saw him going backwards to Bethlehem and she had to laugh."[60]

O'Connor has rearranged the silent testament of the emblemata in the last scene of *Wise Blood*, ending with the image of a pinpoint of light not visible to the naked eye shining through the darkness. In "The Grotesque in Southern Fiction" O'Connor explains that the writer must be "looking for one image that will connect or combine or embody two points; one is a point in the concrete, and the other is a point not visible to the naked eye, but believed by him firmly, just as real to him, really, as the one that everybody sees."[61] Situating Hazel Motes's head in the *vanitas* tableaux inspires a figural interpretation of events in the novel that is rather more like "Old Testament prefiguration" and which "points forward to the incarnation and the proclamation of the gospel, but also [to] latter events, for they are not the ultimate fulfillment, but themselves a promise of the end time and the true kingdom of God."[62] This skews our "modern view of historical development" in which the "provisional event is treated as a step in a broken horizontal process."[63] Figures inviting this kind of interpretation become "tentative" and are "prophecies of something that has always been, but which

[59] Marshall Bruce Gentry, "Wise Women, Wise Blood," *Wise Blood: A Re-Consideration*, ed. John J. Han (New York: Rodopi, 1994) 324.

[60] Ibid., 123.

[61] O'Connor, *Mystery and Manners*, 42.

[62] Erich Auerbach, *Mimesis* (New York: Meridian Books, 1959) 58.

[63] Ibid., 59.

will remain veiled for men until the day when they behold the Saviour *revelata facie*, with the senses as well as in the spirit."[64] The moments of pause in the narrative of *Wise Blood* in which the reader is confronted by the *vanitas* are "eternal and timeless," pointing "not only to the concrete future, but also to something that has always been and always will be."[65]

ENOCH EMORY: IN THE BELLY OF A WHALE: MONTAGE, ASSEMBLAGE

The waste of the world becomes my art. Kurt Schwitters, 1930s[66]

O'Connor changes her pictorial perspective when writing about Enoch Emory in *Wise Blood.* Enoch is featured in filmic montages. By inserting the idea of a camera between her character and her audience, O'Connor permits "the audience to take the position of a critic without experiencing any personal contact with the actor."[67] Enoch's and Hazel's pictorial renditions operate in opposition to one another in the way that painting does to film. "The painter," Benjamin writes,

> maintains in his work a natural distance from reality, the cameraman penetrates deeply into its web. There is a tremendous difference between the pictures they obtain. That of the painter is a total one, that of the cameraman consists of multiple fragments which are assembled under a new law. Thus, for contemporary man the representation of reality by the film is incomparably more significant than that of the painter, since it offers, precisely because of the thoroughgoing permeation of reality with mechanical equipment, an aspect of reality which is free of all equipment.[68]

[64] Ibid.

[65] Ibid.

[66] Michael Nyman, "Classical Music: Collector's Items," *The Guardian* (July 9, 2004) *www.theguardian.com.*

[67] Walter Benjamin, *Illuminations*, trans. Harry Zohn (New York: Schocken Books, 1968) 228.

[68] Ibid., 234.

This enables O'Connor to use the flickering images of Enoch Emory as comic relief to the doggedness of Hazel Motes. The audiences' response to Enoch can be predicted and controlled because of the "fusion of visual and emotional enjoyment with the orientation of the expert"—the director—or the writer, in this case.[69] The filmic quality of Enoch's scenes forces him to appear as a replica. Hence his rituals. Enoch's wise blood forces him to repeat his behavior day after day in ritualistic sequence, just as if it were replayed over and over again on film. As Benjamin describes it, he loses the aura that comes with "presence." "This situation may be characterized as follows: for the first time—and this is the effect of the film—man has to operate with his whole living person, yet forgoing its aura. For aura is tied to his presence; there can be no replica of it."[70]

Benjamin points out that the stage actor, who has presence, performs for an audience and responds immediately to that audience. In this way, Hazel Motes, the street preacher, is the consummate stage actor. His audience offers immediate rejoinders and retorts. Hazel is a presence among them. Enoch's ritualistic behavior just unrolls and is reproduced every day as if he were held prisoner on the movie screen. In this way, he is doomed. He is doomed to repetition and doomed as an obverse John the Baptist to prepare the way for the "new jesus" and then to be sacrificed. It would seem that here again we see the influence of West's *The Day of the Locust.* That novel opens at quitting time on a Hollywood movie lot. As the main character, Tod Hackett, walks to his car, he passes among movie extras dressed like hussars, an army of cavalry, and Hanoverian light horse guards. Time and space, illusion and reality are collapsed on a movie lot. Everyone and everything is a replica a simulacrum. The composition of scenes in West's novel begins to take on the look of stereotypical movie scenes. Stereotypical plotlines are played out until it becomes difficult to determine what is real, if anything.

O'Connor opens chapter 8 of *Wise Blood* with Enoch Emory responding to the instinctual promptings of his "wise blood," attempting to obey the chaotic urges and forces that inhabit and control him. Until Hazel Motes arrived in Taulkinham, Enoch had functioned in a vacuum without anyone to pay attention to his daily ritual. Hazel's arrival has aroused in Enoch the hope of a guide, the hope of some meaning in his empty life.

[69] Ibid.
[70] Ibid., 229.

When he comes upon Hazel preaching about a "new jesus" outside of a movie theater, his imagination is inflamed and he commences a formalistic sanctification process. The entire rite is encapsulated in a filmic montage sequence spurred on by Enoch's blood. "Enoch's brain was divided into two parts. The part in communication with his blood did the figuring but it never said anything in words. The other part was stocked up with all kinds of words and phrases."[71]

The montage serves to visually reveal what is occurring in the part of Enoch's brain that "never says anything in words" by employing the medium of image. "Montage," writes Sam Rodhie, "simply is the joining together the different elements of film in a variety of ways."[72] O'Connor's interest in this technique stems from the fact that the "film strip is made of still frames that when projected at a set speed of twenty-four frames a second, give the illusion of movement and continuity. Film has to reconcile these contrary directions of stillness and movement, continuity and rupture."[73]

This description of montage also sounds a great deal like a comic strip. In fact, the storyboard for any film sequence looks very much like a comic strip. In Enoch's case, however, O'Connor means for the reader to connect the frames as comic strip fragments that have been blended into the wholeness of filmic montage. The idea of film montage is furthered by the fact that Enoch lives his life as if he were performing for an audience. Though that audience might be pictures on the wall of his room or the monkeys in the zoo, it is an audience, nonetheless. The audience that concerns O'Connor, however, is the reader, and she focuses her reader's eye as a camera lens, distorting objects, figures, and common rituals, exposing them as simulacra, thereby demonstrating the hollowness at Enoch's center, at the center of the city, and at the center of the novel.

The way visual language created social myths was under scrutiny in the early 1950s. In postwar America, there was a cultural war being waged. It was the constant barrage from the advertising agencies for control of the American psyche. The advent of television in 1949 enabled advertisers to enter the living rooms of America and bombard the consumer with image after image, spawning a new level of reality and creating a "need" for the products being advertised. In her letter to "A" on September 8, 1956, Flan-

[71] O'Connor, *Collected Works*, 49.

[72] Sam Rhodie, *Montage* (Manchester, UK: Manchester University Press) 1.

[73] Ibid.

nery O'Connor writes enthusiastically about *The Mechanical Bride* (1951), Marshall McLuhan's book that examines the cultural effects of advertising. McLuhan calls this visual language "the folklore of industrial man, so much of which stems from the laboratory, the studio, and the advertising agencies."[74] These visions, provided by inventions, films, or advertisers, create a "whirling phantasmagoria [that] can be grasped only when arrested for contemplation."[75] Scenes from the picaresque "ministories" in *Wise Blood,* like those in a film, are arranged frame by frame, formulating a "filmic ekphrasis to illustrate how ultimately determining are artificial systems of signs."[76] These frames open a door to the times in which they were written.[77] We will examine how the Enoch Emory washstand sequence fulfills McLuhan's formula for folkloric quality of a filmic visual text.

WASHSTAND SEQUENCE

When the sequence opens, Enoch is found semi-fasting in preparation for the task that is set before him. The powerful urges brought on by his "wise blood" have doomed him to uncomfortable behaviors, but he is powerless to do anything about them. He develops a new frugality. He stops stealing. He begins a ceremonial cleansing of his room, starting "with the least important thing and [working] around and in toward the center where the meaning" is.[78] The center of meaning responsible for this urgency is the washstand, a "tabernacle-like cabinet which is meant to contain a slop-jar." Not owning a slop-jar, but having "a certain reverence for the purpose of

[74] McLuhan, *The Mechanical Bride*, v.

[75] Ibid.

[76] Mack Smith, *Literary Realism and the Ekphrastic Tradition* (Universtiy Park: Penn State University Press) 214.

[77] Jon Lance Bacon correlates the writings of McLuhan with the writing of *Wise Blood*: The relation between salesmanship and selfhood receives its fullest treatment in the novel O'Connor published one year after McLuhan published *The Mechanical Bride*. In *Wise Blood*, O'Connor depicts a society pervaded by advertising and marketing techniques. Her depiction is satirical, and the target of her satire is much larger than the urban South, which provides the setting for the novel. *Wise Blood* represents her critique of American consumer culture, whose period of greatest expansion coincided with her literary career. Bacon, "A Fondness for Supermarkets," 27.

[78] *Wise Blood*, 132.

things and since he didn't have the right thing [or the slop jar] to put in it, he [leaves the cabinet] empty."[79] This cabinet is Enoch's connection to the "mystery." He dreams "of unlocking the cabinet and getting in it and then proceeding to certain rites and mysteries."[80] Enoch has the desire to exist in the gold-painted repository that has begun to resemble a grotesque replica of a monstrance. He imagines himself occupying the same space as the icon—to be physically enclosed in the sacramental space. In Catholic ritual, it is inside the monstrance that the host is transubstantiated into the body of Christ, and it is into this tabernacle-like structure Enoch eventually places the "new jesus," which does not transform, but remains a conglomeration of what it is—dust and trash, the substance of death, not life. Before he can prepare the washstand for whatever mysterious rite is being required of him, however, Enoch finds it necessary to deal with an audience that continuously watches him day and night as if he were on film. These ever-present watchers abide in the three pictures hanging on the walls of the room. The first, one which is and feared by Enoch, is of a moose in the wild. For Enoch, this moose bears the human qualities of an irritating "roommate"—a "smug face" and an insufferable "look of superiority."[81] The moose picture is framed "in a heavy brown frame with leaf designs on it" which add "to his weight and self-satisfied look."[82] Based on a "sudden intuition," Enoch realizes "that taking the frame off him [the moose] would be equal to taking the clothes off him (although he didn't have on any) and he was right because when he had done it, the animal looked so reduced that Enoch could only snicker and look at him out of the corner of his eye."[83]

In order for the ritual to proceed, the moose must be "dehumanized" by being stripped of his "clothing." This is a foreshadowing of Enoch's own dehumanization by stripping off his own clothing and donning the gorilla suit.[84] Adopting Gonga as a role model suggests "that Enoch's own identity,

[79] O'Connor, *Collected Works*, 74.

[80] Ibid.

[81] Ibid., 75.

[82] Ibid.

[83] Ibid.

[84] The suit, according to Bacon, "has less to do with animal nature than with consumer culture. In *Wise Blood*, forms of advertising and marketing envelop the self, submerging it in a world of salable objects" (Bacon, "A Fondness for Supermarkets," 32). Enoch finds himself "helpless to resist the appeal of a movie poster,

grounded in his own experience, is unimportant."[85] In chapter 1, we considered the influence of the humor of the cartoons of George Price and how he often decorated the walls of his drawn domiciles with pictures of clothed animals that looked disdainfully on the human activities occurring within the cartoon panel. Since Enoch is certainly a comic figure in *Wise Blood*, his behavior appears cartoonish and ridiculous but should not be dismissed as meaningless.[86]

The other two pictures are both on calendars that Enoch leaves hanging on the wall. The one that hangs over his bed, his favorite, is an illustration of "a small boy in a pair of Doctor Denton sleepers, kneeling at his bed, saying, 'And bless daddy,' while the moon [looks] in at the window."[87] We are reminded of Enoch's first conversation with Hazel, in which he reveals that his "daddy," who looks like Jesus, has never given him a moment of love and has kicked him out on his own. As a young child, he was deprived of the most basic human needs—love and safety. Even though O'Connor clearly states in her correspondence that Enoch should not be analyzed, it is not difficult to believe that she includes this picture to aid in the believability of Enoch's eventual complete shedding of humanity. Personification of elements of nature, like the cloud that leads Hazel and Sabbath Lily, often serve as the eye of God on the proceedings in O'Connor stories (much like it did for the Israelites in the desert). The picture of the moon looking through the picture of a window performs as a reminder of God, but for poor Enoch, God is never real, only a paper representation, a paper moon.[88] Again, O'Connor illustrates Enoch's lack of "aura." The

he is likewise vulnerable to the ways in which advertising validates personal identity or withholds validation" (Ibid., 31).

[85] Ibid., 31.

[86] The act of removing the picture frame further illustrates the difference between O'Connor's depiction of Hazel and Enoch. Hazel is always framed, thereby retaining his "aura," while Enoch literally cannot be framed by the cabinet, and even his "moose" audience loses its "aura" and "presence" as well (Benjamin, 229).

[87] O'Connor, *Collected Works*, 75.

[88] "Paper Moon," 1933. Music by Harold Arlen, lyrics by E. Y. Harburg and Billy Rose.

Say, its only a paper moon
Sailing over a cardboard sea
But it wouldn't be make-believe
If you believed in me.

moon is a paper representation in the filmic montage in which Enoch is only a fragmented representation of a comic sidekick.

The third picture is on a calendar from the American Rubber Tire Company. It is a woman wearing a tire. Equating the woman with the object being sold is another example of the world of advertising The calendar, in its small way, is playing with turning desire into need by offering a tire that is embracing a naked woman. The strange thing about this picture is that it is positioned across from the moose, where Enoch thinks the moose only "pretends not to see it."[89] It would seem that even though the moose has been denuded, he still retains his personhood for Enoch. A similar triad formulates around Enoch when, early on, he is interrupted by Hazel Motes while he (Enoch) is about one of his daily rituals—that of sitting in the bushes watching women swimming in the pool that is also in the park surrounding the zoo where he works. On this day, he positions himself so he can watch Hazel's face as one of the women, her suit "half off her in front," tries to catch his eye. "King Jesus!" Enoch whispers when Hazel will have none of it and walks away.[90] The three are frozen in a tableau similar to that replicated in Enoch's bedroom by Enoch, the woman wearing a tire, and the moose. There is no difference in Enoch's mind between his conditioned response to the paper figures and his conditioned response to Hazel and the bathing woman.[91] This, again, is because O'Connor has created him as a

Yes, it's only a canvas sky
Hanging over a muslin tree
But it wouldn't be make-believe
If you believed in me.
Without your love
It's a honky-tonk parade.
Without your love
It's a melody played in a penny arcade.
It's a Barnum and Bailey world
Just as phony as it can be
But it wouldn't be make-believe
If you believed in me.

[89] O'Connor, *Collected Works*, 76.

[90] Ibid., 48.

[91] Baudrillard writes, "It is no longer a case of imitation, nor of reduplication, nor even of parody. It is rather a question of substituting signs of the real for the real itself, that is, an operation to deter every real process by its operational double,

celluloid figure without "aura" or "presence." Enoch is caught in Baudrillard's "system of death,"[92] and O'Connor uses the medium of montage to walk him (and us) through to its conclusion.

The next part of the montage shows Enoch as a sort of obsessive dark creator. We watch him constructing an assemblage out of a washstand. He decorates it with the purchases he has bought using the money he has saved because of his newfound frugality. He paints it with gilt and hangs the chintz curtains from it. As he works, the washstand becomes transformed. The fact that Enoch is performing this task, submitting to the demands of his "wise blood," depicts him as possibly the tool of the powers of evil. Up to this point, Enoch has performed the duties of the comedic sidekick to Hazel's humorless, driven lead. We have been privy to Enoch's ritualistic observances already, and this new behavior foreshadows some sort of darkness to come. Enoch now takes the shape of an Igor or an Iago. He is a "hollow man" performing an empty ritual and creating a hollow vessel:

> *Shape without form, shade without colour,*
> *Paralysed force, gesture without motion.*[93]

Time passes as it does in a montage, and after the passage of some days, Enoch awakens knowing that this is the day his "wise blood" is going to let him know what to put in the cabinet. All day he tries to ignore his blood, but after work, it leads him into town to the Walgreen's Drugstore. Walgreen's is presented here as a virtual cathedral built for worship by the American consumer of simulated reality; in essence, Enoch. He "is motivated by an internal compulsion he does not understand. At the same time, however, the external stimulus of advertising determines the particular manner in which his internal compulsion will be expressed."[94] Enoch works his way "to a rumbling noise which [comes] from the center of a small al-

a metastable, programmatic, perfect descriptive machine which provides all the signs of the real and short-circuits all its vicissitudes." Jean Baudrillard, *Simulations*, trans. Paul Foss, Paul Patton, and Philip Beitchman (Los Angeles: Semiotext(e), 1983) 4.

[92] Ibid., 4.

[93] T. S. Eliot, "The Hollow Men."

[94] John Lance Bacon, *Flannery O'Connor and Cold War Culture* (Cambridge, UK: Cambridge University Press, 1993) 118.

cove that formed the entrance to the drug store. Here was a yellow and blue, glass and steel machine, belching popcorn into a cauldron of butter and salt."[95] Participating in a grotesque communion parody, an unholy Eucharist, Enoch accepts the "host" (popcorn) and almost accepts the "wine" (lime-cherry surprise) but bolts instead. He cannot even complete this unholy communion because its completion would give him an unholy "aura."

His blood carries him along: "I don't want to do it he was saying to himself. Whatever it is I don't want to do it. I'm going home. It'll be something I don't want to do. It'll be something I ain't got no business doing.... It'll be something against the law, he said. It's always something against the law. I ain't going to do it, he said and stopped."[96]

It is interesting that the interior monologue here is not punctuated so that no form is applied to still the motion of the montage gesture. The blood has stopped him in front of a movie theater sporting a poster illustrating "a monster stuffing a young woman into an incinerator."[97]

THE MOVIE THEATER SEQUENCE

Enoch tells himself over and over that he is not going in, and yet, as the "two doors [fly] open...he [finds] himself moving down a long red foyer and then up a darker tunnel and then up a higher, still darker tunnel. In a few minutes he [is] up in a high part of the maw, feeling around, like Jonah, for a seat."[98] In this Enoch montage, O'Connor has concocted the surreal mixture of images of religious ritual, pop culture, and consumerism that make up the world of the first part of his brain—the part that doesn't think in words. However, she is not finished. Enoch, like Jonah, has tried to escape his destiny, but he must now sit in the belly of the whale (the movie thea-

[95] O'Connor, *Collected Works*, 77.

[96] Ibid., 78.

[97] Ibid. This image might refer to Richard Wright's *Native Son*, in which we watch the transformation of Bigger into a monster. Enoch would probably be attracted to the way Bigger takes power over his sordid existence.

[98] Ibid., 79. Referencing Jonah here takes us backward into the Old Testament story. Because of this reference, one wonders if Enoch's destiny, like that of Judas in relation to Jesus, is to enable the salvation of Hazel Motes regardless of what it costs Enoch himself.

ter) and contemplate. Even though Enoch vows, "I ain't going to look at it,"[99] he finds he must watch three movies.

The first movie is called *The Eye* and is about a mad scientist who removes necessary body parts while his victim is sleeping. In the 1936 film *The Invisible Ray*, Boris Karloff "is transformed into a murdering, radiation-poisoned megalomaniac as he hunts down his enemies and projects death rays at them from his eyes (glaring from under a soft felt hat)."[100] As he watches this film, "Enoch pulled his hat down very low and drew his knees in front of his face; only his eyes looked at the screen."[101] Enoch is mirroring the movie poster of Boris Karloff that accompanied this film in 1936. By choosing this film, O'Connor features the eye in the way of a montage artist. "Eyes" and seeing are thematic elements in *Wise Blood*, but though the eye imagery usually appears in conjunction with Hazel Motes, by featuring a celluloid eye, O'Connor is taking the symbol "out of its original context [in the novel] and [it has been] fractured and integrated into a different space and form configuration, [and because of this] it acquires a plastic quality it did not have in the original."[102] The reader's eye is seeing Enoch, whose eyes are focused on a movie screen that features Boris Karloff's made-up radiation-poisoned eye. It is at once a representation of a representation of a representation, producing a hyperreality which is "henceforth sheltered by from the imaginary, and from any distinction between the real and the imaginary, leaving room only for the orbital recurrence of models and the simulated generation of difference."[103] The "system of death" continues.

[99] Ibid., 79.

[100] "Although he usually played a grotesque monster, Karloff starred as experimental physicist Dr. Janos Rukh in this film; after traveling to Africa with his colleague Dr. Benet (Bela Lugosi) and becoming infected by radiation (Radium X) in a meteor of the nebula Andromeda, Karloff was transformed into a murdering, radiation-poisoned megalomaniac as he hunted down his enemies and projected death rays at them from his eyes (glaring from under a soft felt hat)." John Colton, *The Invisible Ray*, directed by Lambert Hillyer (Universal City, CA: Universal Pictures, 1936, http://www.filmsite.org/sci-fifilms.html).

[101] O'Connor, *Collected Works*, 79.

[102] Romare Bearden, "Rectangular Structure in My Montage Paintings," *Leonardo* 40/3 (2007): 291–300, 298.

[103] Baudrillard, *Simulations*, 4.

The second film, *Devil's Island Penitentiary,* is a prison movie. Paul Mason, in his essay "Men, Machines, and the Mincer: The Prison Movie," writes: "Central to the prison movie is the concept of the prison as a machine: the 'system' with its impenetrable sets of rules and regulations which grind on relentlessly. The effect of such a mechanistic depiction of punishment is to highlight both the individual fight for survival and the inherent process of dehumanization which comes with incarceration in the system."[104]

Enoch himself has been imprisoned at Rodmere Boys Training Academy, where he was expected to rigidly perform. Even as he watches this film, his body is being forced to respond mechanically to his "wise blood," which imprisons him and will not let him leave. He is virtually an automaton, an excellent example of the victim of the mechanized dehumanized society, the signs of which are carefully placed by O'Connor throughout the novel. O'Connor, however, does not afford Enoch any pity. She writes that Enoch "is a moron and chiefly a comic character. I don't think it is important whether his compulsion is clinical or not."[105] It would seem to be important to the novel that it is not clinical. It is necessary to sacrifice Enoch to ensure the salvation of Hazel Motes.

The third picture is called *Lonnie Comes Home* and features a baboon named Lonnie (an imitation of *King Kong*) who saves orphan children from a fire and is awarded a medal for his efforts. This plotline follows that of the 1949 film *Mighty Joe Young.*[106] Enoch replicates Joe Young's jerky stop-motion movements as he tries to resist the urges of his "wise blood."[107] In "the end a nice-looking girl gave him [the ape] a medal. It was more than Enoch could stand."[108] Again, an animal is lauded when Enoch's existence

[104] Paul Mason, "Men, Machines, and the Mincer: The Prison Movie," August 1998. http://cap-press.com/sites/pj/articles/Prison.htm, 4.

[105] O'Connor, *Mystery and Manners,* 116–17.

[106] This film did not feature a man in a gorilla suit like in the 1933 film *King Kong,* which was made by the same producers. The gorilla from Africa featured in *Mighty Joe Young* was created by Ray Harryhausen using stop-gap animation.

[107] A notable scene in the movie occurs when the gorilla is being displayed in the Cocoanut Grove nightclub and he runs amuck into the crowd of gawkers. Again, I think the power of this animal would draw Enoch to him even though Enoch professes hatred and disdain.

[108] O'Connor, *Collected Works,* 79.

on the bottom rung of the social ladder is ignored. At this point, Enoch dashes down the tunnels, out of the theater into the street, resigned to follow his "wise blood." He comes upon Hazel Motes preaching from the hood of his car. Hazel speaks as if he is delivering a message directly to Enoch:

> Listen here. What you need is something to take the place of Jesus, something that would speak plain. The Church Without Christ don't have a Jesus but it needs one! It needs a new jesus! It needs one that's all man, without blood to waste, and it needs one that don't look like any other man so you'll look at him. Give me such a jesus, you people. Give me such a jesus and you'll see how far the Church Without Christ can go![109]

Enoch knows just where that new jesus can be found, and he has prepared a tabernacle for that unholy of unholies right in his room! Enoch Emory is Hazel's only convert. He now knows his destiny and he hurries back to the "heart of the city" where the new jesus resides, thus ending the montage.

The Enoch montage offers insight into the forces and urges that animate Enoch Emory, and by presenting this segment of his story as a montage, the reader is propelled forward in the throes of those forces as well. A collage is more stationary while a montage, by its very nature, demands movement. Are we ever able to delineate those "forces?" Are they a result of early religious training—empty ritual? Are they due to evil supernatural forces (i.e., the devil)? Or are they caused by psychological impairment—Boys Training School?—brought on by an animalistic nature? Arguments have been made that support each of these conclusions. What we do know is that Enoch is composed of all of them, and all of them propel him.

In a larger sense, Enoch, influenced by products, advertising, and the movies, as well as the urges of his wise blood, is a close-up of one of the sheep-like characters created by West in *The Day of the Locust.* In fact, the Hazel Motes/Enoch Emory buddy or sidekick duo is not unlike that of Tod Hackett and Homer Simpson. Tod visualizes, Homer responds to his urges. No matter what he says, Hazel Motes cannot rid himself of the visuals that populate his dreams. Enoch, borrowing from movies, cannot help but re-

[109] *Wise Blood,* 140–41.

spond to his wise blood, which seems schooled in Catholic ritual. These two represent one of O'Connor's pairings of the literal and the visual. Enoch is literal in the sense that he follows form without belief. Hazel is visual because he essentially believes he is Christ-haunted. In the pictorial creation of these two characters, O'Connor has taken us from the fifteenth century to the mid-twentieth century in order to refine and expand her message. Readers are able to travel far beyond the frame of the pictorial text because of what is included inside the frame, revealing, as Derrida argues, the lack in the picture. This lack, this hollowness is illustrated by O'Connor in pictures.

Chapter 3

Women of *Wise Blood*: Assemblages of Objects

This was omitted on my new theory that you could omit anything if you knew that you omitted and the omitted part would strengthen the story and make people feel more than they understood.
—Hemingway[1]

We are able to study Flannery O'Connor's creative process in a way that would, in all probability, not be possible were she writing today on a personal computer. O'Connor's way of writing and rewriting backstory, retailoring scenes and points of view in a manner reminiscent of Hitchcock's revolving camera, presents the reader of the manuscript with multifaceted and engaging female characters, predecessors to the women that populate her short stories. Reading the 2,000-plus pages of the *Wise Blood* manuscript reveals the young author's great concern about the power of advertising in craftily shaping the perceptions, needs, and desires of mid-century women. The *Wise Blood* women are poor. They fall below the grid of advertiser's demographics. Yet when O'Connor measures them against the criteria imposed by women's magazines, Ruby Wickers (Hazel Motes's sister), Annie Lee Jackson Wickers (Hazel's and Ruby's tormented mother), Leora Watts (beautician, receptionist, and Hazel's lover), and Sabbath (a Tarwateresque street evangelist, replete with visions) fall short and appear as humorous grotesques living on the fringes of society. These female characters are greatly altered in the published form of the novel or, as in Ruby's case, erased completely. Solidly constructed, the *Wise Blood* manuscript women embody a social and cultural significance that is recognizably, contextually American.[2] O'Connor carves and shapes these women much as she did her linotype cartoons, and as a consequence, what remains is women composed as poetic assemblages of symbolic, sometimes fetishized objects or products

[1] Ernest Hemingway, *A Moveable Feast, Restored Edition* (New York: Scribner, 2009) 71.

[2] Women living in the margins exist throughout American Literature. Examples include Hawthorne's *The Scarlet Letter,* Miller's *The Crucible.*

that resonate as part of shared American material culture. These images unite into a composite that represents pages of manuscript writing. This elevates the image until it stands apart in the narrative, rivaling those advertising creations so prevalent in the culture. W. J. T. Mitchell writes, "Magical attitudes toward images are just as powerful in the modern world as they were in the so-called ages of faith,"[3] encouraging one to think that this is exactly why O'Connor, the scholar of Catholicism, would perfect this mode of writing.

My fascination with the ensemble of women in the *Wise Blood* manuscript is not because they have been banished to an existence in a file folder in Milledgeville, Georgia. Rather, my fascination is with O'Connor's process as she incrementally weaves her original ideas into her published characters. The way the women are featured or framed and the meager props that accompany them in the novel is reminiscent of the undergraduate cartoons in which O'Connor honed her gestural messages early on. As discussed in chapter 1, the PhD cartoon alone highlights the stories of many women's lives in that the positioning of the dancers, the very inclinations of their heads and the placements of their arms on the shoulders of their partners, tells small stories of their lives and relationships. The lives of the *Wise Blood* women are rendered visually in the same way as those of the dancers in the cartoon. Annie Wickers, Ruby, Sabbath, and Leora are framed in the narrative and presented visually accompanied by an assortment of discarded objects.

Hazel's and Ruby's troublesome and complex mother, Annie, of the manuscript, whose husband's sporadic visits result in the production of one doomed offspring after another, becomes in the published *Wise Blood* a set of riveting mother-centered objects: eyeglasses, a chifforobe, a bat-like crea-

[3] W. J. T. Mitchell writes in *What Do Pictures Want?*, "My argument here is that the double consciousness about images is a deep abiding feature of human responses to representation. It is not something we 'get over' when we grow up, become modern, or acquire critical consciousness. The specific expressions of this paradoxical double consciousness of images are amazingly various. They include such phenomena as popular *and* sophisticated beliefs about art, response to religious icons by true believers *and* reflections by theologians, children (*and* parents) behavior with dolls and toys, the feelings of nations and populations about cultural and political icons, reactions to technical advances in media and reproduction, and the circulation of archaic racial stereotypes" (Mitchell, 8).

ture rising from a coffin. Leora, in the manuscript, is a careworn young woman who has been on her own and has supported herself with an array of jobs since her early teens. She appears in the published novel as a collage of body parts viewed from varying perspectives—a knee, an elbow, toenail clippings. Only with Sabbath is it possible to actually witness the writerly transformation to Sabbath Lily in the manuscript as she morphs from street evangelist, whose mangled feet shuffle in an old pair of men's shoes (Sabbath) into the young girl that appears at Ruby's party in tiny high heels ready to dance (a first rendition of Sabbath Lily).

These women exist in a strangely stylized world where the flow of language is punctuated with "for sale" and "buy this." It is the language of the sales "pitch" designed to create desire. Desire in both the manuscript as well as the published version of this book are held up for inspection through the female gaze. On the very first page of the novel, Hazel is accurately assessed by Mrs. Wally Bee Hitchcock right down to the price tag that still dangles from his newly purchased suit: "'I guess you're going home,' she said, turning back to him again. He didn't look, to her, much over twenty, but he had a stiff black broad-brimmed hat on his lap, a hat that an elderly country preacher would wear. His suit was a glaring blue and the price tag was still stapled on the sleeve of it."[4]

Planting that price tag on Hazel's suit, as well as Mrs. Hitchcock's assessment of it ("The suit had cost him $11.98. She felt that that placed him.")[5], situates him in the milieu of visual advertising that infiltrates *Wise Blood*.[6]

[4] O'Connor, *Collected Works*, 3.

[5] Ibid.

[6] Madison Avenue admen designed marketing campaigns to be featured on television and in women's magazines targeting the post-WWII American housewife who had begun to symbolize a new "American way of life." This process, according to Betty Friedan, in 1963 writing in *The Feminine Mystique*, was devastating to American women: "The public image, in the magazines and television commercials, is designed to sell washing machines, cake mixes, deodorants, detergents, rejuvenating face creams, hair tints. But the power of that image, on which companies spend millions of dollars for television time and ad space, comes from this: American women no longer know who they are. They are sorely in need of a new image to help them find their identity" (Friedan, 72)."

The omission or silencing of the *Wise Blood* women as they appear in the manuscript has been a subject for discussion by various O'Connor critics. Katherine Hemple Prown, in *Revising Flannery O'Connor: Southern Literary Culture and the Problem of Female Authorship*, wrote specifically about the type of silencing imposed by the culture of the male authors that mentored the young Flannery O'Connor and published her work.[7] According to Prown, by erasing and altering these early female characters, O'Connor was displaying "her allegiance to the disembodied male intellect"[8] and in this way aligning herself with the Southern Agrarians who were adamant that the Southern white male literary tradition should be preserved and that this preservation could only be carried out by repressing African Americans and women.[9] Prown writes that by "banishing female characters, silencing female voices, and redirecting her satirical gaze from men to women, O'Connor reshaped her work to appeal to a literary and critical community built on the gender-based and racial hierarchies that had characterized southern culture."[10]

I contend that these women are not erased but remain in the text of the novel represented as collages or arrangements of objects in pictorial moments in the text of *Wise Blood*. In truth, much of the narrative backstory found in the manuscript concerning these characters has been omitted but is validated by an awareness that, to quote Hemingway, "the omitted

The economic and political power of advertising along with its influence on writers is acknowledged by Flannery O'Connor, herself, in her essay "The Fiction Writer & His Country." She writes, "Unless we are willing to accept our artists as they are, the answer to the question, 'Who speaks for America today?' will have to be: the advertising agencies" (*Mystery and Manners*, 34). She points out that not only do advertisers create consumers, but they also create writers.

[7] Andrew Lytle, one of the designers of the Agrarian's creed *I'll Take my Stand*, presided over the final version of the *Wise Blood* manuscripts. At the time, Lytle was overseeing the last revision of his own novel, *The Velvet Horn*, every page of which is awash in phallic imagery. There was no place in this strict Southern Agrarian definition of art for a sympathetic portrait of Ruby, Annie, Sabbath, and Leora, embarrassingly authentic women.

[8] Katherine Hempel Prown, *Revising Flannery O'Connor: Southern Literary Culture and the Problem of Female Authorship* (Charlottesville: University of Virginia Press, 2001) 50.

[9] Ibid., 70.

[10] Ibid., 3.

part would strengthen the story and make people feel more than they understood."[11]

THE LEGACY OF ANNIE LOU JACKSON WICKERS

References to Annie Lou Jackson Wickers in the *Wise Blood* manuscript are scarce, but if we scratch the surface of Hazel Motes and his sister, Ruby (whose story is told in "A Stroke of Good Fortune"), we find Annie enthroned at the core. Annie is a woman who has borne eight children, four of whom have survived. She is consumed by the knowledge that she is cursed by God because of premarital sex with her husband, Lemmuck Wickers, an older deaf man who wanders in and out of her life, showing up now and again to impregnate her. The curse festers and takes form and lodges within Annie alongside the other inhabitants (her babies) that come and go, some surviving some not. Because of this symbiotic relationship, Annie knows sin. She knows it intimately. She knows its ravages when she holds yet another dead baby. This knowledge informs her in the raising of her surviving children.

Hazel leaves Eastrod and ventures into the Army armed with his mother's eyeglasses. He plans to use them to spot sin before it takes hold of him. When some of the other soldiers invited him to go out with them, "he took his mother's glasses out of his pocket and put them on. Then he told them he wouldn't go with them for a million dollars and a feather bed to lie on."[12] He dons his mother's glasses again when he flings the new jesus out of the fire-escape door. The significance of seeing through his mother's eyes is inescapable, but what does establishing Annie's gaze accomplish? To begin with, it already has been established in the text that Annie seems to be omniscient. When Hazel slinks back home after viewing a peep show at the fair, she knows that he has been committing a sin before she even lays eyes on him. We know that in Hazel's mind, she seems to be one of the undead. In his dreams, she swoops out of her coffin, taking the form of a bat. Wearing his mother's glasses, establishing the scene through Annie's gaze, Hazel looks at the tableau framed by the mirror: himself, Sabbath Lily, and a dried-up mummy—another in the series of dead babies that appears in the

[11] Hemingway, *A Moveable Feast*, 71.
[12] O'Connor, *Collected Works*, 12.

novel. The glasses at that moment focus the scene within Annie's unbending vision of sin. [13]

Annie, in Hazel's mind, equals furniture. O'Connor first had Hazel, newly discharged from the Army, ask Ruby about the whereabouts of Annie's snuffbox. However, the chifforobe that once held Annie's clothes was the furniture O'Connor settled on to represent mother and home. The three objects—glasses, coffin, and chifforobe—form the assemblage that is the Annie Lou Wickers of *Wise Blood.* The juxtaposition of these resonant objects not only keeps Annie alive in Hazel's mind, but also conjures her in the minds of readers.

RUBY: THE MECHANICAL BRIDE[14]

We will begin our look at how O'Connor's manuscript backstories and cultural messages concerning the women who were her contemporaries were, in fact, represented pictorially by examining the case of Ruby Wickers, who is removed from the published version of the novel and is given a short story of her own, "A Stroke of Good Fortune." I further contend that the Ruby themes have not been removed from the novel and that they exist embodied in the narratives of other characters in the published text.[15]

One of the books in O'Connor's library was *The Mechanical Bride* by Marshall McLuhan. The book is a compilation of advertisements taken from both magazines and newspapers. Each ad is accompanied by an essay written by McLuhan discussing the effect of the ad on the American consumer. The very title of the book ties it to the way women are particularly and relentlessly targeted by advertising and how women are constantly made to feel guilty and inadequate for their lack of or failure to provide their families with certain designated products. "To purchase gadgets that

[13] I have used elements from both the manuscript and the published text here to formulate my interpretation. Just the death of one of Annie's children, Hazel's brother, is mentioned in *Wise Blood.* The lineage of dead babies becomes important in Ruby's story, "A Stroke of Good Fortune."

[14] *The Mechanical Bride: Folklore of Industrial Man* is a study of popular culture written by Marshall McLuhan in 1951.

[15] Much of this introduction was taken from an article, "An Untapped Legacy: Flannery O'Connor's Ruby in 'A Stroke of Good Fortune' and in the Manuscript of *Wise Blood*," I wrote for *The Flannery O'Connor Review*, 2010.

relieve this drudgery and thus promote domestic affection is, therefore, a duty, too. And so it is that not only labor-saving appliances but food and nylons ('your legs owe it to their audience') are consumed and promoted with moral fervor."[16]

Ruby Wickers, Hazel's sister, is a woman, with an unwieldy, embarrassing body; a woman who, regardless of her consumption of women's magazines or her accumulation of products, finds herself unable to measure up to the 1950s ideal. Though deleted from the final version of *Wise Blood,* Ruby is rewarded with a short story of her own, "A Stroke of Good Fortune." The Ruby of the short story is essentially the same character as the Ruby of the manuscript, but in "A Stroke of Good Fortune," she appears in a manner that, like a literary *tromp l'oeil,* both freezes her *in* and detaches her *from* her cultural milieu. The question is, then, based on what we have discerned from the way O'Connor employs the pictorial, to what effect does O'Connor perform the silencing and repackaging of this female character who dominates the early versions of *Wise Blood*? The manuscript Ruby stands as a sort of "everywoman" who is not wealthy or educated or even wise. She continues to exist, as Peter Brooks describes, as a "text of muteness": a silent text that is conveyed by "tableau and gesture."[17] Portrayals of mid-century women from whom "the spoken word is rarely used toward the formulation of significant messages"[18] abound. Examples range from Arthur Miller's Elizabeth Proctor to Updike's Janice Angstrom. Flannery O'Connor's Ruby merits a place in their company. Speaking with profound gesture and in domestic tableaux, the sacrificial actions of these women are often confused and offer no evidence of linear reasoning when displayed alongside those of their male counterparts. They embody a kind of force that proves destructive to the nuclear family.[19] By closely examining the manuscript Ruby—the word "made flesh"—along with the short story Ruby, who, in becoming a virtual collection of objects, becomes the word it-

[16] McLuhan, *The Mechanical Bride*, 33.

[17] Ibid., 56.

[18] Brooks, *The Melodramatic Imagination*, 63.

[19] In Arthur Miller's *The Crucible*, 1953, Elizabeth Proctor bears her husband's guilt. In Updike's *Rabbit, Run*, published in 1960, Janice drunkenly drowns her baby. O'Connor, writing in the early 1950s has the manuscript Ruby acknowledge her pregnancy, but try to erase the baby's existence using the "scientific" paste sold to her by a druggist, thusly causing her own demise.

self, I will assess whether anything has been lost by the omission of Ruby from *Wise Blood* and whether the Ruby who appears in "A Stroke of Good Fortune" differs greatly from the manuscript Ruby. I will then determine exactly what part O'Connor's pictorial sign language plays in this process.

I begin my analysis, appropriately, with a picture: Picasso's *Girl before a Mirror.* Flannery O'Connor's cursory mention of Picasso, in a letter to Janet McKane written in 1963, does not reveal how great an interest she may have had in the artist[20] but does reveal her awareness of his existence in regard to Chagall, an artist in whom she was quite interested. Barry Moser, when writing about the undergraduate cartoons, ties the style of the PhD cartoon specifically to this picture by Picasso.[21] For this study we are going to extend that comparison to Ruby Wickers.

After having erased Ruby from *Wise Blood,* where her compelling story began to override O'Connor's essential message, she is granted her own stage in "A Stroke of Good Fortune," which appears in O'Connor's first short story collection, *A Good Man Is Hard to Find.* The published Ruby, when compared with the manuscript Ruby, vividly demonstrates the development of O'Connor's pictorial writing style. In the telling of one afternoon of Ruby's life, O'Connor wields her typewriter like a scalpel and hones the story down to an assembled series of objects that define her main character with concrete images—a mirror, collard greens, steps, and a pair of green shoes. She uses objects to create visual signs that form an illustrative poetry that speaks semiotically to the perceptions, to the senses, and to the human spirit, and, consequently, establishes extended platforms of meaning.

[20] In this letter, O'Connor is reminiscing about a television interview that she saw with Marc Chagall. She writes, "Chagall said in the simplest way possible that his greatest influence was his mother.... And when Chagall speaks of 'the Spaniard' does he mean Picasso do you suppose?" (O'Connor, *Habit of Being,* 531).

[21] "Indeed," Barry Moser writes, "it is all a matter of gesture. O'Connor also had a strong natural sense of composition that becomes evident after studying the prints. The overall pattern of 'Oh, well, I can always be a PhD.,' is a good example. She divides the rectangle into many near repetitive black shapes, contrasts them with smaller, similar shapes in white, and then throws in a series of circle-like shapes and bold angular stripes—all in all it reminds me, distantly, of Pablo Picasso's *Girl Before a Mirror* (1932)." (Moser, "Working Backward," ix).

RUBY IN "A STROKE OF GOOD FORTUNE"

As the story begins, the first object confronting the reader is a mirror which provides a moment of self-contemplation for Ruby as she pauses before ascending the stairs to her apartment on the top floor. Northrop Frye sees the modulation "of the mirror image" is employed by a writer to bring readers "to the pictures, tapestries, and statues which so often turn up near the beginning of a romance to indicate the threshold of the romance world".[22] The romance in this story is laced with irony. Based on her mother's experiences, Ruby, who is pregnant, comes to terms with the fact that she may well die in childbirth. Unlike the sacrificial mothers of romance, Ruby resents giving up her life for her child's and ends the story in dejected acceptance. O'Connor uses the mirror to frame Ruby's reflection, which shows "her head balanced like a florid vegetable at the top of the [grocery] sack"[23] she is holding and with "a gritty collard leaf" stuck "against her right cheek."[24] O'Connor has designed a virtual vegetable collage or still life featuring Ruby's face as the main vegetable. The finely detailed brushstrokes that painted the manuscript Ruby have been reduced and distilled into this moment when the published Ruby observes her face juxtaposed with a collection of "florid" vegetables. A "short woman, shaped nearly like a funeral urn"[25] is the phrase that places the object O'Connor uses to describe Ruby's body. The choice of this one object presents Ruby as a doomed carrier of death, a "suffering human body," O'Connor's "densest symbol."[26]

The face of Picasso's *Girl* is not teetering on top of a bag of groceries, but, like Ruby, the mirror *Girl* does have a green leaf-like fragment over her

[22] Northrup Frye, *The Secular Scripture,* (Cambridge, MA: Harvard University Press, 1976) 109.

[23] In chapter 1, in reference to the grocery store scene in "The Crop," I mentioned O'Connor's cartoon drawing of a coed carrying a bag of groceries that appeared in the 1945 *Spectrum*, the yearbook for Georgia College for Women. The girl's face is balanced on top of the overflowing bag as if she herself were a commodity. The caption is "Where our pennies go." This picture seems to have stayed with O'Connor, and it comes to fruition as Ruby stands in front of the hall mirror in "A Stroke of Good Fortune."

[24] O'Connor, *Collected Works*, 184.

[25] Ibid.

[26] John D. Sykes, *Flannery O'Connor, Walker Percy, and the Aesthetic Revolution* (Columbia: University of Missouri Press, 2007) 5.

right cheek. She, in a Cubist manner, is constructed from geometric fragments. In Cubist artwork, objects are analyzed, broken up, and reassembled in an abstract form. Clement Greenberg, in his essay "Collage," writes that Cubists were concerned

> with obtaining sculptural results by strictly nonsculptural means: that is, with finding for every aspect of three-dimensional vision an explicitly two-dimensional equivalent, regardless of how much verisimilitude might suffer in the process. Painting had to spell out rather than to deny the physical fact that it was flat, even though at the same time it had to overcome this proclaimed flatness as an aesthetic fact and continue to report nature.[27]

It is this flatness that is of concern in this examination of O'Connor's pictorial text. In chapter 1, I discussed how the depiction of flatness in the PhD cartoon brought all of the girls onto the same plane, unlike the *New Yorker* illustration, which was drawn to suggest alienation and depth. This alteration of the figure ground continuum is important to analysis and to discernment of O'Connor's purpose. Like Ruby, Picasso's *Girl* has a body shaped like a funeral urn. The girl outside the mirror is embracing her own image in the mirror. The image in the mirror is painted with darker hues, the face shaded, suggesting a "night-self": "By setting a conventional day-self over a night-self, Picasso is able to provide a time capsule of an entire life. He reduces a full-length novel (or movie) like Madame Bovary to a single image of great intensity. By juxtaposition and contrast, he is able to 'say' a great deal and to provide much intelligibility for daily life."[28]

The image of the girl in the mirror is essentially a Cubist representation of a representation of the real, constructed "in accordance with the laws of the very object to be posited in being (ship, house, carpet, colored canvas or hewn block). This exigency of its generic concept takes precedence over everything else; and to make the representation of the real [manuscript Ruby] its essential end is to destroy it."[29] Carla Gottlieb writes in her essay "Picasso's 'Girl before a Mirror'" that in this painting Picasso is not necessarily discovering "new themes" but his "originality resides" in the "way he treats

[27] Clement Greenberg, "Collage," *Art and Culture*, from *Art News* (September 1958) np.

[28] McLuhan, *The Mechanical Bride*, 80.

[29] Maritain, *Art and Scholasticism*, 57.

the old ones."[30] This sort of statement could be made about O'Connor as well, as evidenced by the way she used upended clichés in her cartoons as well as the putting forth of her theological agenda.

It is important to take note of just exactly what the mirror accomplishes, both in Ruby's case and in the case of Picasso's *Girl*.[31] In both cases, the mirror distorts. Gottlieb writes that the reflected and rearranged image painted by Picasso looks "benighted—ghostly and fearsome as the image of a human being" and that the girl sees herself as a kind of *memento mori*, evidenced by the bone-like striations across her body. The picture suggests death-in-life. O'Connor's rendition of Ruby is that of a tired young woman pausing before she must ascend the stairs to her third-floor apartment.

> Ruby came in the front door of the apartment building and lowered the paper sack with four cans of number three beans in it onto the hall table. She was too tired to take her arms from around it or to straighten up and she hung there collapsed from the hips, her head balanced like a big florid vegetable at the top of the sack. She gazed with stony unrecognition at the face that confronted her in the dark yellow-spotted mirror over the table. Against her right cheek was a gritty collard leaf that had been stuck there half the way home. She gave it a vicious swipe with her arm and straightened up muttering, "Collards, collards," in a voice of sultry subdued wrath. Standing up straight, she was a short woman shaped nearly like a funeral urn. She had mulberry-colored hair stacked in sausage rolls around her head but some of these had come loose with the heat and the long walk from the grocery store

[30] Carla Gottlieb, "Picasso's Girl before a Mirror," *The Journal of Aesthetics and Art Criticism* 24/4 (Summer 1966): 509–18, 509. Gottlieb further writes, "With an artist of such a frame of mind, it is not astonishing to find in his works unconscious similarities as well as conscious references to allegorical subjects and symbolism, these favorites of the past ages. But they will be rendered in novel ways and hence can be overlooked."

[31] Ibid., Gottlieb: "The canvas portrays a young and beautiful girl in the act of surveying herself in a oval mirror which reflects her likeness in a distorted way: it lengthens her nose while shortening her cheek and jowl; it colors the face in chalky lilac tones; it replaces the eye's almond shape with a maroon circle; it transforms the flush upon the cheek into an orange sickle; and it covers the forehead and upper portions of the nose with a jarring carmine of red."

> and pointed frantically in various directions. "Collard greens!" she said, spitting the word from her mouth this time as if it were a poisonous seed.[32]

O'Connor suggests the idea of death-in-life with the mere phrase "shaped nearly like a funeral urn." Ruby is described throughout as an assortment of groceries and the reader is somewhat amused by the contemporary *momento mori.* The collard green leaf is wilted. The groceries are processed and preserved in cans. There seems to be nothing alive caught within the frame of the mirror. Both women, on either side of the mirror, seem to be pausing for a moment of double consciousness, a moment of "reflection" and self-awareness and recognition of both a conscious and subconscious "inner world."[33]

WISE BLOOD MANUSCRIPT RUBY

What, then, is the omitted text that exists in the *Wise Blood* manuscript Ruby, subject of O'Connor's grocery collage? Throughout this document, O'Connor paints the pastoral terrain of Ruby's body with fine intimate strokes, emphasizing shapes and lines and creating a Modern feminine abstraction which brings to mind an O'Keefe flower or landscape painting. Ruby's story is presented in fragments, in fits and starts through the memories and reminiscences of the males that surround her and through her own interior monologue. Her story ebbs and flows in a fashion that is circular—the fashion that Luce Irigaray would later describe in her essay "The Sex Which Is Not One" as exhibiting a kind of distinct femininity: women being "within themselves.... And if you ask them insistently what they are thinking about, they can only reply: Nothing. Everything."[34] Because of the fact that, according to Irigaray, women exist "in the little-structured margins of a [male] dominat[ed] ideology, as waste, or excess,"[35] the female imaginary will appear in strange fragments that do not seem to translate into the cultural whole, because that cultural whole is male. O'Connor's altered writing style, sans Ruby, in the published *Wise Blood* resembles the art of

[32] O'Connor, *Collected Works,* 184.

[33] Gottlieb, "Picasso's Girl," 511.

[34] Luce Irigaray, *The Sex Which Is Not One* (Ithaca, NY: Cornell University Press, 1985) 29.

[35] Ibid., 30.

assemblage or collage rather than the feminized, sexualized pastoral landscape of the manuscript. The novel becomes a *bildungsroman* featuring a male protagonist. The emergence of what eventually is a signature style for O'Connor—that of assembling emblematic objects that evoke layers of meanings concerned with urbanization, Christianity, and consumerism—manifests her novel as a compacted symbolic form with image, feeling, and ambiguity; in essence, a poem. This movement from the particularly feminine voice to that of a detached sexless narrator occurs in a silent space that exists between folders 148j and 149[36] of the manuscript and leaves no place for the manuscript Ruby and her love of MIRACLE products, her cumbersome, undesirably pregnant body in the highly stylized final version of the novel.[37]

In the *Wise Blood* manuscript, O'Connor uses Ruby's voice to reveal the subtle shaping of an American woman's life by the "culture industry," as defined by Horkheimer and Adorno in their *Dialectics of Enlightenment*, and to detail the insidious nature of the cultural milieu that engulfed women of the postwar years. Ruby's past makes her a prime target for the marvelous claims of advertisers. During her early life, she finds her own way in rural Georgia, virtually alone, moving through a jungle of leering men, avoiding her insane, sometimes violent father, who hides behind trees and follows her, and hiding from a stern fundamentalist mother (Annie Lee Jackson Wickers), all the while trailed and observed by her little brother, Hazel. After her mother dies and Hazel is conscripted, Ruby is left at home as the sole caretaker of her invalid father. O'Connor experiments with a variety of versions of this father's character, and none of them is very attractive. In all of the versions, he has been away from home, has come back to die, and is incommunicable and paralyzed. In a letter to Hazel, Ruby writes that her

[36] Stephen G. Driggers, Robert J. Dunn, and Sarah Gordon, *The Manuscripts of Flannery O'Connor at Georgia College* (Athens: University of Georgia Press, 1989) 71.

[37] There is no explanation of what occurred at this juncture in the life of the young writer. However, reading the *Wise Blood* manuscripts and listening to the voices that have been edited, both O'Connor's and Ruby's, opens an inviting window to the 1950s for modern readers, particularly female readers. Looking through this window to a seemingly simpler time in American history, and listening to the plenary voice of Flannery O'Connor, can shed light on female participation in the discourse of the twenty-first century.

father can no longer move his hands and feet and that she has found work in Cate's store in Eastrod in order to put food on the table, but her one consolation is a twenty-eight-year-old salesman, Bill Hill, who takes her on a drive every Saturday and with whom she goes steady. She then describes a strange event involving a vision of a veiled woman and a floating hearse that has upset her and that reveals another "shard" or fragment of her "female imaginary."[38] Eventually, Bill Hill asks Ruby to marry him and move to town—to Taulkingham. She leaves and she never looks back. O'Connor uses this letter to open for the reader the strange mystical interiority that defines Ruby. She has not internalized her mother's and Hazel's fundamental religiosity, but instead depends on signs and omens to guide her actions. This might well explain her easy acceptance of a life defined by a glossy page or a screen in a darkened theater.

Because of a past fraught with violence and despair, the *Wise Blood* manuscript Ruby is only able to define herself in the unfamiliar urban setting using the criteria of home decorating and of the ownership of household products provided by Bill Hill, her husband, seller of MIRACLE products. In creating Ruby, O'Connor has constructed a woman who literally embodies the emptiness and void created by the advertising agencies and who is attempting to fill that void with consumerism: in essence, more products equal less emptiness. As viewed through the tiny window of Ruby's apartment, the world that takes shape in between the flashes of a neon light advertising a MIRACLE[39] is a world of and about women. In the personage of Ruby, O'Connor embodies, at once, the absurdity and desperation in the life of a postwar American woman of the lower class. Lacking any other guidebook, women like Ruby studied women's magazines and movies in an attempt to climb the social ladder—to become part of the coveted American middle class. It is with the advent of her new life with Bill Hill that Ruby finds an orbit in the patriarchal universe. The role of "housewife," just the sort of housewife decried by Friedan, is the role that she can fill. Fortunately, Bill Hill's sales have packed her kitchen with household gadgets that can serve as her props in this role. These props or objects that O'Connor places in the Hill's apartment in Taulkingham tell the story of Ruby's attempts to realize her dream.

[38] Irigaray, *The Sex Which Is Not One*, 30.

[39] It is interesting that this is the name of the products sold by Harry Greener in *The Day of the Locust*.

Ruby's plans seem to be working well for her until her body betrays her or, in her opinion, until Bill Hill betrays her. She becomes pregnant. She now is thrust back into that fragmented marginal past. It is at this point, according to Driggers and Dunn, the drafts for "Woman on the Stairs" or what would become the short story "A Stroke of Good Fortune" appear in the *Wise Blood* manuscript. Growing up, Ruby almost daily hears her mother recite a litany of the names of the children that Annie Lou Jackson Wickers had borne dead or who had died before the age of two. Childbearing has always been associated with death for Ruby. In the manuscript story, Ruby is now no longer a "wife" with "pretentions of independence" but a woman with a body who is "forc[ed] to share [her] mother's vulnerability...the horrifying biological destiny of child bearing."[40] She makes the decision to erase the baby she is carrying—to just make it go away. The word abortion is never uttered. Dr. Fischer, the druggist to whom she has appealed for help, adeptly as any Madison Avenue adman, praises her for being a "modern" woman and offers a "scientific" way to solve her problem. This line of thought appeals to Ruby, who has applied that very premise to choosing products in designing her kitchen. In her marginal notes, and with the portentous dream appearance of a baby hanging by a silk stocking, O'Connor indicates that both Ruby and the baby are destined to die.

O'Connor has reduced the manuscript narrative of Ruby's life to a reflection framed by a mirror and composed of an exhausted woman's face surrounded by grocery products. The choice of a mirror as *parergon* poses Ruby as she comes face-to-face with her reflection, her doppelgänger. On the "real" side of the mirror, O'Connor has given us Ruby's body shape and the style of her unnaturally colored hair. In the mirror we see her face surrounded by products in a manner reminiscent of an advertisement in a woman's magazine. This moment of pause in the narrative evokes feelings in the same manner as that accomplished by Picasso with his *Girl before a Mirror*. Ruby's choice of canned beans and her disdain for the fresh collards reveals her love for modern mass-produced, well-packaged products. Those food packages represent her new life with Bill Hill. The collard leaf sticking to her face reminds Ruby of a time when she was not able to afford the colorfully labeled cans from the grocery store. Her family depended on working in a garden for food. The food that was not packed in clean sterile pack-

[40] Westling, *Sacred Groves and Ravaged Gardens*, 148.

ages came with dirt attached. She left that life behind when she ran away with Bill Hill...or so she thought. Even though the mirror into which she peers reflects her up-to-date hairstyle, Ruby will always carry the legacy of the past inside of her like she carries a collard green on her right cheek. She is like one of those cans of beans—brightly packaged on the outside, but just beans on the inside. Her funeral-urn body is very similar to that of the Picasso *Girl* and presents an object wrought with ambiguity that serves as an emblem encasing the layers of violence, rejection, superstition, fear, and dread that O'Connor painted in the *Wise Blood* manuscript while landscaping Ruby. In its place, in the foreground, stands a funeral urn, a death-in-life image, that is the embodiment of all that *is* Ruby, a representative of a long line of women who have climbed these steps before her and who will climb them after she is gone. Ruby is at a crossroads. Does she have a spiritual center somewhere hidden by the objects that compose her? That, I think, is the question O'Connor leaves with us at the end of the story.

LEORA WATTS: ASSEMBLY-LINE LOVE-GODDESS[41]

THE IMAGE IN THE GLASS

She turns and looks a moment in the glass,
Feature a picture
Her brain allows one half-formed thought to pass:
"Well now that's done: and I'm glad it's over."
When lovely woman stoops to folly and
Paces about her room again, alone,
She smoothes her hair with automatic hand,
And puts a record on the gramophone.[42]

An Ivory Flakes advertisement is included in Marshall McLuhan's 1950 essay "Love-Goddess Assembly Line." The ad begins, "The Girls who get the calls...the girls who get the rings...are the girls who are in the know.... So we show you the inside story of one who has a *way* with her clothes."

[41] McLuhan, *The Mechanical Bride.* In "The Waste Land," Eliot makes the encounter between the clerk and the typist callously mechanical.

[42] Eliot, *The Waste Land*, 46.

This ad calls upon a "culturally constructed and shared idea to evoke individualized, self-related cognitions (self-schemas, possible selves, role selves, autobiographical memories, etc.) that favorably influence the viewer's reactions to the ad."[43] The norms and schema at work in this ad all center on beliefs, shared by both men and women, about the female body. Furthermore, McLuhan makes the case that this ad evidences the "interfusion of sex and technology"[44] by presenting a girl's body as a collection of interchangeable parts implicative of that great American achievement—the assembly line. The girl is referenced not by name, but by a number—her phone number. The answer to the question, "'What makes a gal a good number?' is simply 'looking like a number of other gals....' Just as success and personality know-how consist of recipes and formulas for reducing everybody to the same pattern, we seem to demand, in harmony with this principle, that love goddesses be all alike."[45]

According to the Ivory Flakes assessment, her undies must be "daisy fresh"; she must have a "smooth, smooth figure"; her legs must be "head-turning"; and her clothing must be colorful and bright.[46] Another thing that is necessary to the Love-Goddess construction is the illusion of innocence. It would not do to desire a girl who was not herself "fresh" and pure. The ad conveys this by having one half of the girl accompanied by all of the female embellishments. She is wearing a flowery dress. There is a romantic candelabrum on the mantelpiece behind her. There are fresh flowers on the table in front of her. The pedestal of the table on the left side of the picture actually blocks any sight of her leg. The right side of the picture reveals what we all know to be true. Under the "fresh" girlish exterior of that "girl-next-door" there is a bra, girdle, and garters holding up the sexy nylon stocking on that long beautiful leg. Of course she is wearing heels. Even if your figure falls short, you can "smooth" it with these undergarments. The implication is that after the lights are out and the smoothing garments are removed, it does not matter anyway—all women have the same usable parts. It is important, however, that the undergarments, like the girl, be "fresh"—hence,

[43] Anne M. Brumbaugh, "Sources and Cues in Advertising and Their Effects on the Activation of Cultural and Subcultural Knowledge on the Route to Persuasion," *Journal of Consumer Research* 29/2 (September 2002): 258.

[44] McLuhan, *The Mechanical Bride*, 94.

[45] Ibid., 96.

[46] Ibid., 95.

the need for Ivory Flakes. The selling here is that of "fresh" body parts covered by "fresh" garments. To be seen with such a harmoniously constructed, intoxicating piece of work is a "sure sign that you [the American male] are clicking on all cylinders."[47] This Love-Goddess construct is so familiar in the American lexicon that O'Connor addressed the legs ("a big white knee"), the clothing (the "pink nightgown that would better have fit a smaller figure"), and freshness (her yellow hair and greasy white skin) in her composition of Mrs. Leora Watts. The advertisement that Hazel reads on the wall of a bathroom stall does use a name to reference Mrs. Watts. However, then she is identified by a number, "60 Buckley Road," and objectified as a bed, "The friendliest bed in town."

In chapter 2 of *Wise Blood*, Leora Watts first appears actually "as a collection of body parts,"[48] who is "a physical presence only."[49] Katheryn Hemple Prown writes that the "*Lea*" (my emphasis) of the manuscript "rivals [Hazel] as a protagonist, whereas in the published novel she merely serves, in the role of prostitute Leora Watts, as a temporary antidote to his uncontrollable religious impulses."[50] Prown further contends that "the dominant voice that characterizes her [O'Connor's] published fiction versus the muted voice that speaks in her manuscripts—pervaded O'Connor's personal and professional lives and remains key to an understanding of her work."[51] Marshall Bruce Gentry argues that because Hazel later poses the question, "What do I need with Jesus?" and immediately adds the explanation, "I got Leora Watts,"

> we might indeed see some godly qualities in Mrs. Watts [that Hazel, because of the distortion in his mind at the time, does not see]. Alongside the satire the narrator directs at her, then, we can perhaps see in Mrs. Watts some of the power—and perhaps at

[47] Ibid.

[48] Robert Donahoo, "O'Connor and *The Feminine Mystique*: The Limitations That Reality Imposed on the Subject of the Feminist Business: Re-Reading Flannery O'Connor," *On the Subject of the Feminist Business: Re-Reading Flannery O'Connor*, ed. Teresa Caruso (New York: Peter Lang, Inc., 2004) 23.

[49] Gordon, *The Obedient Imagination*, 105.

[50] Prown, *Revising Flannery O'Connor*, 7.

[51] Ibid., 14.

least a pinpoint of light—of the sort that is suggested by her name.[52]

Whether she provides a "pinpoint of light" or not, there are deeper powers ebbing and flowing in the moment of Leora's appearance in the novel. Gordon, Gentry, and Prown all make convincing arguments. Juxtaposing Leora with Jesus in Hazel's mind suggests something more, and the *Wise Blood* manuscript does provide a "key" to the understanding of Leora. The fact that O'Connor introduces Leora as a caricature, a collage of body parts, and an assemblage of objects makes a reading of the text that is Leora an exercise in pictorial analysis. In the moment that the narrative pauses and Hazel views first the collage of body parts, next, the assemblage of objects on the bureau, and, lastly, Leora, complete, in the "yellowish" glass of the mirror—that moment contains the essence of the story of Lea found in the *Wise Blood* manuscript. Though, rather than mute Lea's voice as Prown contends, O'Connor has elected to express that voice stylistically employing pictorial text.

WISE BLOOD MANUSCRIPT LEA

In folders 39 to 44 of the manuscript, O'Connor writes and rewrites the scene of Hazel Motes, a discharged WWII soldier embarking from the taxi upon his arrival at his sister Ruby's apartment. He approaches a porch where a blonde-haired woman is seated, slowly swinging back and forth on a porch swing. In each rewriting of this scene, Hazel mistakes the woman for his sister, Ruby; he does not seem to remember what she looks like. Lea is this woman, and at this point, her looks are not unlike those of the published Leora. With each revision, however, she becomes more and more attractive until finally, in folder 45, Hazel thinks of her as beautiful. It is here, I think, that O'Connor decides to construct a Love-Goddess. Folder 57 features a scenario where Hazel rises early in the morning, puts on his black wool hat, and goes down to the third floor and knocks on Lea's door. Wearing a kimono, she opens the door wide and Hazel walks right into her apartment, which consists of one room featuring a hanging light bulb shaded by a paper bag, a bed on one side, and a stove and sink on the other. He fumbles around trying to make it clear what he has come for and they both

[52] Gentry, "Wise Women, Wise Blood," 314.

fall on the bed. The last image in this particular revision is the black wool hat at the foot of the bed.

Folders 80a–c are redrafts of that early-morning visit written from Lea's point of view. Lea is startled by the sight of Hazel, lying prone, asleep in the porch swing when she opens the door to retrieve her bottle of milk from the doorstep. The reader is treated to a physical description of Hazel Motes and to Lea's internal argument about whether he could qualify as "cute" or not. Lea picks up her milk, returns to her apartment, checks her cleavage in the mirror, begins to make breakfast, and leaves her door open a crack so that she can hear Hazel if he stirs. Lea returns to the mirror to apply her makeup, and O'Connor writes and rewrites what she sees there—sometimes in stream of consciousness, sometimes in the narrative voice. What she sees in the mirror terrifies Lea. Again, O'Connor calls upon Freud by confronting Lea with her doppelgänger.[53] It is both her own face and something else—something terrifying. For her entire life, she has had this sort of out-of-body experience. As she sits there, her entire life runs through her mind. She is the daughter of a fallen Baptist minister. She runs away from home at 16 with a man who promises her a job at a beauty parlor in Macon. In the end, there is no job and she realizes she probably never even knew the man's real name. Writing this backstory from Lea's point of view makes this a different kind of novel from the stylistic published version of *Wise Blood.* Prown is right. Because of the stylistic techniques, however, Lea's *presence* continues to exist in the final rendition of the novel.

MRS. LEORA WATTS: THE PUBLISHED VERSION

The published introduction to Lea/Leora begins this way. Sinfulness is Hazel Motes's intent when he disembarks from the train. It is the only way he can escape the "wild ragged figure" of Jesus moving "from tree to tree in the back of his mind."[54] In this quest, Hazel's first stop is the "MEN'S TOILET. WHITE," where he encounters the name of Mrs. Leora Watts written on the bathroom wall. "He went into a narrow room lined on one side with washbasins and on the other with a row of wooden stalls. The walls of the room had once been a bright cheerful yellow but now they were more nearly green and were decorated with handwriting and with various detailed

[53] "The Uncanny."

[54] O'Connor, *Collected Works*, 11.

drawings of the parts of the body of both men and women."[55] On the wall of his stall, he reads:

> Mrs. Leora Watts!
> 60 Buckley Road
> The friendliest bed in town!
>
> Brother[56]

In this novel, Hazel Motes seems to be always moving, even in dreams when he is asleep—sitting backward on the train, walking back and forth the length of the train station, and finally in the taxi on the way to "the friendliest bed in town!" At this point, a pause occurs in the narrative as Hazel is dropped off by the taxi and stands, stilled, on porch of Mrs. Watts's house, where a "warm glow" of light shines "in the front window" behind which she inhabits her friendly bed.[57] It is from this vantage point that the nervous Hazel examines Leora in the manner in which he would a collage, his eyes moving from body part to body part and then finally resting on the entirety of the vision as reflected in a mirror.

> He went up on the front porch and put his eye to a convenient crack in the shade, and found himself looking directly at a large white knee. After some time he moved away from the crack and tried the front door. It was not locked and he went into a small dark hall with a door on either side of it. The door to the left was cracked and let out a narrow shaft of light. He moved into the light and looked through the crack.[58]

Mrs. Watts was sitting alone in a white iron bed, cutting her toenails with a large pair of scissors. She was a big woman with very yellow hair and white skin that glistened with a greasy preparation. She had on a pink nightgown that would better have fit a smaller figure.[59] When Leora ignores him standing in the doorway, he walks into the room. "He went in and stood looking around him. There was nothing much in the room but the

[55] Ibid., 15.
[56] Ibid., 16.
[57] Ibid., 17.
[58] Ibid.
[59] Ibid.

bed and a bureau and a rocking chair full of dirty clothes. He went to the bureau and fingered a nail file and then an empty jelly glass while he looked into the yellowish mirror and watched Mrs. Watts, slightly distorted, grinning at him. His senses were stirred to the limit."[60]

Mrs. Leora Watts, sitting on her bed calmly clipping her toenails and grinning, brings to mind Manet's 1863 painting entitled *Olympia*. To the public "who thronged to the salon of 1865 where *Olympia* was first shown, she embodied sin, both moral and artistic. In spite of her name which implied legitimate descent from the mountain of the gods she seemed to most spectators not a comfortably acceptable nude but a naked, provocative tart."[61] What seemed so embarrassing about Olympia was her "bold acceptance of her own nudity" and "the challenge of her impertinent little face."[62]

If the only sight that we had been provided of Leora was that of her entire body framed by the mirror, we could assume that O'Connor presented her in this way to evoke the historical interpretation of Manet's prostitute in the way that she did with Hazel Motes and the *vanitas* still life. In the case of Leora, however, the collage-like offering of body parts and the objects assembled on her bureau are part of the *composition* that is Leora. The fact that Leora's story is told by objects as well as by the picture in the mirror sets her apart from Manet's *Olympia* and moves analysis of the pictorial technique from the nineteenth to the twentieth century. In collages being created in the fifties, such as those by Romare Bearden, body parts are often exaggerated and composed of a variety of materials.[63] The viewer of such a collage is at first inclined to move her eyes from limb to limb rather than to take in the body as a whole. This reinforces the idea of the body as a

[60] Ibid.

[61] Mina Curtiss, "Manet Caricatures: *Olympia*," *The Massachusetts Review* 7/4 (Autumn 1966): 725–52, 727.

[62] Ibid., 728.

[63] It is interesting to note that "Bearden had struggled with two artistic sides of himself: his background as a

'student of literature and of artistic traditions, and being a black human being involves very real experiences, figurative and concrete' (Witkovsky 1989: 266), which was at combat with the mid-twentieth century 'exploration of abstraction' (267). His frustration with abstraction won over, as he himself described his paintings' focus as coming to a plateau" (Romare Bearden).

construction of separate, but interchangeable, parts. Since Leora is viewed through Hazel's eyes, this, as Sarah Gordon points out, robs Mrs. Watts of her personhood and puts her in the same category as the carnival girl in a coffin which the twelve-year-old Hazel Motes had to pay a nickel to view. He remembers her looking like a "skinned animal." This early experience made a profound impression on the young Hazel, and when he decides to lose his virginity, and since he considers sex a sin, he is on the lookout for a prostitute. A prostitute is Flannery O'Connor's satiric version of a Love-Goddess—an upended version—of course. O'Connor has presented her to us in exactly the same way that Ivory Flakes marketed the "fresh" girl. This marketing technique of deconstructing and then reconstructing the female body was rampant in mid-century America. In 1950, Al Capp conducted a similar exercise—vending a woman's body part by part for the purpose of engaging readers of his cartoon strip *Li'l Abner*. O'Connor, reader of magazines and newspapers and connoisseur of comics, could not have missed this.

On November 13, 1939, *Life Magazine* featured a picture of Mrs. Guinn Granbury wearing shorts and showing her kneecaps, which seemed to have faces like cherubs. Readers sent in photographs of various family members who also had kneecaps that looked like faces. Contests began to spring up across the United States in which women competed for the label of prize kneecaps. Eleven years later, in 1950, Al Capp used the idea of the quest for the best face-like kneecap in an unprecedented yearlong storyline in which Li'l Abner falls in love with the picture of a girl's knee that seems to sport a face. Falling in love with a knee seems absurd, but McLuhan contends this is not necessarily so: "In a specialist world it is natural we should select some single part of the body for attention. Al Capp expressed this ironically when he had Li'l Abner fall desperately in love with the pictorial scrap of a woman's knee."[64] Li'l Abner explains it this way, "It got a kinda **expreshun** on it—but how kin yo' fall in love of th' expreshun on a gal's **knee?**" He answers his own question, "Why **not**?—some boys falls in love wif th' expreshun on a gal's **face. Ah** is a knee man!!" He looks out of the cartoon frame at the reader and explains, "This torn pitcher of a gal's knee were in th' bindin' of mah 'Fearless Fosdick' comical book. Soon's ah finds th' **rest** o' her—ah'll **marry** her!! Ah loves her madly—on account she got

[64] McLuhan, *The Mechanical Bride*, 98.

such a (sigh) sweet expreshun on her knee!!"[65] We know that the young Flannery O'Connor was a cartoon aficionado and we can safely assume, I think, that she followed newspaper comics as well as the cartoons in the *New Yorker*. In the last comic strip of the series, readers are treated to a picture of the fully assembled picture of Li'l Abner's Love-Goddess. It is a poster announcing the appearance of "Lillian Bustle—the 195 lb. bundle of Joy starring in 'The Merry Whirl of 1902' at the New Opera House."[66] In some ways, Lillian Bustle looks like a stereotypical dancehall girl. She is wearing a strapless tiny costume which snugly fits over voluptuous breasts and hips that billow above and below her miniscule waist. It is important, however, in any construction of a Love-Goddess that the illusion of girlish innocence is created. In so doing, Al Capp has given Lillian a frilly parasol, a bow around her neck, and layers of ruffles that encircle her lower hip area. She is wearing long gloves that cover her arms but do not have any hands (suggesting the further seductive baring of body parts), a garter around her right thigh, and, of course, high heels. Here again, we see the assemblage of Marshall McLuhan's Love-Goddess: she is (hilariously, I'm sure) identified by a number—her weight, "195 lb."; she has been presented as an assortment of perfect body parts—a "bundle of joy." At this point in the yearlong adventure, Li'l Abner finds himself in the old opera house, where he reconstructs the poster on the stage floor, and he wonders aloud,

> She was at th' **NEW** opera house in **1902!!** Wonder whar she is, **NOW?**
>
> [A voice answers him from the darkened theater.]

[65] Al Capp, *In Search of the Perfect Woman...Li'l Abner: Dailies. Volume 16. 1950*, (Princeton, NJ: Kitchen Sink Press, 1993) 15. And so Li'l Abner sets out "obsessed by an idiotically conceived project, following an impractical plan of action, blundering into a series of desperate life threatening adventures with various corrupt and depraved villians" (Frank Stack, "Introduction," *In Search of the Perfect Woman*, 5). Frank Stack's description of Capp's project sounds somewhat like the plot of *Wise Blood.* Stack sums up Capps's "epic" as a "noble try" at an "all-encompassing critique of American society" (Stack, *In Search of the Perfect Woman*, 6). He ends his essay with the declaration, "Al Capp created The Great American Comic Strip." The Li'l Abner comic strip ran for forty-three years from 1934 to 1977.

[66] Ibid., 166.

She's **still** here, Honey!!

??—But, this is th' **old** opera house!!

[*Mise en scene* and in the foreground, we see the rather ample derriere of a cleaning woman scrubbing the floor on her hands and knees. In the background, Li'l Abner is on his knees onstage, arms outspread, and shirtless, a pose which displays his bulging pectorals.]

Opera houses **change**, in 48 years—and so do beautiful showgirls. **I'm Lillian Bustle!!**

?!—So **yo'** is **Lillian Bustle!**—th' bootiful chorus gal whose kneecap ah fell in love with becuz it had sech **a sweet ex-preshun!!** Wal—gulp!—ah is **still** loyal to yore kneecap. Ah will marry **it**—an' th' **rest** o' yo' kin-sob!!—come along!!

I may have lost my figger, Dearie—but my kneecap is still **just** as pretty!!

Yo' is wrong Ma'm!! [In the fore ground of this panel Li'l Abner is putting his coat and hurriedly leaving.] Y'ars of scrubbin' floors done **wore away** th' lovely expreshun on 'em. Goo'bye!!

[Lillian Bustle is in the background, again *mise en scene*, standing in the puddle created by her floor scrubbing.]

Sigh-h!!—I guess they are a li'l tired-lookin'. G-Good-bye Dearie!![67]

Lillian Bustle's face, in the last panel of this yearlong saga bears the lines of regret, of a certain innocence. She stands watching Li'l Abner scurry out of the theater. She is overweight, double chinned, breasts sagging, legs thickened, and she wears a torn and patched dress. If one examines just the singular panels of the collection of comic strips that make up the Lillian Bustle story, it becomes evident that any panel that features a part of Lillian's body also features a recognizable part of Li'l Abner. We are very aware that the story is being told through Li'l Abner, the voyeur. Though Al Capp

[67] Ibid., 166–67.

upends the Love-Goddess cliché in a way that is comedic at the expense of aging, overweight women, I argue that O'Connor does not use Mrs. Leora Watts as comic fodder in the same way. The text that is Leora is a text that gives voice to class and gender discrimination. I base this contention on a pink nightgown, a nail file, and an empty jelly glass. These items provide the illusion of innocence that McLuhan deemed necessary as one of the interchangeable parts of this construction.

The only chair in her room is filled with cast-off dirty clothes, suggesting that even though her bed is the *friendliest* in town, friendliness is not defined by sitting and chatting. This kind of relationship with other people has fallen by the wayside in Leora's life. The ill-fitting pink nightgown that she wears is, most certainly, part of O'Connor's satirical take on the Love-Goddess assemblage as described by McLuhan. In the 1950s, pink "baby doll" or "shortie" pajamas were the rage. Putting Leora in an ill-fitting pink nightgown serves two purposes. On the surface, the idea of a pink, frilly nightgown on an aging, overweight, not-too-clean prostitute would be funny to O'Connor's readers,[68] particularly those who appreciated the reveal of Al Capp's Lillian Bustle, reduced to a scrubwoman on her hands and knees, overweight and in rags at the end of the comic-strip saga.

Quite frankly, employing this kind of humor is what urges feminist critic Katheryn Hemple Prown to make the claim that O'Connor attempted "to ally herself with a masculinist[69] theory and literary cultural tradition" and that she carried out a "gradual silencing of a female-sexed voice" that dominated the manuscript.[70] However, Leora's pink nightgown makes a different kind of statement, one that can be validated (but does not need to be) by the "sexed" voice of Lea in the manuscript. In the 1940s and '50s, the idea that pink[71] was a feminine color took on popularity. "*Dior* pink"

[68] Imagine this sort of garment on Manet's *Olympia*.

[69] Prown writes, "By *masculinist*, I mean any political, cultural, or literary construct that privileges male subjectivity, perpetuates an androcentric world view, endorses patriarchal social relations, and denies or obscures female subjectivity and agency" (2).

[70] Prown, *Revising Flanner O'Connor*, 2.

[71] Interestingly, before this, there is some evidence that it was the other way around. Pink was masculine and blue was feminine (Marco Del Giudice, "The Twentieth Century Revival of Pink-Blue Gender Coding: A Scientific Urban Legend?" *Archive of Sexual Behavior* 41 (2012): 1321–23).

became a catch phrase in fashion, and Mamie Eisenhower loved the color so much that it was "often referred to as 'Mamie Pink.'"[72] Choosing a color for Leora, and making that color pink, makes a comedic as well as a cultural statement. The comedy, again, is obvious. I contend, though, that making this color choice addresses ideas beyond the obvious, outside of the frame, and reflects, as Marshall Bruce Gentry explains, O'Connor's "psyche" or how "the parts of the psyche other than conscious intellect are involved in the creation of [her] fiction.... She probably would not have become a great writer if she had not been comfortable with the idea that there are important things in her fiction of which she is completely unaware."[73] One of the pleasures of reading the 2,000-plus pages of the *Wise Blood* manuscript is that we can chart the ideas that O'Connor had while creating a specific character. Leora starts out pretty much like she appears in the published version of the novel, but then O'Connor writes a compelling backstory for her, the gist of which I have described previously: she finds it necessary, at age 16, to escape an untenable situation at home and runs off with the first man who will promise her a different life. She, of course, is used and abused by this man just as she has been by her father. The pink nightgown would have fit this more hopeful young version of Leora. She, aware of color trends by means of women's magazines, would certainly have chosen pink. We can only surmise what is not told about the years that intervene between the young girl who sits in front of her mirror applying eye makeup and the vacant-faced woman viewed in the mirror by Hazel Motes, resident

[72] Amy Burger, "Preserve the Pink: How to Enhance the Retro Bathroom's Charm," *St. Louis Post-Dispatch*, September 2, 2011. "Mamie Eisenhower loved the color so much that she redecorated the private quarters in the White House in pink—so much that reporters called it the 'Pink Palace,' and the bathroom in her Gettysburg retirement home was pink down to the cotton balls. For this reason, the color was often referred to as 'Mamie Pink'" (Burger).

[73] Marshall Bruce Gentry "O'Connor as Miscegenationist," *Flannery O'Connor in the Age of Terrorism: Essays on Violence and Grace*, eds. Avis Hewitt and Robert Donahoo (Knoxville: University of Tennessee Press, 2010) 191. Gentry writes, "Some literary criticism is written as if everything O'Connor ever wrote were a sort of term paper, in which everything there is intended and almost everything has its documentable source" (191). He goes on to make a strong argument on how the concept of the *Johari Window* applies to creative writing and to O'Connor specifically.

of "the friendliest bed in town." Standing at Leora's bureau, Hazel Motes fingers "a nail file and then an empty jelly glass while he look[s] into the yellowish mirror and watch[es] Mrs. Watts slightly distorted, grinning at him. His senses were stirred to the limit."[74] Regardless of whatever trappings of femininity Mrs. Watts has left behind, we know she still cares about her nails. Hazel first views her clipping her toenails. The lone nail file on her bureau and the clippers in her hand attest to the fact that there is some semblance of female vanity that still resides in Leora. Dominant fashion trends of any decade stimulate discussion and research, and nail treatment in the 1940s and 1950s is distinctive and quite recognizable. At some time in her life, any woman could quite possibly own a manicure kit. The fact that Leora possesses only two items that would have been included in such a kit speaks of the poverty and bleakness of her life. Neither "Lea," who yearned for a job in a beauty parlor,[75] nor "Laverne,"[76] secretary to a podiatrist, both earlier renditions of the diminished Mrs. Leora Watts, would have displayed such attenuated circumstances. The empty jelly glass only serves to further this impression. The actual existence of the jelly glass on the bureau suggests a kind of domesticity that we do not usually associate with Mrs. Watts. There was once jelly in that glass that must have been purchased as a grocery item. The jelly glass humanizes Leora. Maybe she makes peanut butter and jelly sandwiches. Given the distorted smile Hazel views in the "yellowish" glass of the mirror, the glass must have been brought into the bedroom from a kitchen, in all probability filled with some type of alcohol. Seeing Leora in this way gives us the impression that she is looking out of the frame at us in the way that the PhD girl did in the undergraduate cartoon. This, however, is not the case. The PhD girl is looking right at us, ready to jump out of that cartoon panel alive and engaged in the swirl of life. Due, most likely, to whatever was in the jelly glass, Leora's eyes are not focused—distorted. She is static and captive in her framed mirror, a sort of death-in-life positioning.

The woman of reduced means that exists on the outside of society has often been fodder for American literature: Hester Prynne,[77] Sarah Good and

[74] O'Connor, *Collected Works*, 17.

[75] File 80b *Wise Blood* Manuscript, O'Connor Collection, Georgia College.

[76] "A Stroke of Good Fortune."

[77] Hawthorne, *The Scarlett Letter*.

Sarah Osborne,[78] Sethe and Pilate,[79] Myrtle Wilson,[80] to list just a few. Hazel Morse,[81] the main character of Dorothy Parker's most famous story, "Big Blonde," published in 1929, is one of these women. Hazel Morse's hair and body build replicates that of Mrs. Leora Watts. She is "is severely disappointed in her marriage and, perhaps primarily for that reason, goes through a succession of men, all of whom bore her. She attempts suicide and fails, ending up, at the story's conclusion, returning to drink as her solace."[82] One could conjecture that the life of Hazel Morse, captured by Dorothy Parker, is very similar to what is not said about the span of time that occurs between the young Lea of the manuscript and the old-age Leora Watts. What I consider remarkable about the Parker story is the pictorial moment when Nettie, Mrs. Morse's maid, views her as she has arranged herself the morning after overdosing on "veronal tablets."

> But when she [Nettie] had done the living-room and stolen in to tidy the little square bedroom, she could not avoid a tiny clatter as she arranged the objects on the dressing table. Instinctively, she glanced over her shoulder at the sleeper, and without warning a sickly uneasiness crept over her. She came to the bed and stared down at the woman lying there.
>
> Mrs. Morse lay on her back, one flabby, white arm flung up, the wrist against her forehead. Her stiff hair hung untenderly along her face. The bed covers were pushed down, exposing a deep square soft neck and a pink nightgown, its fabric worn uneven by many launderings; her great breasts, freed from their tight confiner, sagged beneath her armpits.[83]

[78] These women exist in the court documents of the Salem Witch Trials. In 1953, Arthur Miller included them in *The Crucible*, which was first called *The Chronicles of Sarah Good*.

[79] Toni Morrison, *Beloved* and *Song of Solomon*.

[80] F. Scott Fitzgerald, *The Great Gatsby*.

[81] Sarah Gordon posits that this similarity of character names between Hazel Motes and Hazel Morse is nothing short of "remarkable."

[82] Gordon, *The Obedient Imagination*, 63.

[83] Parker, "Big Blonde," 169.

Again, just as we did with the PhD cartoon, we have an example of O'Connor adjusting, changing, rearranging, and emphasizing elements that exist in another artist's (Parker's) depiction so that in her pictorial arrangement they tell a different story. Just as Parker does, O'Connor's image of Leora is viewed by another character while he (Hazel) or she (Nettie) handles the personal items on the "bureau" or "dressing table," respectively. Instead of having Hazel Motes look backward over his shoulder at Leora, O'Connor uses a mirror to frame her, which means that Hazel is, in fact, "seeing" her backward. Also, O'Connor limits the items on the bureau to two and uses them as part of the text that is Leora. O'Connor uses the pink nightgown in a way that suggests the "great breasts, freed from their tight confiner" rather than describing them specifically. Hazel Morse's bed serves as a virtual coffin since she has so carefully planned her demise and the discovery of her body. Even though Leora's bed has been described as "the friendliest" in town, it is in this bed that Hazel has a flashback of the naked woman in a coffin he viewed in a carnival sideshow that he attended with his father. The men in the tent "were looking down into a lowered place where something white was lying, squirming a little, in a box lined with black cloth. For a second, he thought it was a skinned animal and then he saw it was a woman. She was fat and she had a face like an ordinary woman except there was a mole on the corner of her lip, that moved when she grinned, and one on her side."[84]

Of course Hazel experiences this hypnogogic memory while he is in bed with Leora Watts because Leora's bed holds her and those who enter it in the grip of a certain death. It is both the death of spirituality that Hazel desires and the death of sensuality that accompanies the Assembly-Line Love-Goddess. In this moment, Hazel subconsciously realizes that Leora's actions are machine-like and mechanical, like those of Eliot's typist, and when he is done, she goes about her business as usual. It is after this realization that he moves on to a different kind of sexual encounter with the young Sabbath Lily Hawks.

Dorothy Parker's pictorial text creates a sort of portrait of Mrs. Hazel Morse that is viewed by Nettie looking back "over her shoulder"[85] at a kind

[84] O'Connor, *Collected Works*, 35.

[85] The implications of that backward look are too complex to be discussed here. The fact that Nettie is an African American earning her living by creating the

of still life, at Mrs. Morse splayed in a death-in-life pose. O'Connor's pictorial moment, however, is designed in a very modern way. Her tableau includes a framed "picture" seen through the eyes of a viewer, Hazel Motes, who is, of course, also a character in the drama, as well. His handling of the objects on the bureau serves to link them and him to the text of the tableau. Robert Rauschenberg invented the idea of presenting this kind of collection, as such, in the mid-1950s. He called it a "combine," which was "a form of painted assemblage using found objects" which "evolved naturally from the collage basis of his earlier work."[86] We visualize Leora much the same manner. She enters our awareness seen through the male gaze as a collage of body parts that take shape in the "yellowish glass" of the mirror connected to the objects on the bureau beneath the mirror again by Hazel, who is at once a voyeur and a client. This collection of figures and objects provides the composition of O'Connor's Love-Goddess tableau or assemblage.

SABBATH LILY HAWKS: AN ALL-AMERICAN BELLADONNA

Here is Belladonna, the Lady of the Rocks,
The lady of situations.[87]

The metamorphosis of Sabbath Motes to Sabbath Lily Hawks is a fascinating procedure that can be traced in the *Wise Blood* manuscript in ways that the development of Ruby and Leora cannot. Ruby is eliminated completely from the novel and is rejoined "as is" in "A Stroke of Good Fortune." There is a period of time missing between the young Lea of the manuscript and the old Leora of the published version of *Wise Blood.* In the transformation of Sabbath, however, we can follow physical changes as O'Connor's thought processes progress, particularly by following the changes in her footwear, which evolves from a cast-off, scuffed pair of men's shoes to a tiny pair of high heels fit for dancing, neither of which exist in the final version of Sabbath Lily.

illusion of living for the dead-in-life drunken Mrs. Morse is a matter that demands explication, but not in this work.

[86] Marco Livingstone, *Pop Art: A Continuing History* (New York: Thames & Hudson, 2001) 22.

[87] Eliot, *The Waste Land*, 39.

SABBATH MOTES: THE MANUSCRIPT SABBATH

Flannery O'Connor's vision of herself as a modern prophet, albeit female, allows her to create a female to bear her prophetic message in her initial drafts of *Wise Blood*[88]. Adding a female to the literary equation, writes Nancy Armstrong in *Desire and Domestic Fiction*, introduces "a whole new vocabulary for social relations, terms that attach precise moral value to certain qualities of mind."[89] Armstrong defines the "whole domain over which our culture grants women authority: the use of leisure time, the ordinary care of the body, courtship practices, the operation of desire, forms of pleasure, gender differences, and family relations."[90] Historically, preaching is another way that marginal and otherwise "othered" women can speak out in a patriarchal context. Huldah, Miriam, and Anna, biblical female prophets, all live and prophesy from domestic spaces, Deborah, the judge, being the exception.[79] Sarah Gordon writes, "The final version of Sabbath therefore fits the stereotyped or the paradigmatic female who is an obstacle in the male's spiritual quest. It matters not that Sabbath, presented as a caricature of the femme fatale, exudes no real sensuality or eroticism."[91] I contend that the

[88] Karl Martin, "Flannery O'Connor's Prophetic Imagination," *Religion & Literature* 26/3 (Autumn 1994): 33–58. Martin makes the compelling argument that O'Connor regarded her own voice as prophetic. He writes: "When therefore, O'Connor wrote, 'The prophet is a realist of distances...' and the 'prophetic vision' is 'peculiar to any novelist' (O'Connor, *Collected* Works, 817), she was expressing a key element of her aesthetic theory and religious faith. She was also expressing a carefully formulated understanding of her role as a writer. As a writer O'Connor believed herself a prophet. When she identified herself as a writer who sees 'from the standpoint of Christian orthodoxy' (804), she clarified the distinctiveness of her prophetic vision in the modern world" (33).

[89] Gordon, *The Obedient Imagination*, 4.

[90] Nancy Armstrong, *Desire and Domestic Fiction* (New York: Oxford University Press, 1987) 26. Because of that "prophetic imagination" attributed to her most eloquently by Martin, Bruggemann, and Asals, and in concert with biblical precedent, in her creation of Sabbath Motes, O'Connor builds on the Hawthorne form by combining the domestic sphere. In fact, it is in the domestic dominion that the young Sabbath Motes, in much the same way as the young Tarwater, is shaped and molded in accordance with her future mission. O'Connor's domestic dominions are laced with violence, pain, and loss.

[91] Gordon, *The Obedient Imagination*, 98.

original designation of Sabbath Motes as prophetic message bearer has not been altered, and that the key to this can be found in the analysis of the scene where Sabbath Lily holds the "new jesus" in her arms during yet another pictorial pause in the narrative text. Before we examine this particular moment, it is important to explore the Sabbath of the manuscript.

Sabbath Motes, as a nursling, was baptized by fire when she was carried out of her burning home in the arms of her mother's lover, Sedman, a man who was considered either Jesus or the Devil incarnate, depending on who was telling the story. The fire was set by Sabbath's father upon discovering the two lovers together. Sedman, undamaged by the flames that devoured Sabbath's mother, shared the child's upraising with a crazy woman, Miss Webbie Lee, who some people said was just out of the sanitarium. Miss Webbie Lee performed her maternal duties either by forgetting Sabbath's existence and almost causing her to starve to death for lack of mother's milk or by focusing obsessive attention upon her every move and even following her up and down the hallways of her school. Like the young Tarwater, Sabbath Motes hears the whispered voice of a Stranger hiding behind a fence. He tells her she is the ugliest woman alive, but she knows she is not and walks on. Obviously, this is "a startlingly different Sabbath, one who, for a time at least, occupied a central space in the novel and on whom a great visionary burden was laid."[92] She is a powerful woman whose "strange power, especially the power of her gaze, is repeatedly emphasized in the [*Wise Blood*] drafts."[93] Sabbath's speech is otherworldly. She speaks in metaphor and pronouncement. In all probability this is due to the fact that she exists in actuality with one foot in the world of the streets of Taulkinham and the other in the spiritual world of her visions, which often feature a weeping Jesus. She is the vessel for His message—"Jesus will bear your pain."

Sabbath's congregation is in constant motion. People willfully come and go, singly and in groups on the streets of Taulkinham, through which Sabbath moves in no particular direction, passing out religious pamphlets, stopping and starting, O'Connor writes, like a horse that is being led. In fact, there is direct correlation between this woman and a horse, as O'Connor caricatures her with equine features—large bones, a mulish face, her eyes slanted backward like a horses'—rather like some of the characters

[92] Ibid.
[93] Ibid., 111.

found in her early cartoon drawings. An assortment of dispirited pieces of clothing, both male and female, hang from her broad frame forming a collage of pieces that, when collected on her body, jar the visual sensibilities as well as the gendered context, making the perception of any sense of accord in her adornment impossible. Though faded, her blouse is a feminine satin—soft, silky, draping—reminiscent of a more frivolous time or perhaps just a cast-off from a more frivolous person. Her skirt has been made by cutting and sewing a pair of man's trousers and reshaping them into a female garment. Her socks—black—and her shoes—a man's—discarded. Enoch Emory comments that he has a pair just like them but he never thought he'd see them on a woman. Enoch and Hazel first catch sight of Sabbath Motes while they are standing in the street listening to the spiel of a street vendor selling potato peelers. At first they see a tall woman led by a small man along the margins of the crowd, passing out pamphlets. The woman suddenly ceases her evangelizing and pushes herself forward through the group of people to watch intently the man in a straw hat and pheasant shirt demonstrate the peelers. The crowd drifts away leaving Sabbath, Hazel, and Enoch still attentive to the sales pitch. She reaches into her pocket and pulls out a knotted handkerchief from which she extricates two quarters. She holds out the money to the salesman, saying, "Give me one of them." He irritably informs her that the peeler sells for "a buck fifty." Hazel, watching the woman closely, thinks he sees her hand begin shaking as she withdraws it and she orders the man accompanying her—her father Asa—to give the salesman fifty cents more—he refuses and leads her off. Just as in the published version, Hazel buys a peeler and follows the woman and man in order to present it to her. In the street scenes, Sabbath carries a croker sack from which she feeds her followers (Hazel and Enoch) with sandwiches—just jelly, no chicken, and in which she keeps the vegetable peeler and the religious pamphlets. These objects, which form an assemblage of resonant artifacts, appear and reappear in the various drafts as strange ciphers that punctuate Sabbath's interactions with the other characters. In the published version, it is telling that Sabbath Lily desires a kitchen utensil when she has no kitchen in which to peel her potatoes. The 1950s kitchen was the heart of the home. In the fledgling world of the TV sitcom, it is the place of the woman—the heart of the family. In 1959, it was commodified and presented to Nikita Kruschev by Richard Nixon as a visual symbol of the American way of life. It is the place where Hazel Motes hugged the chifforobe that formerly held his mother's clothes. It is what

Sabbath Motes of the manuscript has and Sabbath Lily does not. Attaching herself to the nebulous Hazel Motes, "playing house" seems to be Sabbath Lily's only hope of attaining that kitchen. When Hazel buys the potato peeler and presents it to each of the Sabbaths, he is presenting her with an object from the world of the 1950s woman—a world created just for her by advertisers. Sabbath Lily immediately begins to scheme, but Sabbath Motes tosses the peeler in the croker bag to be taken to her kitchen, which serves for her as a domestic space of refuge and where she can see the roosters in the backyard from her backdoor.[94] She retreats to this kitchen when Asa and neighbors bring in a drunk and sick Hazel Wickers from off the street. They have placed him in what one would think is her most intimate domestic space—on Sabbath's bed, but it is in the kitchen that the reader is allowed to experience a vision through Sabbath's consciousness.[95] Up to this point readers have only Asa's description of Sabbath in the throes of ecstasy, but here we are seeing the prophetic images sent by God through her eyes, creating an uncharacteristic communion between character and reader. Controlling the panic she feels by images of the invasion of buzzing of flies circling, as it were, Hazel's deadened body, Sabbath stabilizes herself by shedding tears for Jesus. She imagines two of her selves facing one another and she is suddenly aware of the duality that Asals describes as between Jesus and self. In this manner she is able to stabilize and to minister to the suffering Hazel Motes. The "rather compelling description of Sabbath's struggles in this passage," Sarah Gordon writes, "certainly provides a full portrait of a female visionary."[96] Sabbath Motes offers the possibility of a redemptive female presence in *Wise Blood* and elsewhere where her spirit animates a cast of O'Connor's prophetic characters.

[94] When I read about this kitchen in the *Wise Blood* manuscript, I could not stop myself from picturing it as the kitchen at Andalusia in Milledgeville, Georgia, which is intact and open to the public today. Every time I visit, I imagine Flannery and Regina O'Connor sitting around the small wooden table having their morning coffee.

[95] Frederick Asals claims the type of transformative visionary writing that happens in the passages that describe Sabbath's visions would be characteristic of O'Connor's later writings (Asals, *The Imagination of Extremity*, 207).

[96] Gordon, *The Obedient Imagination*, 112.

SABBATH LILY HAWKS

Chapter 3 of (the published) *Wise Blood* opens with a view of the sky. "The black sky was underpinned with long silver streaks that looked like scaffolding and depth on depth behind it were thousands of stars that all seemed to be moving very slowly as if they were about some vast construction work that involved the whole order of the universe and would take all time to complete. No one was paying any attention to the sky."[97]

This representation of a universe that bears the evidence of an eternal order is juxtaposed with a street scene where a group of bystanders are not looking at the sky, but are watching the demonstration of a potato peeler by a street salesman. Sabbath Lily and her father Asa Hawks, a "blind" street evangelist, are a part of that assembly. By creating Sabbath Lily as a child of 15, O'Connor links her to the ranks of literary fifteen- or sixteen-year-old girls who navigate a fallen world and live by their wits—Richardson's Pamela, Rousseau's Julie, Miller's Abigail Williams, Morrison's Denver, Dickens's Little Dorrit, and Harriet Jacob's slave girl.[98] It is important to this text to note that this is *not* one of O'Connor's prepubescent narrators or experientially stifled PhD women. Sabbath Lily stands alone in the O'Connor lexicon of female characters. In the short stories, we hear about the adventures of girls of this age, but only in a second-hand way (i.e., Mrs. Freeman's daughters).[99] Even though she is also not the female prophet of the manuscript, Sabbath Lily does have a message to relate that is, in its way, darkly prophetic. When she "preaches" to Enoch and Hazel, her sermonette is very similar to that of Sabbath Motes's except that when delivered by Sabbath Motes, the story has an eerie otherworldly quality, and when delivered by Sabbath Lily, it is rather like the narration of the plotline of a horror movie or a Poe story. The tale in Sabbath Lily's mouth takes a place in the modern world where it stands as a reflection on or metaphor for the fallen world—the landscape of the wasteland.[100]

[97] O'Connor, *Collected Works*, 19.

[98] *Pamela, Julie or the New Heloise, The Crucible, Beloved, Little Dorrit, Diary of a Slave Girl.*

[99] "Good Country People."

[100] Sarah Gordon writes, "The influence of Eliot's 'Waste Land' on O'Connor's first novel is unquestioned. In 1984 Sally Fitzgerald argued that, although certainly Poe and West and Sophocles had influenced *Wise Blood*, 'it was

> "Listen," she said in a louder voice, "this here man and woman killed this little baby. It was her own child but it was ugly and she never give it any love. This child had Jesus and this woman didn't have nothing but good looks and a man she was living in sin with. She sent the child away and it come back and she sent it away again and it come back again and ever' time she sent it away, it come back to where her and this man was living in sin. They strangled it with a silk stocking and hung it up in the chimney. It didn't give her any peace after that, though. Everything she looked at was that child. Jesus made it beautiful to haunt her. She couldn't lie with that man without she saw it, staring through the chimney at her, shining through the brick in the middle of the night."[101]

Along with this story and Sabbath Lily's other stories, it is easy to imagine that her early life has not been much different than Sabbath Motes's. It seems clear here that she, herself, has suffered abuse and neglect of some kind and her desperation to seduce Hazel Motes comes from the fact that Asa has told her he is leaving her behind and she will have to find a way to fend for herself essentially on the streets.[102]

Sabbath Lily, like Eliot's Belladonna, is a "lady of situations" who would "adopt any posture, deploy any weapon—even her neurosis—in the game of seduction."[103] We first meet Sabbath Lily, her knit cap pulled down tight around her ears, on the outskirts of a crowd handing out pamphlets in

Eliot and his "Waste Land" who provided for [O'Connor's first impetus to write such a book as *Wise Blood* at all]' ("The Owl and the Nightengale")" (Gordon, *The Obedient Imagination*, 102).

[101] O'Connor, *Collected Works*, 28.

[102] In "Wise Women, Wise Blood," Marshall Bruce Gentry writes that Sabbath Lily's "sense of desperation seems justified when one notices how little Hazel reacts to her tale of the evil grandmother. And Sabbath's sense that she is unloved becomes especially poignant when one considers the moral she draws from her tale of the dead baby hanging in the chimney: that 'good looks' are insufficient—they 'ain't enough' (*Collected Works*, 29). Sabbath surely feels she is ugly and that, even if she were not ugly, no amount of comeliness would be enough to make anyone love her" (Gentry, "Wise Women, Wise Blood," 321).

[103] Philip Sicker, "The Belladonna: Eliot's Female Archetype in *The Waste Land*," *Twentieth Century Literature*, 30/4 (Summer 1978): 769–808, 425.

the wake of Asa Hawks, who is wearing dark glasses and carrying a white cane. She notices Hazel Motes in the crowd just as he notices her, and she begins (in Hazel's words) giving him "the eye." Staring hard at Hazel Motes, the first words out of her mouth to him, her eyes glittering "like two chips of green bottle glass," are "I seen you."[104] She immediately initiates her "game of seduction" which begins (as it has for young women for thousands of years) by ignoring him. Love-struck, he buys her the potato peeler and follows her across town to give it to her. Again, Li'l Abner and his global quest for the perfect woman come to mind. Hazel's quest, accompanied by his verbose sidekick Enoch Emory, allows O'Connor to introduce the "unreal city" of Taulkinham and some of its residents. She propels these characters through comic advance-retreat "situations," essentially performing the moves of an age-old courtship ritual, not unlike those portrayed in the PhD cartoon, until, finally, the time comes when Hazel and Sabbath Lily both decide (separately) it is time to "seal the deal" and consummate the seduction. O'Connor composes a pictorial cartoon panel of the seduction scene. In it we see Sabbath Lily pull out the weapons, familiar to every American girl, or every girl, for that matter, in an attempt to lure her prey into her web. The car provides the frame for her cartoon panel. The action begins while Hazel, again in motion, driving the car, seemingly led by a cloud shaped in the stereotypical "image of God," is on his way out of the "unreal city" into the pastoral countryside, the place where he feels at home. He, like any American boy, is testing his new car

> to see how well it worked on the open road. The sky was just a little lighter blue than his suit, clear and even, with only one cloud in it, a large blinding white one with curls and a beard. He had gone about a mile out of town when he heard a throat cleared behind him. He slowed down and turned his head and saw Hawk's child getting up off the floor onto the two-by-four that stretched across the seat frame. "I been here all the time," she said, "and you never known it." She had a bunch of dandelions in her hair and a wide red mouth on her pale face.[105]

[104] O'Connor, *Collected Works*, 22.
[105] Ibid., 66.

The frame freezes Sabbath Lily lounging in full seduction regalia and we experience a Thurber-esque moment. Marshall McLuhan has provided a kind of yardstick by which to measure this mythical seduction mode, which is particularly American—the Coke ad, Abraham Lincoln's mother, and a Ziegfeld girl. Now, the American girl as portrayed by the Coke ads has always been an archetype. No matter how much thigh she may be demurely sporting, she is sweet, nonsexual, and immaturely innocent. Her flesh is firm and full, but she is pure as a soap bubble. She is clean *and* fun loving.

> In short, she is a cluster-symbol which embraces at one extreme Abe Lincoln's "All that I am and all that I hope to be I owe to my darling mother," and, at the other, Ziegfeld's dream of the glorified American girl as a group of tall, cold, glittering mechanical dolls. The gyrations and patterns assumed by these dolls in a revue is intended to convey, if not Beatific Vision, at least a Jacob's Ladder of angelic hierarchies linking earth and heaven.[106]

In the way of the cartoonist, O'Connor has chosen just two unmistakable identifying characteristics—the "bunch of dandelions in her hair" and Sabbath Lily's "wide red mouth—to illustrate her satirical unending upending of the mythical modern American girl-next-door. (Sabbath literally lives next door to Hazel Motes in Mrs. Flood's boarding house.) Embarking on her seduction scheme, Sabbath, operating within her means, is trying to look alluring like the girls in the ads. Where a girl in an advertisement places a gardenia behind her ear, Sabbath Lily dons a weed. In fact, she perches a "bunch" of dandelions in her hair. One wonders, just where would a "bunch" go? How would she hold it in place—bobby pins, a rubber band? Any way the imagination configures it, a "bunch" would be strange and unwieldy springing out from her head. In the late 1940s, women were wearing more luxurious hairstyles that featured hair accessories: ribbons, clips, bobby pins, and flowers. Sabbath Lily was on the cutting edge of style, but, of course, she could only use what she had at hand—dandelions. In the creation of the upended Sabbath Lily as Belladonna of the wasteland, makeup becomes very important as the word "'belladonna' refers to

[106] McLuhan, *The Mechanical Bride*, 118.

a cosmetic made from the toxic leaves of the plant used to dilate the pupils of the eyes of women. The modern mind is inclined to associate the use of such a cosmetic with seduction and prostitution (painted women)."[107] In O'Connor's stripped-to-the-bone fashion, she only adorns the character's lips. In the late 1940s, all shades of red lipstick were popular and it was important that lips looked sensual, full, soft, and inviting. If a girl's lips did not quite measure up, she could draw in fullness using her lipstick. This practice could account for O'Connor's use of the word "wide" as a descriptor for Sabbath Lily's red mouth. Sabbath Lily is a predator, lurking in the backseat of the car, ready and waiting to devour Hazel Motes with her wide red lips. Her behavior is familiar, predictable, and studied. Her very existence depends on the trapping of Hazel Motes, and she is willing to stop at nothing to accomplish this.

Sabbath Lily, the cartoonish "lady of situations," is reminiscent of O'Connor's undergraduate cartoons, but Eliot's "Belladonna" is also described as "Lady of the rocks," which recalls da Vinci's painting of the Madonna and child entitled *Virgin of the Rocks*. The da Vinci depicts the Madonna and Christ Child in a moment of repose framed by a rocky grotto and accompanied by John the Baptist and an angel. Sabbath Lily's moment of repose occurs closed in the shared bathroom of a boarding house. Sabbath retreats to her "grotto" carrying the bundle that has just been handed to her by Enoch Emory. She opens it and there is a pause in the action of the novel which O'Connor actually measures in minutes. Sabbath Lily sits on the side of the bathtub and stares at "what is in her lap."

> Two days out of the glass case had not improved the new jesus' condition. One side of his face had been partly mashed in and on the other side, his eyelid had split and a pale dust was seeping out of it. For a while her face had an empty look, as if she didn't know what she thought about him or didn't think anything. She might have sat there for ten minutes without a thought, held by whatever it was that was familiar about him. She had never known anyone who looked like him before, but there was something in him of everyone she had ever known, as if they had all been rolled into one person and killed and shrunk and dried.
>
> She held him up and began to examine him and after a minute her hands grew accustomed to the feel of his skin. Some of

[107] Sicker, "The Belladonna," 424.

> his hair had come undone and she brushed it back where it belonged, holding him in the crook of her arm and looking down into his squinched face. His mouth had been knocked a little to one side so that there was just a trace of a grin covering his terrified look. She began to rock him a little in her arm and a slight reflection of the same grin appeared on her own face. "Well I declare," she murmured, "you're right cute, ain't you?"
> His head fitted exactly into the hollow of her shoulder. "Who's your momma and daddy?" she asked.[108]

Something happens to Sabbath Lily in these ten minutes of silent repose. She is changed. She is not transfigured or transformed, but rather within her a merging has taken place. Enclosed in the bathroom of a boarding house, she begins to take on the characteristics of the archetypal female—the mother—the Madonna. She, however, is a dark Madonna, a Madonna in a fallen world cradling a dead baby that resembles "everyone she had ever known." This mummy, this "hollow man," is all that this modern Madonna has to offer to the world. Sabbath Lily is not a sanctified virgin, however. In fact, she is "both a victim and a seductress."[109] Her liaison with Hazel is a kind of prostitution—a calculated sexual coup in which the payoff will provide a kind of security for her, a "place to be," even if that place is a rat-colored car with a plank for a back seat. She emerges as an upended Madonna—a "Belladonna," which is Eliot's "poetical label for this woman...an archetype of his own naming which he inserts into Madame Sosotris' Tarot pack. Her name is well chosen, for the belladonna is actually a poisonous plant—a modern substitute for the hyacinth and a fitting flower to grow in the wasteland. This 'Lady of the Rocks' appropriately inhabits a landscape of 'red rock' and 'stony rubbish.'"[110]

Marked by the fire through which Sabbath Motes of the manuscript is carried as a child, at this moment Sabbath Lily truly becomes a universal image, a vessel, a crucible. She holds an amalgamation of all of the women of *Wise Blood*, all of the American women who have wandered the wasteland on the margins in American literature. She is O'Connor's "Belladon-

[108] O'Connor, *Collected Works*, 104.
[109] Sicker, "The Belladonna," 427.
[110] Ibid., 424.

na," her modern woman, reproductively sterile, sexually mechanical and calculated.[111] The last time that we see Sabbath Lily, she is looking in a mirror at "what is" and figuring how to "fix" it.

> In the minutes of Sabbath Lily' repose, Hazel Motes had awakened with a plan. It had come to him like his decision to buy a car, out of his sleep and without any indication of it beforehand: he was going to move immediately to some other city and preach the Church Without Christ where they had never heard of it. He would get another room there and another woman and make a new start with nothing on his mind.[112]

At the same time that Sabbath is figuring out her next move, Hazel is preparing to run away and to reinvent himself...again. While packing his duffle, he manages to avoid touching the Bible "that had sat like a rock in the bottom of the bag for the last few years."[113] Digging his hand into the bag, he touches the case that contains his mother's glasses. He cannot stop himself from opening it and putting the glasses on. Immediately, "the wall that he was facing moved up closer and wavered."[114] The movement of the wall signals that Hazel Motes, along with the reader, has left the "actual" and has moved into a mystical or Divine province: the anagogical realm. Readers, positioned behind Hazel's shoulder, as it were, see on that wavering wall a mirror that serves as a palimpsest between reality and the Divine.

> There was a small white framed mirror hung on the back of the door and he made his way to it and looked at himself. His blurred face was dark with excitement and the lines in it were deep and

[111] Ralph Wood describes Sabbath Lily as one of the "antihuman forces that would come to dominate late modern life.... Though Sabbath appears to be a nymphomaniac, there is a certain innocence about her sexuality.... She thus plays the role of a hell-bound slattern who might as well enjoy the ride. We can surmise that Sabbath Hawks is far from an erotomaniacal nihilist because of the fierce and instructive ghosts, as O'Connor called them, that still haunt her. She is obsessed, for example, with the murder of a child, a killing she reports as though it belonged to someone else, when it clearly pertains to her own experience" (Woods 237).

[112] O'Connor, *Collected Works,* 105.

[113] Ibid.

[114] O'Connor, *Wise Blood,* 186–87.

> crooked. The little silver-rimmed glasses gave him a look of deflected sharpness, as if they were hiding some dishonest plan that would show in his naked eyes. His fingers began to snap nervously and he forgot what he was going to do. He saw his mother's face in his, looking at the face in the mirror. He moved back quickly and raised his hand to take off the glasses but the door opened and two more faces floated into his line of vision; one of them said, "Call me Momma now."
>
> The smaller dark one, just under the other, only squinted as if it were trying to identify an old friend who was going to kill it.[115]

The murky images in the mirror appear to be not unlike a doubly exposed photograph, revealing simultaneously the existence of the actual and the anagogical. Inside the white frame, first and foremost, there is Hazel, inhabited and haunted after literally donning his mother's "gaze" in the form of her glasses. The scope of our vision widens, and we see that Hazel has been joined by Sabbath Lily, holding the mummified "new jesus." We have before us a dark pantomime of the Holy Family. Horrified at the revelation of this "vision," Hazel smashes the mummy against the wall and throws it out the door. The shrunken man's head pops and the mummy is exposed as an assemblage of "trash…[that] spray[s] out in a little cloud of dust,"[116] bearing wordless witness of the broken condition at the center of the modern world, as well as marking the center of this emotionally charged novel. Sabbath Lily shouts, "You've broken him and he was mine! You didn't have to throw him out, I might have fixed him!"[117] Sabbath Lily, as Belladonna, "lady of situations," disregards the fact that the mummy is filled with trash, obviously dead—long dead—and yearns to "fix" him. The Madonna offers the Christ Child to the fallen world; Belladonna can offer only a pile of trash, a dust pile. This is O'Connor's snapshot of the modern condition as it is.

The women of *Wise Blood*, more often than not, have been considered as comic relief. While O'Connor casts a satiric eye on most of her charac-

[115] O'Connor, *Collected Works*, 105–106.

[116] Ibid., 106.

[117] Ibid.

ters, these women are imbued with both satire and subtle nuance. O'Connor has used the pictorial techniques of assemblage and collage to design Leora and Sabbath Lily so that they stare out at us from the pages of the novel and demand that we, as readers, heed their complexity and hear their voices. The backstories in the manuscripts verify that she had these nuanced characters in mind as she painstakingly created the *Wise Blood* women. We cannot ignore the textual signals that O'Connor placed before us.

Chapter 4

Snapshot: The Prophet with the "Camera Eye"

A "Realist of Distances"

The prophet is a realist of distances, and it is this kind of realism that you find in the best modern instances of the grotesque.[1]

This chapter will examine Flannery O'Connor's pictorial text from the perspective of both style and technique. In *The Violent Bear It Away*, she adopts the mode of the medium photography in a way that differs slightly from what she has done previously with linotype, painting, assemblage, and drawing. Thus far, we have examined the evolution of O'Connor's pictorial text by considering the meaning conveyed by the arrangement of figures in a single-panel cartoon and the contextual significance found in literary tableaux, montage, and assemblage. In this chapter, we will examine O'Connor's use of the pictorial "camera eye." Shaping the pictorial text in the novel by using the conventions of photography creates a sense of instantaneity and reality largely because of the properties of the medium itself. Mid-twentieth century photography had a built-in sense of duality, since, during this time, every amateur photographer received her developed photos accompanied by a negative. As one stared into these negatives, one could imagine an altered or parallel reality—one that is very like but inverse of our own. The very nature of photographic "reality" comes into play in this novel as well. Can we ever trust that a photograph is merely freezing time, or is there always something more—some hint of another reality? Sensibility of these properties of the medium—the "camera eye," a dual nature, and the questions about reality—provided a veritable base upon which O'Connor structured her pictorial pauses in *The Violent Bear It Away*. Her purpose for fashioning the verbal snapshots that punctuate this narrative is to make plausible the existence of a Divine reality that exists alongside the reality

[1] *Photography Changes Everything*, ed. Marvin Heiferman (New York: Aperture, 2012).

that we know. Already embedded in the choice of a snapshot are the characteristics she needs to fuel this effort to show the reality of the Divine—to create a sense of wonder at the miraculous which threads through everyday life. In order to scrutinize her pictorial technique, then, we must begin by looking at the properties of each of the elements and how their combination in her textual snapshots lifts the veil for a second revealing of a Divine Plan that is terrible and, more often than not, inexplicable.

THE "CAMERA EYE"

In his novel *The 42nd Parallel*, John Dos Passos introduces "a device he called the Camera eye" which reveals "the uncanny effect of the camera's eye on the writer's field of vision." The stylistic device owes a debt to "the prevalence of photographs" in "the world of the brownie snapshot" and presents in the narrative a new sort of time, a *stopped time*, a fragmented and reassembled time, [like that which is] visible in Duchamp's *Nude Descending a Staircase*." These "fissures in time's narrative flow, which the photograph calls to our attention, have left expanding and disquieting gaps in our perceived notions of reality, of a familiar and stable world."[2] O'Connor's particular use of the verbal snapshot allows her to call into question the very fabric of reality in her second novel, *The Violent Bear It Away*. It allows her to not only stop or fragment time in her pictorial pauses, but to move backward and forward in a way that diverges from that painterly technique employed in *Wise Blood*. "At key moments," Jill Baumgaertner writes, "—often at the height of a story's crisis, sometimes at a moment of foreshadowing—O'Connor clicks the camera and catches a strange picture. In the seventeenth century, these would have been called *emblems*; the fictive moment containing them, the emblematic moment."[3]

Seventeenth-century "emblems were the pictorial representations of scriptural truth—highly exaggerated yet literal."[4] By using photographic technique to refine her pictorial pauses in the narrative, O'Connor is able to reveal the presence and the influential power of a Divine realm that exists simultaneously with the historical or concrete realm in which we all live. In the emblematic moment both realms become crystalized, concrete, and

[2] Wright Morris, "The Camera Eye," *Critical Inquiry* 8/1 (Autumn 1981): 1.

[3] Baumgartner, *A Proper Scarring*, 20.

[4] Ibid.

readers are able to "see" clearly as the two spheres converge. This revelatory event is often followed by an interpretation of this Divine snapshot. These moments are short and the reader is left wanting a greater understanding of what exactly she has just witnessed.

Photography—seeing events through the camera eye—was on O'Connor's mind as she worked out the first drafts to *The Violent Bear It Away*. The camera is an ever-present object in these drafts of the scenes of this novel. The main character in the early manuscript is a young boy, a serious reader of newspapers who, much like in descriptions of O'Connor's father, Edwin O'Connor, almost always wears a camera hanging around his neck. As the story commences, we find the boy standing over a burning cross that has appeared overnight in his father's rock garden. This image, appearing and reappearing, dominates the early pages of the manuscript of *The Violent Bear It Away.* John Martin, the boy, is the schoolteacher John Martin Rayber's oldest son, and he appears only in the manuscript, not in the published version of the novel. He is a collector of snapshots, particularly those that document catastrophic events, either man-made, like automobile accidents, or acts of God, like hurricanes. He classifies them under headlines of his own design. An only child, in whom his parents expend a great deal of expectation, John Martin has begun to dream of defying them and becoming a shoe salesman. John Martin Rayber Sr., a self-defined radical, encourages the young John Martin to take numerous pictures of the burning cross in case the newspaper reporters, whom he has already called about the incident in his rock garden, might need them. He is secretly pleased that his particular brand of humanism has evoked this visual eruption of hatred.[5] John Martin Jr., the boy behind the camera, eventually

[5] The Rayber family consists of Rayber Sr., a teacher in these early drafts, his wife, Rufus Johnson, an ex-con whom Rayber is trying to rehabilitate, and John Martin (Rayber Jr.), when Francis Marion Tarwater arrives on the scene bearing many of the same characteristics that he has in the published novel. Eventually, Johnson disappears from the text, destined to become the club-footed juvenile delinquent in "The Lame Shall Enter First," and John Martin morphs into a boy called B. K. who is still carrying a camera, but rather than taking news-worthy photos, he is obsessed with manipulating his family into posing for snapshots, in tableaux. He behaves as a writer might, arranging his characters *mise en scene,* in the confines of a snapshot, or as a cartoonist might, arranging her characters to fit the strictures of a single-panel cartoon. Of course, young Tarwater will have none of B.

leaves the manuscript revisions. However, I contend that the camera eye never really leaves the novel. The confinements of the snapshot remain embodied and embedded in O'Connor's pictorial narrative of events in the novel.

Images in the published novel are often arranged as if viewed through the "camera eye." The feeling that someone is watching him pervades the thoughts of Francis Marion Tarwater as he sits on Rayber's doorstep after having set his great-uncle's house on fire. He cannot look up at the stars of which he "was unpleasantly aware...[because] they seemed to be holes in his skull through which some distant unmoving light was watching him. It was as if he were alone in the presence of an immense silent eye."[6] The young Tarwater, who has nowhere else to go, has been drawn to this spot by some invisible force. Rayber opens the door, steps aside, and in that moment Tarwater experiences a snapshot-like vision of Bishop, Rayber's mentally impaired son, who will never function above the level of a five-year-old. In this flash of anagogic awareness, the boy envisions Bishop simultaneously in two realms: the historical present and the mystical somewhere else.[7]

> Tarwater was not looking at him [Rayber]. His neck had suddenly snapped forward and he was staring straight ahead over the schoolteacher's shoulder. He heard a faint familiar sound of heavy breathing. It was closer to him than the beating of his own heart. His eyes widened and an inner door in them opened in preparation for some inevitable vision.
>
> The small white-haired boy shambled into the back of the hall and stood peering forward at the stranger. He had on the bottoms to a pair of blue pajamas drawn up as high as they would go, the string tied over his chest and then again, harness-like, around his neck to keep them on. His eyes were slightly sunken

K's maneuverings and eventually the camera disappears from the manuscript. B. K. morphs into Bishop and the only photos that make the final cut in the published novel are those that are composed as part of a material reality—news photos, a photo of Bishop's mother.

[6] O'Connor, *Collected Works,* 385.

[7] O'Connor describes this awareness as having "vision that is able to see at different levels of reality in one image or one situation" or that which has "to do with Divine life and our participation in it" (O'Connor, *Mystery and Manners,* 72).

> beneath his forehead and his cheekbones were lower than they should have been. He stood there dim and ancient, like a child who had been a child for centuries.[8]

This pause in the narrative action enables the reader to see Bishop close-up, just as she would if she were holding a snapshot of the boy in her hand. Bishop "peers forward" as he might if someone had been trying to attract his attention to take a picture. In the final sentence of the pictorial moment, O'Connor performs a "qualitative transformation"[9] and establishes the child's simultaneous existence in two realms, the present and in some "ancient" mystical past. The idea of exhibiting these photographic moments in the text of the novel offers the reader an experience similar to that created by the gallery-like atmosphere of *Wise Blood*, where the narrative flows and then pauses, allowing the picture to formulate in the mind of the reader. The photographic moments in *The Violent Bear It Away* differ in that they carry an intimacy between the reader and the pictorial that does not exist within the confines of O'Connor's first novel—a photograph can be held in one's hand. The distance between the world inside the frame and the world outside of it is not nearly as great as that which exists between the gallery visitor and the painting hanging before him. Even if the viewer of a painting is looking at that painting by means of a book of photographs of paintings, Benjamin writes, those reproductions lack "one element: its presence in time and space, its unique existence at the place where it happens to be."[10] The original painting exists in a gallery or a cathedral somewhere and "the situations into which the product of mechanical reproduction can be brought may not touch the actual work of art, yet the quality of its presence is always depreciated."[11] The "aura" of the work of art "withers." The photograph can reside in an album of like personages or objects which rests in the viewer's lap and can be cited at will. Benjamin explains the feeling of familiarity and closeness that results from this as, in this era of reproduction, the "desire of contemporary masses to bring things 'closer' spatially and humanly, is just as ardent as their bent toward overcoming the unique-

[8] O'Connor, *Collected Works*, 388.

[9] Benjamin, *Illuminations*, 225.

[10] Ibid., 220.

[11] Ibid.

ness of every reality by accepting its reproduction."[12] This "destroys" its "aura" by adjusting "reality to the masses and the masses to reality."[13] Understanding this, O'Connor, by emphasizing the duality built into the photograph, is trying to restore the desire for "aura" and authenticity in modern society, grown complacent with reproductions. To O'Connor, the photograph carries with it the aura of the mystical. It is a frame viewed through the camera eye that could hold what seems to be the known, but upon examination could reveal what might not appear to the naked eye.

THE HOMILETIC NOVEL

O'Connor's use of the properties of photography to create a sort of pictorial double vision of the historical and the divine simultaneously structures *The Violent Bear It Away* as a modern homiletic text much like those of the nineteenth-century "evangelical exhorters" who sought to "reorient" readers' "lives according to a typological script where allegory functions to link the personal to the Christian universal and to permit a lived experience of unified historical and biblical time."[14] By evoking this "uniquely American form of literary representation," O'Connor joins these "interventionist" ranks that include a number of Hawthorne's "scribbling women," whose "cumulative work...developed through the narrative strategies and theological innovations as they were adapted to the particularity of New World experience. Designed to draw readers and auditors into the frame of homiletic allegory, this representational system bound an intensely optic imagination with specific Protestant strategies for engaging visual, oral, and literary texts."

Rather than writing allegory in the manner of John Bunyan, O'Connor veers more toward a narrative realism in the establishment of her homiletic text.[15] The determination of the real is what separated eighteenth- and nineteenth-century homiletic realism from its secular counterpart. Homiletic reality "assumes the fallibility of an epistemology degraded by

[12] Ibid., 223.

[13] Ibid.

[14] Jackson, *Word*, 232.

[15] In *The Word and Its Witness: The Spiritualization of American Realism*, Gregory Jackson makes the argument that this type of novel be recognized under the auspices of American literary realism.

humanity's culpability in original sin."[16] This imbues characters with "volition and moral agency [which] contest[s] literary realism's assumption that reality exists apart from experience." In fact, "religious adherents of homiletics assumed personal experience, illuminated by spiritual insight, to be the measure of reality."[17] This evokes a "distinct temporal frame" which exists "alongside diegetic time."[18]

"Characters of the novel," Ian Watt writes, "can only be individualised if they are set in a background of particular time and space."[19] However, time in the homiletic novel can be measured in spiritual events occurring during the individual's lifespan, such as "atonement, conversion, redemption, spiritual rebirth, and above all pilgrimage."[20] This arrangement as employed by O'Connor, however, does not cause confusion in Francis Marion Tarwater, who, to begin with, is not exactly sure of his own age. As is the case with everything else he knows, his knowledge of his age is based on his uncle's measurement of historical time: "His uncle had said he was seventy years of age at the time he had rescued and undertaken to bring him up; he was eighty-four when he died. Tarwater figured this made his own age fourteen."[21] He is not unaware of the concept of historical time, it is just that biblical history exists side by side with material reality. "His uncle had taught him Figures, Reading Writing, and History beginning with Adam expelled from the Garden and going on down the presidents to Herbert Hoover and on in speculation toward the Second Coming and the Day of Judgment."[22]

There is no difference between the visible realm and the spiritual realm for the young Tarwater in the same way that there was none for his great-uncle who raised him. In chapter 8 of *The Violent Bear It Away*, O'Connor shows us, through the eyes of young Tarwater, what it is like when the veil thins and one is able to "see" both "countries," the visible and the invisible. At this point, the boy is denying his mission—to baptize Bishop—so that

[16] Ibid., 9.

[17] Ibid., 11.

[18] Jackson, "Game," 457.

[19] Ian Watt, *The Rise of the Novel: Studies in Defoe, Richardson, and Fielding* (Berkley: University of California Press, 2001) 21.

[20] Jackson, "Game," 457.

[21] O'Connor, *Collected Works*, 331.

[22] Ibid.

the milieu in which he exists is "enveloping him in a strange waiting silence. It seemed to lie all around him like an invisible country whose borders he was always on the edge of, always in danger of crossing. From time to time as they had walked in the city, he had looked to the side and seen his own form alongside him in a store window, transparent as a snakeskin. It moved beside him like some violent ghost who had already crossed over and was reproaching him from the other side."[23] Evidence of this country beyond the veil not only appears in store windows (a significant mid-century appellation), but young Tarwater sees the "silent country" reflected in Bishop's eyes.

This does not hold true for Rayber, who was kidnapped by Mason Tarwater when he was seven years old. Rayber was under the influence of his uncle only a short time as compared with the young Tarwater, who was with him for fourteen years. Rayber speaks with the voice of the "real" world, the world of historical time. It is the voice of the world with which O'Connor's readers are well acquainted. It is the world of science, psychology, testing, and measurement. Rayber is not unaware of the spiritual world and once believed in its realness. He accuses his uncle of ruining his life by introducing him to the Divine Plan:

> "You pushed me out of the real world, and I stayed out of it until I didn't know which was which. You infected me with your idiot hopes, your foolish violence. I'm not always myself. I'm not al..." but he stopped. He wouldn't admit what the old man knew. "There's nothing wrong with me," he said. "I've made myself straight."

Raybur has extricated the belief in the spiritual realm from his consciousness. If occasionally it does erupt, he categorizes it as dreams and fancy. Young Tarwater is the vessel in which spiritual time and diegetic time are in the process of converging, causing violent outbreaks in the boy.

The idea of convergence was basic to O'Connor's interpretation of theology. At the time she was writing *The Violent Bear It Away*, O'Connor was working on the stories that appeared in her second volume of short stories, *Everything That Rises Must Converge*. According to Driggers and

[23] Ibid., 429.

Dunn,[24] the publication date for the title story falls right in the middle of her work on the novel. In choosing this as the title for her book of short stories, in which all of the stories deal with the subject of inter- and intra-human confluence, O'Connor pays tribute to Pierre Teilhard de Chardin's phenomenological theory of spiritual convergence. In opposition to the idea of "survival of the fittest," Teilhard believed in the evolution of consciousness. Matter, in his interpretation, is prepossessed to arrange and rearrange itself into groupings which over time become more complicated. Teilhard contends that as the groupings become more complex, the level of consciousness elevates. Instead of further evolution of the human species, an evolution of human consciousness will take place. O'Connor wanted ultimately to accept Teilhard's "Law of Complexity/Consciousness," stating that all human consciousness would eventually evolve, rise, and converge into one great body of Christ, so consequently she creates characters that "as they gravitate toward the divine milieu, carry out their duty in unison with the fulfilling plan of all cosmic perfection."[25] For O'Connor, however, it is the observation of what happens before that convergence—the "rising" and the violence that ensues—that interests her. She clearly defines the conditions involved in creating a pictorial record of this process when talking to young writers about her own writing:

> I often ask myself what makes a story work, and what makes it hold up as a story, and I have decided that it is probably some action, some gesture of a story that is unlike any other in the story, one that indicates where the real heart of the story lies. This would have to be an action or gesture which was both totally right and totally unexpected; it would have to be one that was both in character and beyond character; it would have to suggest both the world and eternity. The action or gesture I'm talking about would have to be on the anagogical level, that is, the level which has to do with the Divine life and our participation in it. It would be a gesture that transcended any neat allegory that might have been

[24] Stephen G. Driggers and Robert J. Dunn with Sarah Gordon, *The Manuscripts of Flannery O'Connor at Georgia College*, Athens: University of Georgia Press, 1989.

[25] Giannone, 160.

intended or any pat moral categories a reader could make. It would be a gesture which somehow made contact with mystery.[26]

Of course, the gesture "unlike any other in the story" in *The Violent Bear It Away* is the drowning of Bishop and the subsequent rape that follows.[27] In this one novel, O'Connor has given us the voice of the devil, a baptism marked by violence and death, and the rape of a young boy—all images torn from the headlines—headlines like those collected by the boy photographer John Martin of the manuscript, and headlines like those clutched to Mrs. Greenleaf's bosom[28] in the story "Greenleaf": "'Oh Jesus, stab me in the heart!' Mrs. Greenleaf shrieked. 'Jesus stab me in the heart!' and she fell back flat in the dirt, a huge human mound, her legs and arms spread out as if she were trying to wrap them around the earth."[29]

Mrs. Greenleaf praying for the healing of the world uses the newspaper photographs and headlines as evidences of the presence of Satan. In this story, as she does in *The Violent Bear It Away*, O'Connor echoes nineteenth-

[26] O'Connor, *Mystery and Manners*, 111.

[27] In *The Word and Its Witness*, Gregory Jackson addresses this same kind of graphic preaching used by the nineteenth-century Protestants to bring religious narratives to life, creating a cathartic experience for the unbeliever. Elizabeth Cady Stanton, in her autobiography, recalls the preaching of Charles Finney and its indelible effect on her mind even though the event she describes occurs sixty-five years before she published her book. She writes: "One evening he described hell and the devil and the long procession of sinners being swept down the rapids, about to make the awful plunge in the burning depths of liquid fire below, and the rejoicing hosts in the inferno coming up to meet them with the shouts of the devils echoing through the vaulted arches. He [Finney] suddenly halted, and, pointing his index finger at the supposed procession, he exclaimed: 'There, do you not see them!'" (Stanton in Jackson, 258).

Finney's "Edwardsian legacy provides yet another instance of the imaginative capacities Social Gospel audiences possessed for turning visually oriented language into vivid realities" (Jackson, 258). This type of visuality pervades *The Violent Bear It Away.*

[28] Flannery O'Connor, "Greenleaf," *Collected Works* (New York: Literary Classics of the United States, 1988). This short story was published in 1955 again, right in the middle of O'Connor's work on *The Violent Bear It Away.*

[29] O'Connor, *Collected Works*, 506–507.

century evangelist Charles Finney as she exhorts, "There do you not see them!"

In *The Word and Its Witness*, Gregory Jackson uses *Pilgrim's Progress* and *Little Women* to show how the Divine and historic intersect in the characters and events that take place in the homiletic novel. In *The Violent Bear It Away*, O'Connor provides for us two modern-day prophets within whom the two realms converge. Old Tarwater sets the stage for his great-nephew. The Lord has given Old Tarwater "rage of vision."[30] The old man's history is narrated in words that are performed with the cadence and litany of the King James Version.

> [Old Tarwater had been called to be a prophet] in his early youth and had set out for the city to proclaim the destruction awaiting a world that had abandoned its Saviour. He proclaimed from the midst of his fury that the world would see the sun burst in blood and fire and while he raged and waited, it rose every morning, calm and contained in itself, as if not only the world, but the Lord himself had failed to hear the prophet's message. Then one morning he saw to his joy a finger of fire coming out of it and before he could turn, before he could shout, the finger had touched him and the destruction he had been waiting for had fallen in his own brain and his own body. His own blood had been burned dry and not the blood of the world.[31]

The Lord does not spare his chosen. In fact, He tries them sorely. Old Tarwater sees it as his responsibility to relate the story of his transformation over and over to his great-nephew alongside the stories of American history that he chronicles in the process of educating him. As the old man does not hesitate to point out,

> the Lord had seen fit to guarantee the purity of [the boy's] upbringing, to preserve him from contamination, to preserve him as His elect servant, trained by a prophet for prophesy. While other children his age were herded together in a room to cut out paper pumpkins under the direction of a woman, he was left free for the pursuit of wisdom, the companions of his spirit Abel and Enoch

[30] Ibid., 332.
[31] Ibid.

> and Noah and Job, Abraham and Moses, King David and Solomon, and all the prophets from Elijah who escaped death, to John whose severed head struck terror from a dish.[32]

Old Tarwater realizes that it is crucial that the boy be educated in the hardships that accompany the Lord's Service. The boy must be ready when he is called. Readying him necessitates beginning at the beginning and convincing the boy that he has been chosen. The tale of the boy's birth must be repeated as legend—as a tale like the tales from the Bible. The boy was the issue of a whore who was the daughter of a whore. The old man's tale works as planned on the boy, who, "when he walked through the woods and came upon some bush a little removed from the rest,...would stop and wait for the bush to burst into flame."[33] The boy expects his prophethood to begin without the finger of flame that touches the prophet and burns him dry before he is ready to take up his mission. He is sure his mission will be made clear and that he will not be required to follow in the footsteps of his great-uncle.

Besides educating Francis Marion Tarwater in the ways and means of prophecy, Old Tarwater has been commissioned by God to baptize Rayber's "dim-witted" child, Bishop. The boy is pretty sure that this will not be his first mission. *He* is destined for greater things. However the old man's litany plays and replays in the boy's head after his great-uncle has departed from this earth, "Jesus is the bread of life," and, Old Tarwater would add, "as soon as he died, he would hasten to the banks of the Lake of Galilee to eat the loaves and fishes the Lord had multiplied"[34]—forever. The boy turns all of this over in his mind as he digs the hole under a fig tree in which to bury his uncle, "because the old man would be good for the figs."[35] This mention of the fig tree underlines O'Connor's subtle but deft "homiletic practice"[36]—that of designing an event that has meaning in both

[32] Ibid., 340.
[33] Ibid., 355.
[34] Ibid., 21.
[35] Ibid., 343.
[36] In "A Game Theory of Evangelical Fiction," Gregory Jackson writes, "By the term homiletic I mean to caption those specifically didactic texts and practices intended to engage believers in the development of their faith through models alluding to but moving beyond the Bible itself."

realms. The tree brings to mind Jesus's parable of the fig tree in which He warns his disciples, "Know ye that the kingdom of God is nigh at hand."[37] He continues: "Take heed to yourselves, lest at any time your hearts be overcharged with surfeiting, and drunkenness, and cares of this life, and so that day come upon you unawares. Watch ye therefore and pray always that ye may be accounted worthy to escape all these things that come to pass, and to stand before the Son of man."[38]

Adroitly placing us at Old Tarwater's graveside, significantly under a fig tree, O'Connor reveals the "vertical axis of divine causality intersecting the historical axis of human history,"[39] which will be the young Tarwater's destiny regardless of the fact that he abandons his digging, gets drunk, and attempts to hide from the eye of the Lord. These recounted teachings of the old man set the backdrop for the revelations that are rendered in flashes, using a pictorial technique that mimics the snapshots that are to follow in the novel.

WHY DOES O'CONNOR USE THE PHOTOGRAPH AS HER PICTORIAL MEDIUM IN *THE VIOLENT BEAR IT AWAY*?

In the opening to a particular speech in 1936 given in Atlanta at an American Legion Convention, attended by both Mary Flannery and her mother, Edwin O'Connor "directly recalled France, even its language, and then reconstructed, through [his] power of syntax, a moment at the battlefront itself. In this, and in so many other references to France, Ed in his speeches is NOT silent about the burden of memory he had borne from World War I. The little girl could hear her father's inner struggle being turned into controlled rhetoric, feeling into art."[40]

Recognition of the capacity to turn "feeling into art" was one of Edwin O'Connor's greatest legacies to his young daughter. The father, an amateur photographer, was able to deliver to his audiences verbal snapshots of what

[37] Luke 21:31 (King James Version).

[38] Luke 21:34–36 (King James Version).

[39] Jackson, "Game," 455.

[40] William Sessions, "Flannery O'Connor and Freud: The Meaning of Life in Death" (Lecture, Emory University, Aquinas Center, Atlanta, November 19, 2012, 10).

he saw on the WWI battlefield[41] and to verbally fashion a pictorial text which allowed his listeners and little Mary Flannery to share his experiences.

Photographs render reality from a variety of perspectives, allowing for a certain unemotional distance to exist between the narrator and an event. Often, events are narrated with a voyeurism that had become increasingly familiar in the mid-twentieth century when O'Connor was writing. The photographic image changed the way Americans responded to the world. Iconic images that marked turning points in the twentieth century were published in *Look* and *Life* magazines and were delivered to American homes and displayed in grocery stores and drugstores weekly. *Life* "made all of life, literally and figuratively, its province. The photographs revealed a visible world seen and shared by all human beings."[42] These photographs bonded Americans by establishing a sense of common visual history, and the appearance and reappearance of these iconic photos in American history texts ensures the perpetuation of a "real" shared culture. This is the familiar paper world in which Old Tarwater in *The Violent Bear It Away* finds himself an occupant, the sole subject of a "study" submitted by his nephew Rayber to a "schoolteacher magazine." The "stench" of his nephew's behavior has "reached heaven and the Lord Himself had rescued the old man. He had sent him a rage of vision, had told him to fly," taking with him an orphaned infant, Rayber's nephew, his great-nephew, "to the farthest part of the backwoods and raise him to justify his Redemption."[43] The boy Tarwater is raised at Powderhead, his great-uncle's farm, separated from the his-

[41] "The First World War shattered cultural and theoretical as well as human and physical connections. All received aesthetic assumptions, conventions, and productions were stripped, reexamined, and generally found wanting.... Weary of the panoramic, the picturesque, and the rhetorical, contemporary writers valued short, often patterned structures that sometimes experimented with representing time or 'ordinary' characters and subjects capable of being described with 'photographic' objectivity. These modernists...whether interested in shocking, delighting, or instructing, became preoccupied with whatever subjects and techniques would improve 'sight' and 'insight,' with whatever angle or juxtaposition would enable individuals to see '*more*.'" (Jane Rabb, "Introductions: Notes Toward a History of Literature and Photography," *Literature & Photography: Interactions 1840–1990* [Albuquerque: University of New Mexico Press, 1995] xlii).

[42] Wright Morris, "The Camera Eye," *Critical Inquiry* 8/1 (Autumn 1981): 2.

[43] O'Connor, *Collected Works*, 332.

torical world and its imagistic imprint and stimulation, making him a perfect subject for the impact of the visual revelation of the Divine realm. Because of Old Tarwater's schooling, the boy expects his own "burning bush" moment. He has yet, however, to experience the barrage of visual images, photographic and otherwise, that shape the historical world. When confronted with the photographic revelations, he will naturally interpret them as Divine. Revelations occur for both Rayber, who is visually sophisticated, and for the young Francis Marion Tarwater, who is a virtual neophyte in the modern world. He even proves unable to dial a telephone. Divine revelations in the form of verbal snapshots are a text easily read by the modern reader, and by using Rayber as the jaded modern man, another familiar text, O'Connor attempts to mold and shape how her reader interprets what she "sees" in the novel.

The question is, then, how can the adaptation of photographic techniques enable readers to "see" what is not actually there? A number of photographic theorists have weighed in in an attempt to analyze this property of the photograph. Marvin Heiferman, in the book *Photography Changes Everything*, writes, "Sometimes the simplest or smallest photographs are the ones that become the most powerful. Snapshots are like that: a button is pushed; a shutter opens and closes; and an image made in a fraction of a second transforms a moment of everyday life into something special, even magical. Mundane experiences get reshaped into memories."[44]

The crux of Heiferman's statement, and, quite possibly, one of the reasons that O'Connor adopted the photographic image as her pictorial method in *The Violent Bear It Away*, is that viewing the photographic image reshapes experience. Because of this, a spatial distance exists between that which is "known" or remembered and that which really happened, and a photograph exists in that space. An example of this "reshaping" is addressed by Ruth Iskin in her argument that even though Lacan professed to "dislike photographs," his theories on "looking and images" could not have helped but be influenced by "the specific visual media environments and the discourses of his time."[45] Iskin's contention is "that photography made its presence felt indirectly as an unconscious in Lacan's writings on the picture,

[44] *Photography Changes Everything*, ed. Marvin Heiferman, (New York: Aperture, 2012) 127.

[45] Ruth Iskin, "The Light of Images and the Shadow of Technology: Lacan, Photography, and Subjectivity," *Discourse* 19/3 (Spring 1997): 43–66, 43.

as well as his theories on images, primarily the mirror stage, the gaze, and the light. Notions of the 'real,' vision, and the subject were reconfigured in the aftermath of this new mass-media world."[46] W. J. T. Mitchell has termed this heightened interest in the visual in all disciplines as "The Pictorial Turn."[47] The "real," according to Iskin, became structured like its photograph...the "carrier" of what Barthes termed an "intractable reality." She points out that in *Four Fundamental Concepts*, Lacan "emphasizes the gaze rather than the camera when he uses the photography metaphor here, asserting that '...the gaze is the instrument through which light is embodied and through which—if you will allow me to use a word, as I often do, in a fragmented form—I am *photo-graphed.*"[48] Iskin asserts, by hyphenating the split in "*photo-graphed*," that "Lacan linguistically enacts the very split that marks the formation of the subject through the gaze in the mirror."[49] Lacan's "self" needs an instrument like the mirror to imagine itself. Lacan suggests the two-dimensional space of pictures when he writes that "only the subject—the human subject, the subject of desire that is the essence of man—is not, unlike the animal, entirely caught up in this imaginary capture. He maps himself in it. How? In so far as he isolates the function of the screen and plays with it. Man, in effect, knows how to play with the mask as that beyond which there is the gaze. The screen here is the locus of mediation."[50]

The screen—the medium—is separate from the body just as the photograph is separate when held in the hand. The mask serves as the "play" or interpretative space that exists between the gaze of the viewer and the pho-

[46] Ibid., 44.

[47] Mitchell writes, "In Anglo-American philosophy, variations on this turn could be traced early on in Charles

Pierce's semiotics and later in Nelson Goodman's 'languages of art.'" 11–12). He further cites Derrida's "'grammartology,' which de-centers the 'phonocentric' model of language by shifting attention to the visible material traces of writing; or with the Frankfurt School's investigations of modernity" (12). For Mitchell, Wittgenstein exemplifies the "enactment of the pictorial turn" by first beginning his philosophical career with "a 'picture theory' of meaning" and ending it with a renunciation of his earlier "pictorialism" (12).

[48] *Four*, 106. Iskin, "The Light of Images," 47.

[49] Iskin, "The Light of Images," 48.

[50] *Four*, 107. Quoted in Iskin, "The Light of Images," 50–51.

tograph. According to Susan Sontag, this "play" space allows the viewer to redefine reality: "Photographs do more than redefine the stuff of ordinary experience (people, things, events, whatever we see—albeit differently, often inattentively—with natural vision) and add vast amounts of material that we never see at all. Reality as such is redefined—as an item for exhibition, as a record for scrutiny, as a target for surveillance."[51]

In other words, a photograph can show us that what we thought was real essentially is not. A photo renders subjects and objects altered—not as perceived in actuality. In fact, Benjamin writes, "The enlargement of a snapshot does not simply render more precise what in any case was visible, though unclear: it reveals entirely new structural formations of the subject."[52]

Photographic images are "able to usurp reality" in a way that is impossible for painting because

> first of all a photograph is not only an image (as a painting is an image), an interpretation of the real; it is also a trace, something directly stenciled off the real, like a footprint or a death mask. While a painting, even one that meets photographic standards of resemblance, is never more than the stating of an interpretation, a photograph is never less than the registering of an emanation (light waves reflected by objects)—a material vestige of its subject in a way that no painting can be.[53]

The very act of examining an exhibited photograph not only redefines ordinary experience, but reveals "amounts of material that we never see at all"[54]. This quality of the photograph is the quality upon which O'Connor calls in the novel to demonstrate her thesis: "I think that the writer of grotesque fiction...is looking for one image that will connect or combine or embody two points; one is a point in the concrete, and the other is a point not visible to the naked eye, but believed by him firmly, just as real to him, really, as the one that everybody sees."[55]

[51] Susan Sontag, *On Photography* (New York: Farrar, Straus, and Giroux, 1973) 156.

[52] Benjamin, *Illuminations*, 236.

[53] Sontag, *On Photography*, 154.

[54] Ibid., 156.

[55] O'Connor, *Mystery and Manners*, 42.

The articulative photographic instant which O'Connor employs is very much like biblical events in which the Lord would send a message to his people through the means of a burning bush, a pillar of fire, or a rainbow. Both mediums of revelation, the photographic and the biblical, exist outside of time, "always [carry] [their] referents with [them], both affected by the same amorous or funereal immobility, at the very heart of the moving world." A photograph, according to Roland Barthes, is "unclassifiable" and "always invisible: it is never it that we see."[56] Photographs teach us a "new visual code" and "they are a grammar and, even more importantly, an ethics of seeing."[57] The same can be said regarding God's visual sign language. Even the most recalcitrant of Israelites could understand the pillar of cloud which led them by day and the pillar of fire which protected them by night. To know that God was leading them required only a lifting of the eyes. In the twentieth century, "the grain of our experience is identified with photographs" that discover, recover, reclaim, "and at unsuspecting moments collaborate with the creation of what we call history."[58] In fact, "if we pause to look about us for an emblem of our condition, it may be so obvious we overlook it. Not the bomb, nor the computer, nor the black holes in space, but the low and not so lowly photograph. If we are looking for a likeness, that is where we will find it—if we know where to look."[59]

HOW DOES THE PHOTOGRAPHIC MEDIUM SERVE THE PURPOSE OF THE HOMILETIC NOVEL?

For a Divine revelation to be effective, it must be accompanied by a sense of immediacy and a sense of place in the surrounding reality, though such a sense does not always ensure that the viewer's attention will not wander, as in the case of the Israelites, who soon grew accustomed to the cloud and fire. In "The Fiction Writer & His Country," O'Connor addressed the need to carefully fashion the reader's reality:

[56] Roland Barthes, *Camera Lucida*, trans. Richard Howard (New York: Hill and Wang, 1980) 6.

[57] Sontag, *On Photography*, 3.

[58] Wright Morris, "The Camera Eye," *Critical Inquiry* 8/1 (Autumn 1981): 1–15, 4.

[59] Ibid., 11.

> The novelist with Christian concerns will find in modern life distortions which are repugnant to him, and his problem will be to make these appear as distortions to an audience which is used to seeing them as natural; and he may well be forced to take evermore violent means to get his vision across to this hostile audience...you have to make your vision apparent by shock—to the hard of hearing you shout, and for the almost blind you draw large and startling figures.[60]

For the modern reader, the use of narrative pauses and the application of the camera eye provide a way to present a familiar visual text that can be read immediately. As is her fashion, O'Connor reaches backward into the artistic past, to the Impressionistic slice of life, to inform the creation of her particular technique.[61] Her employment of the textual snapshot calls upon the pacing, technique, and discipline of the photographer to give her work the feeling of an Impressionist painting—that is, to make readers feel simultaneously a sense of being both out of the stream of time as well as a sense of the propinquity of place.

[60] O'Connor, *Mystery and Manners*, 33–34.

[61] In the nineteenth century, photography, along with other technological inventions, changed the perception of time. To be able to "arrest motion" with a photograph enhanced the aesthetic of the moment. The idea of instantaneity became aesthetically desirable to the Impressionist painters.

"The new opportunities (and hazards) that photography presented for painting at mid-century required that forward-looking artists contend with photography's aesthetic and philosophical challenges. As a consequence, the avant-garde painters' response to work by photographers...was to adapt or be left behind" (Carol McNamara, *The Lens of Impressionism: Photography and Painting along the Normandy Coast 1850–1874* [Ann Arbor: University of Michigan Museum of Art, 2009] 15–16).

O'Connor addressed the importance of Impressionism to her own perception of story writing in "The Nature and the Aim of Fiction": "Reading a story is at first rather like standing a foot away from an impressionistic painting, then gradually moving back until it comes into focus. When you reach the right distance, you suddenly see that a world has been created—and a world in action—and that a complete story has been told, by a wonderful kind of understatement. It has been told more by showing what happens around the story than by touching directly on the story itself" (O'Connor, *Mystery and Manners*, 79).

By combining the emblematic understatement with the snapshot technique, O'Connor is able to infuse her fiction with a sense of immediacy that implies that the Divine is always operating side by side with reality and, in fact, might well *be* reality. The constructed world, the world that is explained and analyzed by Rayber's "teacher magazines," a world verified on paper, is a world constructed and perceived as a validation of human authority. How, then, does the application of a verbal snapshot in a pictorial pause in the narrative pierce the veil that separates us from the "holy of holies"?

At pictorial moments in the novel, the simultaneously existing two realms are exposed by O'Connor's employment of the verbal snapshot because, as Clarence Laughlin puts it, "every good photograph embodies intensive and controlled seeing. From the methods and procedures of the creative photographer emerges a hyper-reality which transcends the recording of the camera. This hyper-reality consists of the extension of the individual object into a more inclusive and more significant reality—the interior realities of the human mind and the human emotions."[62]

The properties of what Laughlin calls a hyper-reality become, in the hands of O'Connor, a Divine reality. Trappist Thomas Merton, correspondent and spiritual guide to O'Connor, describes this dualistic presentation of reality through the eye of a camera as he writes in his journal on November 19, 1968. He is describing his attempts to capture the sensed essence of a mountain he had been photographing: "The camera does not know what it takes; it captures materials with which you reconstruct, not so much what you saw as what you thought you saw. Hence the best photography is aware, mindful, of illusion and uses illusion, permitting and encouraging it—especially unconscious and powerful illusions that are not normally admitted on the scene."[63]

What Merton is calling illusion turns, in the context of the novel, into reality.

For example, when the scene embodied in the Bishop snapshot opens, we find Rayber ushering the young Tarwater through the doorway and into his house with the words, "You and I will make up for lost time. We'll get

[62] Clarence Laughlin, "The Camera's Methods of Approaching Reality," *College Art Journal* 16/4 (Summer 1957): 297–306, 297.

[63] Thomas Merton, *The Search for Solitude*, 454.

you started in the right direction."[64] As is so often the case with O'Connor, these words take on a double meaning. In this moment, Tarwater is faced with the direction toward which he is being pushed, and it is not down an earthly hallway. Tarwater's eyes have become focused on a point that exists on a plane that Rayber cannot see or even imagine. "His neck suddenly snapped forward," and Tarwater's eyes became glued on a spot located over the schoolteacher's shoulder and framed by the hallway. Note the use of the word "snapped." All of a sudden, distance disappears and the vision becomes "closer to him than the beating of his own heart." What he sees is more alive and real than he is. An "inner door" is opened, providing the "parergon"—for the snapshot of Bishop, which becomes an "inevitable vision"—"neither simply outside nor simply inside."[65] The "lack" that this exposed is the work left undone at his great-uncle's demise: "If by the time I die," he had said to Tarwater, "I haven't got him baptized, it'll be up to you, it'll be up to you. It'll be the first mission the Lord sends you."[66]

Before us stands a child who cannot manage his pajama bottoms and yet, at the same time, is named as mythical—"dim and ancient"—and who provides for Tarwater a hyper-real moment. In a split second, forward motion has been arrested and we see in one glance the image of a handicapped child framed by a hallway superimposed upon a vision of a mythological creature framed by an "inner door." The description of Bishop's pajama pants allows the reader to keep one foot firmly in the concrete world and not to be lured into the ancient or the mystical. This is, in fact, a story that takes place in the modern world. The pajama pants' string is "tied over his chest and then again, harness-like, around his neck to keep them on." What kind of parent would tie a string around his child's neck to hold his pants on while he is sleeping? Bishop is not cared for in his own home, by his own father. Rayber seems unconcerned about his child's safety and, in fact, we find later on in the novel that Rayber has already tried to drown Bishop. He tries to kill his son because he loves him and cannot live with the enormity of this love. Rayber has saved himself from the "state of grace" occasioned by his uncle's proselytizing by attempting to eliminate all emotions and to replace them with rational thinking. He has structured a life from which love has been closed out. All of this is embodied in his placement of that

[64] O'Connor, *Collected Works,* 388.
[65] Derrida, *The Truth in Painting,* 54.
[66] O'Connor, *Collected Works,* 335.

pajama string. Instead of purchasing pajamas that were the proper size for Bishop, Rayber just provides him with a cast-off pair of his own. Finding pajamas in the right size would be an admission that Bishop exists, not just as detritus or as something broken, but as a singular being, perfect in his own right on this earth. Admitting this would open that door, the door that Rayber has been steadily pushing closed ever since his stay with Old Tarwater—the door to love—the overwhelming love that a father feels for his child—that the old man felt for young Rayber—that God feels for his son. The small act of tying that pajama string around Bishop's neck like a noose serves as a sign of how successful Rayber has been at blocking these emotions. To him, Bishop is a cast-off, a mistake, and an encumbrance without whom Rayber would be freed to pursue a defined life surrounded by letters and papers. Rayber keeps the darkness away and organizes his world with pages and pages of manuscript.

The significance of the palimpsestic nature of the picture of Bishop in the hallway is not lost on Francis Marion Tarwater. The past floods into the present, and, for an instant, the text of the actual and the "Marvelous" move into position and coincide within the boundaries of his consciousness.

> Tarwater clenched his fists. He stood like one condemned, waiting at the spot of execution. Then the revelation came, silent, implacable, direct as a bullet. He did not look into the eyes of any fiery beast or see a burning bush. He only knew with a certainty sunk in despair, that he was expected to baptize the child he saw and begin the life his great uncle had prepared him for. He knew he was called to be a prophet and that the ways of his prophecy would not be remarkable. His black pupils, glassy and still, reflected depth on depth his own stricken image of himself, trudging into the distance in the bleeding stinking mad shadow of Jesus, until at last he received his reward, a broken fish, a multiplied loaf.[67]

Tarwater, here, looks backward into the truth of his great-uncle's teachings and forward to a "world of loss and fire all to baptize one idiot child that He need not have created in the first place."[68] The snapshot im-

[67] Ibid., 388–89.

[68] Ibid., 389.

age of Bishop has produced an incarnation in Tarwater in the same way as would a "burning bush" or a "fiery beast." He has now been "called." His fate is sealed. He is destined to skulk along in the "stinking mad shadow of Jesus" for the rest of his life.

HAWTHORNE, O'CONNOR, AMERICAN ROMANCE, AND THE HOMILETIC NOVEL

This mixture of the "Marvelous" and the "actual" using the photographic moment as a pictorial technique uniquely enables the reader to experience the two realms simultaneously and is familiar to O'Connor, the reader of American Romance. Hawthorne, a master of this genre, was one of her favorites. In the preface to *The House of the Seven Gables*, Hawthorne advises the writer of Romance:

> When a writer calls his work a Romance, it need hardly be observed that he wishes to claim a certain latitude, both as to its fashion and material, which he would not have felt himself entitled to assume, had he professed to be writing a Novel.... The former—while, as a work of art, it must rigidly subject itself to laws, and while it sins unpardonably, so far as it may swerve aside from the truth of the human heart—has fairly a right to present that truth under circumstances, to a great extent, of the writer's own choosing or creation. If he thinks fit, also, he may so manage his atmospherical medium as to bring out the mellow lights and deepen and enrich the shadows of the picture. He will be wise, no doubt, to make a very moderate use of the privileges here stated, and, especially, to mingle the Marvelous rather as a slight, delicate, and evanescent flavor, than as any portion of the actual substance of the dish offered to the Public.[69]

In Hawthorne's hands in *The House of the Seven Gables*, the photograph or, in this case, the daguerreotype picture not only captures the "actual," but serves as a doorway to the imaginary and "figure[s] consequently both in plot and in literary theory internalized as a major theme within the

[69] Hawthorne, *The House of the Seven Gables*, 3.

fiction."[70] In the romance, Alan Trachtenberg writes, "Hawthorne's figures play nicely on what by 1851 had become a fairly common experience: that apparent trick of the mirrored metallic face of the daguerreotype image, seeming at once here and gone, a positive and a negative, substance and shadow." He goes on to say that what one sees may very well be "one's own visage flashed back from the mirrored surface".[71] Hawthorne uses the image-capturing capacities of the daguerreotype to open a new way of interpreting reality. In *The House of the Seven Gables*, the daguerreotype enables the characters to "see" the past and present simultaneously, thusly resolving the plot conflict in the novel.

When Holcomb holds the judge's picture out for Phoebe Pyncheon to see, she describes daguerreotype pictures as "dodging away from the eye, and trying to escape altogether."[72] Holcomb agrees with this assessment and goes on to pose his theory that "the sun quite tells another story and will not be coaxed out of it.... There is a wonderful insight in Heaven's broad and simple sunshine. While we give it credit only for depicting the merest surface, it actually brings out the secret character with a truth that no painter could ever venture upon, even though he could detect it."[73] In *The Violent Bear It Away*, O'Connor builds on Hawthorne's lead. The visage in Holcomb's daguerreotype reveals the historical past in that it is used as evidence of the sins of an ancestral nature repeating themselves in the face of Judge Pyncheon—"the truth of the human heart," the revelation of which is attributed to Heaven. The daguerreotype serves as the medium of this "Marvelous" revelation. The past brought forth by O'Connor, while also historical, is divine or spiritual as well. It is a past in which "the fiery eyes of the beast" and a "burning bush" are actual events. The world has not been allowed impingement in Tarwater's education, as it has in Rayber's, and this makes the boy secure in his expectation of his reward—"a broken fish and a multiplied loaf."[74] The two realms divulged by Holcomb's daguerreotype are the historical past superimposed on the realm of the historical actual.

[70] Alan Trachtenberg, "Seeing and Believing: Hawthorne's Reflections on the Daguerreotype in *The House of the Seven Gables*," *American Literary History* 9/3 (Autumn 1997): 460–81, 418.

[71] Ibid., 420.

[72] Holcomb, 125.

[73] Ibid.

[74] O'Connor, *Collected Works*, 389.

The two realms realized by O'Connor are the historical actual, both past and present, and the Divine actual, that realm existing both in a biblical past and a biblical present.

O'Connor's mirroring of the death of Judge Pyncheon in her depiction of the death of Old Tarwater serves to clarify her method for the use of the photographic image by following in Hawthorne's footsteps. Judge Pyncheon's last act is to fling himself into "a great ancestral chair" which was

> the very chair, seated in which, the earliest Judge's New England forefathers—he whose picture still hung on the wall—had given a dead man's silent and stern reception to the throng of distinguished guests. From that hour of evil omen, until the present, it may be—though we know not the secret of his heart—but it may be, that no wearier and sadder man had ever sunk into the chair, than this same Judge Pyncheon, whom we have just beheld so immitigably hard and resolute. Surely it must have been at no slight cost, that he had thus fortified his soul with iron![75]

Old Tarwater, too, a man of iron, dies in his "ancestral" chair as he sits at the breakfast table across from the boy Tarwater. He, too, is surrounded with the material evidence of his ancestry. The old man's ancestry, however, cannot be traced in the historical world. The line from which he is descended can be traced in the biblical realm. His bloodline is the blood of Christ. When Mason Tarwater was called to be a prophet, his human blood was "burned dry and not the blood of the world."[76] Just as Judge Pyncheon has busied himself shaping the life of his cousin Clifford, who inherits the Pyncheon wealth, Old Tarwater has dedicated his life to training the boy who will be his inheritor. On the morning that he died, Old Tarwater rose as usual and prepared breakfast for his great-nephew and then died "before he got the first spoonful to his mouth.... [R]ed ropes appear[ed] in his face and a tremor pass[ed] over him. His eyes dead silver, were focused on the boy across from him."[77] The old man and the boy were surrounded by the material accumulation of the prophet's worldly goods. "The downstairs of their house was all kitchen, large and dark, with a wood stove at one end of

[75] Hawthorne, 168–69.

[76] O'Connor, *Collected Works*, 332.

[77] Ibid., 10–11.

it and a board table drawn up to the stove. Sacks of feed and mash were stacked in the corners and scrapmetal, woodshavings, old rope, ladders, and other tinder were wherever he or Tarwater let them fall."[78]

Obviously, unlike Judge Pynchon, he has accumulated nothing of earthly value. To O'Connor, however, the kitchen is the heart of the house. It was where Hazel Motes's mother worked and slept in *Wise Blood.* The kitchen table is the site where problems, both literal and spiritual, are laid out and examined in many of her short stories. The fact that the downstairs of the old man's house is all kitchen, with a wood stove and a board table butted up against it, speaks of the warmth and sustenance the old man provided for his great-nephew. Since he had kidnapped the boy fourteen years earlier, the old man's life had been dedicated to feeding him, both physically and spiritually ("If the old man had done nothing else for him, he had heaped his plate. Never a morning he had not awakened to the smell of fatback frying"[79]), providing him with a skill that would sustain him (tending the still), and creating for him "a place to be" that was safe and secure—essentially a home. "They had slept in the kitchen until a bobcat sprang in the window one night and frightened his uncle into carrying the bed upstairs where there were two empty rooms. The old man prophesied at the time that the stairsteps would take ten years off his life."[80] Upon the soon-to-be-stilled body of the Judge, Hawthorne makes an assessment of the cost of fortifying one's soul with iron. O'Connor, on the other hand, leaves it to her readers to assess the gain of fortifying one's soul whose blood has been "burned dry and not the blood of the world." The Judge will have his reward, his legacy determined by that image superimposed on his dead body, viewed in the daguerreotype picture. At the end of O'Connor's novel, we find that Mason Tarwater's reward will be exactly what he expected—to sit on a hill with the multitudes being fed from a single basket, his hunger sated by the "bread of life."

STUDIUM

In order to have terminology for analysis of the dualistic nature of the photographic moments in the text of the novel, we will adopt Roland Barthes's

[78] Ibid., 335.
[79] Ibid., 430.
[80] Ibid., 335.

terminology to explain and map the terrain of the duality that is intrinsic to interpretation. Barthes calls the cursory examination of a straightforward historical photograph as conducting a *studium.* This might be the kind of informative photo that appears in the newspaper or in a history book. Barthes characterizes the term this way, "It is by *studium* that I am interested in so many photographs, whether I receive them as political testimony or enjoy them as good historical scenes: for it is culturally (this connotation is present in *studium*) that I participate in the figures, the faces, the gestures, the settings, the actions."[81] These particular photographs are singularly significant and referent to the historical cultural world. According to Barthes, they reflect the photographer's intentions, and "a contract between creators and consumers"[82] is manifested by them. Consumers will be informed and educated along the guidelines set out by the photographer—the creator in this case. In *The Violent Bear It Away*, O'Connor avows that even if the photograph appears as a true documentation of events, even if it appears in the newspaper, it may well not bear witness.

An example of this occurs in chapter 6. The narrator recounts the events that take place "one terrible afternoon" when Rayber took Bishop to the beach with the intent to drown him. The drowning never happens because Bishop unexpectedly struggles, expending "a "primeval rage to save" himself.[83] When Rayber comes to his senses after "a moment of complete terror in which he envisioned his life without the child,"[84] he calls for help and carries the limp body out of the water. A photographer happens to be in the right place at the right time to snap pictures of the "breaking news" situation. He is able to provide his paper and its readers with a heart rending human-interest story (truth be damned). Readers "see" what they are led to "see." According to Roland Barthes, the subject, while remaining a subject, is turned into an object, into the other, or into a "total-image."[85] By "total-image," Barthes means that the viewer of a subject in a photograph has an awareness of the death of that subject. The subject's "total" existence on two planes, in two realms, becomes evident. Barthes goes on to explain this duality. Many photographs exist within the framework of history. A

[81] Barthes, *Camera Lucida*, 26.

[82] Ibid., 28.

[83] O'Connor, *Collected Works*, 418.

[84] Ibid., 419.

[85] Barthes, *Camera Lucida*, 14.

great number of newspaper photos fall into this category. To the viewer, these photos are generally interesting and require "a kind of general enthusiastic commitment, but without special acuity."[86] However, these photographs are often staged and illusive, as is the newspaper photo that was taken in the aftermath of Rayber's failed drowning attempt.

Rayber had planned the drowning in advance and had taken Bishop to a beach 200 miles away so he could return to his life unencumbered but "bereaved"[87] when the incident was over and the deed was accomplished. Second thoughts spur a cry for help.

> The beach which he had thought empty before had become peopled with strangers converging on him from all directions. A bald-headed man in red and blue Roman striped shorts began at once to administer artificial respiration. Three wailing women and a photographer appeared. The next day there had been a picture in the paper, showing the rescuer, striped bottom forward, working over the child. Rayber was beside him on his knees watching with an agonized expression. The caption said, OVERJOYED FATHER SEES SON REVIVED.[88]

In citing this one incident and in describing its accompanying photograph, O'Connor neatly indicates the fictive, constructed reality that is often present in a newspaper photograph. In this way she disregards the Impressionistic idea of photography as a slice of the "real," essentially—the truth. We know from the narrative that Rayber is certainly in agony regardless of the caption's description of him as "overjoyed." What might strike the reader and the viewer of the photo is the rescuer with his "striped bottom forward, working over the child" while Rayber observes. The placement of the figures in the space of the photo (like in the single-panel cartoon) suggests that Rayber has attained the distance from his son with which he feels comfortable. He has conquered the wave of terror that overtook him when Bishop was swept away and is kneeling, watching the owner of the "striped bottom" as he ministers to his son. We know that his "agonized expression" is evidence of a complex depth of agony that includes the awareness of his own attempt to murder his son. O'Connor uses the venue

[86] Ibid., 26.
[87] O'Connor, *Collected Works*, 418.
[88] Ibid., 419.

of this novel to probe the boundaries of reality as constructed by the complacency of reproduction media, exemplified, in this case, by the newspaper photo of the rescue, and, earlier in the novel, in the "teacher magazine" story.

PUNCTUM

The next of Barthes's terms that I am borrowing is *punctum*. Explaining this term, Barthes calls photography "a kind of primitive theater, a kind of *Tableau Vivant*, a figuration of the motionless and made-up face beneath which we see the dead."[89] "Seeing the dead," according to Barthes, is seeing more than was intended in either the performance of an actor or in a photograph. When, according to Barthes, a second element "breaks or punctuates the *studium*",[90] the existence of this element or interpretative gesture might well be a surprise to the photographer, as it might to an actor in the *tableau vivant*. However, because of the break or punctuation in the *studium* of the photograph, another reality appears, one that features an "entirely new structural formation of the subject."[91] Barthes describes this as an element in the photograph rising and shooting out of it like an arrow piercing the viewer and inflicting a "wound." He calls these wounding jabs the *punctum*: "for *punctum* is also: sting, speck, cut, little hole—and also a cast of the dice. A photograph's *punctum* is that accident which pricks me (but also bruises me, is poignant to me)."[92] The idea of a *punctum,* and the determination of exactly what that punctum is in a photograph, enables us to make a step-by-step analysis of the compositions of the verbal snapshots inserted by O'Connor into her narrative. I think she uses the "BORN IN A CAR WRECK" litany to begin implanting the double consciousness of the *studium* and *punctum* in her readers' minds. The sensationalism of the newspapers is suggested again in *The Violent Bear It Away* by the continuous recitation of the events surrounding young Tarwater's birth. Each time the narrative appears in the text, it is accompanied by the prediction that the young boy, chosen by God to survive, is destined to become a prophet. These recitations, not unlike those which might appear in a tabloid, become

[89] Barthes, *Camera Lucida*, 32.
[90] Ibid., 26.
[91] Benjamin, *Illuminations*.
[92] Barthes, *Camera Lucida*, 27.

part of the legend that surrounds such a character, whether he be biblical or mythical. The young Tarwater, reciting the details of his birth, relates that his mother and grandmother

> along with his grandfather, had been killed in the automobile crash, leaving only the schoolteacher alive in that family, and Tarwater himself, for his mother (unmarried and shameless) had lived just long enough after the crash for him to be born. He had been born at the scene of the wreck.

In this instance, which occurs early on in the novel, O'Connor has clearly united the historical and the Divine in one picture. She could make a safe conjecture that the *punctum* of such a picture—a survivor being carried away from a flaming accident—had at some point entered her readers' lexicon. This image was and is still today very popular in film as well as in newspaper photos.[93] By repeatedly imparting this story, O'Connor demonstrates how such a dramatic pictorial demonstration of the circumstances surrounding the boy's birth could well carry two interpretations—i.e., exist in two realms. Young Tarwater is very proud

> that he had been born in a wreck. He had always felt that it set his existence apart from the ordinary one and he had understood from it the plans of God for him were special, even though nothing of consequence had happened to him so far. Often when he walked in the woods and came on some bush a little removed from the rest, his breath would catch in his throat and he would not stop and wait for the bush to burst into flame. It had not done it yet.[94]

It is important that the reader begin to view such incidences in the book with a double consciousness, just as Tarwater himself does. O'Connor uses this exemplification to prepare us for what follows pictorially.

[93] It is interesting to me how much the description of this wreck resembles Andy Warhol's *Car Crash* paintings that began to appear in 1962.

[94] O'Connor, *Collected Works*, 355.

A SERIES OF VERBAL SNAPSHOTS

We will now commence on a chronological tour of the pictorial text designed and framed as verbal snapshots that O'Connor employs to lift the veil between the two realms and to enhance the homiletic nature of *The Violent Bear It Away*. Young Tarwater is positive that he will be called to carry on the Lord's work in the city. This revelation had come to him two or three years before when he accompanied his uncle to visit a lawyer. Finding himself in an urban environment for the first time, he is overwhelmed with the sheer number of people in the streets. As he walks along, his head "jerks backward after each passing figure."[95] He finds that "their eyes didn't grab at you like the eyes of country people."[96] In a "burst of light" he sees that the city is a place of evil and that "that these people [are] hastening away from the Lord God Almighty. It was to the city that the prophets came and he was in the midst of it."[97] He begins to rail at his uncle for hurrying on about his business and for not preaching to this multitude. His uncle replies, "If you been called by the Lord, then be about your own mission."[98] The boy backs away. This is the boy's initial revelation—perhaps even his "call," delivered briefly in the fashion of a snapshot and accompanied with the requisite "burst of light." In the next scene, we find the boy in the lawyer's office looking out of the window, and readers are treated to the panorama of his mission field: "the floating speckled street moving like a river of tin below."[99] He vows that when he returns, "he [will] set the city astir, he [will] return with fire in his eyes."[100] This is the first time that the young Tarwater sees with double vision through the "camera eye." The first snap is a sidewalk shot from the perspective of a young child. We "see" figures frozen in a tableau that indicates activity and movement. From a child's perspective, some of these figures would be truncated and fragmented; in fact, no figure would really be complete as the boy and his great-uncle passed. Various body parts, providing a sense of modern life, would be momentarily captured in his frame of reference, providing the *punctum* of

[95] Ibid., 345–46.
[96] Ibid., 346.
[97] Ibid.
[98] Ibid., 347.
[99] Ibid.
[100] Ibid.

this verbal picture. In a flash, the boy sees into the "other country," the Divine realm, and sees that all of these people are "hastening away from the Lord God Almighty." His mission field has become clear to him.

To picture the sheaves to be harvested, O'Connor snaps an overhead shot of the undulating mass of humanity viewed from the window of a skyscraper. This vantage point is reminiscent of aerial reconnaissance photography[101] employed in wartime. In fact, the boy does imagine himself a "warrior" for the Lord. As he leans out of the window, the boy says to himself, "When I come for good, I'll do something to make every eye stick on me, and leaning forward, he saw his new hat drop down gently, lost and casual, dallied slightly by the breeze on its way to be smashed in the tin river below."[102] Along with his mission, the Divine presence has delivered a foreshadowing of the boy's fate as he is smashed in his struggle first to avoid and then to fulfill his assignment.

After his great-uncle's demise, the young Tarwater is drawn back to the city and to his uncle's doorstep, where he receives an opening of an "inner-door" and the divine revelation about Bishop's part in his destiny discussed previously. Upon the young Tarwater's arrival at his door, Rayber, ever the schoolteacher, decides to reeducate the boy, to undo what the old man had done, and to make the boy his own. This begins with educational walks through the city with both boys, Tarwater and Bishop, visiting all of the wonders of the historical world—art galleries, movie theaters, supermarkets, the post office, the water works, and city hall. For four days nothing happens. The only things that seem to interest Tarwater are a red car in a showroom window and the tall building that he recognizes having visited on that long ago visit to the lawyer with his great-uncle. The boy keeps moving forward, searching...until suddenly he

> had stopped with a kind of lurch backwards in front of a grimey garage-like structure with two yellow and blue painted windows in the front of it, and had stood there, precariously balanced as if he were arresting himself in the middle of a fall. Rayber recognized the place for some kind of Pentecostal tabernacle. Over the door was a paper banner bearing the words, UNLESS YE BE BORN AGAIN YE SHALL NOT HAVE EVERLASTING

[101] Rabb, xlv.

[102] O'Connor, *Collected Works*, 347.

> LIFE. Beneath it a poster showed a man and woman and child holding hands. "Hear the Carmodys for Christ!" it said. "Thrill to the Music, Message, and Magic of this team!"[103]

Through Rayber's eyes we are able to watch young Tarwater in the throes of a flash of Divine reality. O'Connor has composed this picture in a manner similar that in her early cartoons. In the background she provides a very basic sketch of a church—"garage-like structure" with two stained-glass windows. Rayber comments as one would if one were holding a photograph in his hand. His *studium* locates the structure in the context of the historical world. It is a Pentecostal tabernacle. Pentecostal denotes a particular kind of primitive or simplistic worship—a purer unadulterated gospel than that which might be preached in a church more richly ornamented. The word tabernacle again carries us back to the biblical times—or rather it brings those times forward into the present. Rayber's utterance has placed the building that serves as a backdrop in both the spiritual and the historical realm. Above the door, what might well be the *punctum* for the young Tarwater appears. It is a paper banner that provides the caption to the photo, a message which could not be clearer. One must be born again to have eternal life. But what does it mean to be born again? The evidences of the meaning of the phrase "born again" have been included in the text of this novel. It is exemplified in the ancestral lives of the prophets that have been listed over and over again—Daniel, Jonah, Elijah, Elisha. It has been exemplified in Old Tarwater's recounting of his own burning clean. This is the history that the boy knows. The message is intended for him, and, by the way he reacts physically, we can assume it has pierced him in the heart. The banner is made out of paper—subject to the wind, to the rain, to age. In the historical world, the message is fleeting, as is the property of a photograph, but it remains impressed in Tarwater's heart and in O'Connor's book.

Anticlimactically, below the banner is a poster bearing the picture of a family of evangelists promising "Music, Message, and Magic!" This advertisement falls far short of the message imprinted on the banner above it. It is the construction of a human mind, an enticement that includes the word "Magic," and because of this word, there are hints of a fourth "M"—Money. Why would a family of evangelists advertise themselves as a magic show? Bigger attendance—bigger offering. It's show business.

[103] Ibid., 398.

Rayber himself provides for readers a picture of the effect that the words on the banner have on young Tarwater. After separating himself from Rayber and Bishop, the boy walks away on the farthest edge of the sidewalk. Rayber thinks, "He wore his isolation like a mantle, wrapped it around himself as if it were a garment signifying the elect."[104] The isolation of a prophet is such a garment: "And he said, Verily I say unto you, No prophet is accepted in his own country."[105]

After this incident, Rayber, the schoolteacher, bides his time. Unable or unwilling to accept the revelatory evidence of boy's figure that is before his eyes, he remains certain that Tarwater will eventually reveal "what interests him." He remains alert after he has ordered everyone to bed, and his vigilance is rewarded when he hears the front door open and close. He throws on a trench coat over his pajamas and, barefooted, follows Tarwater through the darkened streets. Readers picture the boy's furtive progress through Rayber's perspective as "he turns off his hearing aid and pursues the dim figure as if in a dream."[106] As he turns a corner, he sees that Tarwater has stopped and is standing in the middle of a block looking in a store window: "Tarwater's face was strangely lit from the window he was standing before. Rayber watched curiously for a few moments. It looked to him like the face of someone starving who sees a meal he can't reach laid out before him. At last something he *wants*, he [Rayber] thought, and determined that tomorrow he would return and buy it."[107]

Determining what it is that Tarwater desires, Rayber is sure, will enable him to have power over the boy and ultimately to root out the old man's teachings and save him from a life outside of the "real world." In the execution of this snapshot moment, O'Connor has changed the reader's perspective. We are viewing Tarwater from a distance, more specifically from a darkened staircase, where Rayber is hiding, that enables us to see the boy's face but not what he is looking at framed in the show window. The boy's face is lit "strangely" as we conduct our *studium* of his *studium*. Because we have been conditioned from the medium of light, the snapshots that have occurred previously in the book, O'Connor only needs to use that one word to indicate that we, again, are going to see the parting of the curtains and

[104] Ibid., 399.

[105] Luke 4:24 (King James Version).

[106] O'Connor, *Collected Works*, 405.

[107] Ibid., 406.

that a revelation is at hand. It is this strange light that serves as the *punctum*. "Tarwater reached out and touched the glass and then drew his hand back slowly. He hung there as if he could not take his eyes off what it was he wanted. A pet shop, perhaps, Rayber thought. Maybe he wants a dog. A dog might make all the difference. Abruptly the boy broke away and moved on."[108] Rayber is in his glory. Now this is behavior that he can measure and explain. So far, the boy has resisted his efforts to collect analytic data. As soon as the boy is sufficiently down the street, Rayber rushes to the window ready to celebrate his victory and is sorely disappointed. "The place was only a bakery. The window was empty except for a loaf of bread pushed to the side that must have been overlooked when the shelf was cleaned for the night. He stared, puzzled, at the empty window for a second before he started after the boy again. Everything was a false alarm, he thought with disgust."[109] O'Connor has manipulated the perspective so that the *punctum* rises up from the page and pierces our readerly hearts! How can Rayber have lived with the old man, have been trained by him, baptized by him, and not be able to recognize the boy hungers for the "bread of life"? The handwriting is on the wall—on the wall of the Pentecostal tabernacle—literally in a storefront show window. Tarwater is being "weighed in the balances, and found wanting."[110] He wants to reach out for the bread, but he cannot bring himself to make the commitment—to offer himself for the burning clean—to be born again. What Rayber sees is only a day-old, forgotten loaf destined to stale overnight. To us, and to Tarwater, it is *mise en scene.* It is central to this novel, and it appears in a verbal snapshot exactly on the middle page of the book.

Rayber, having again turned on his hearing aid, continues to follow the boy and watches him disappear into a building. "As he reached the place, singing burst flatly against his eardrums. Two blue and yellow windows glared at him in the darkness like the eyes of some Biblical beast. He stopped in front of the banner and read the mocking words, UNLESS YE BE BORN AGAIN...."[111] The boy has been drawn into the belly of the beast. The veil has finally been lifted for Rayber in the darkness of night, he is able to witness firsthand the battle for the boy's soul. He maneuvers him-

[108] Ibid., 406–407.

[109] Ibid., 407.

[110] Daniel 5:27 (King James Version).

[111] O'Connor, *Collected Works,* 407.

self to a window where we readers, along with the schoolteacher, are able to peer into the body of the whale—to hear what long ago was imparted to Jonah, one in the ancestral line of prophets leading forward to the boy. He is looking in on an anteroom whose door to the stage was left open. He cannot see the audience. A man is on stage introducing an evangelical speaker that is a little girl, the youngest member of the Carmody Family.

Lucette Carmody, the child evangelist, who "simply by the sight of her," Rayber could tell, "was not a fraud," hobbles into the spotlight on "thin legs twisted from the knees."[112] She turns her gaze on Rayber who is watching her through the window:

> He stared back at her. Her eyes remained on his face for a moment. A deep shock went through him. He was certain the child had looked directly into his heart and seen his pity. He felt some mysterious connection was established between them.
>
> "'My Word is coming,'" she said, turning back to face the glare, "'my Word is coming from the house of David, the king.'"[113]

At this point, the perspective changes, and Rayber, framed by the window, has become the subject of the snapshot that the reader is able to examine from Lucette's point of view. Only, the next words spoken, utterances emanating from Lucette's mouth, are not her words. O'Connor uses the double quotation marks to indicate that Lucette is speaking ex-cathedra. She is speaking the words of the Lord. Rayber, in the bushes, at the window, is now on Holy Ground—on God's playing field—in Lacan's space of the "mask," between the gaze and the "screen." Of course, Rayber uses this space to "mask" what is clearly happening and in his mind creates a scenario where Lucette is appealing to him to "save" her from the life her parents have imposed on her. During this reverie, O'Connor enables the reader to simultaneously see Rayber, as the initiator of the gaze, to see his creation of the "mask," and to see Rayber as the subject of God's gaze. Interrupting his reverie, Lucette shrieks, her/God's eyes focused on Rayber: "I see a damned

[112] Ibid., 411.
[113] Ibid., 412.

soul before my eye! I see a dead man Jesus hasn't raised. His head is in the window but his ear is deaf to the Holy Word!"[114]

Outside the window, Rayber's head, "as if it had been struck by an invisible bolt [flash, *punctum*], dropped from the ledge." Lucette continues to shriek: "Are you deaf to the Lord's Word? The Word of God is a burning Word to burn you clean, burns man and child, man and child the same, you people! Be saved in the Lord's fire or perish in your own! Be saved in...."[115] Rayber turns off his hearing aid and from this point on in the novel, he receives no more pictorial revelations. He has consciously severed the connection. Throughout the novel, so far, readers have witnessed Rayber's struggle to silence the old man's words instilled in his boyish heart. Until this point he has not been successful. Events in the present, particularly after the arrival of the young Tarwater, would transport him back to the time he spent at the old man's feet, listening and believing. The seed, as the old man would say, was planted, but Rayber associates the fact that the old man never came for him with the indifference of his parents and spends the rest of his spiritual and emotional life transferring his faith to the learning embodied in his beloved books and papers. Deliberately turning off his hearing aid, silencing Lucette's words, indicates that there will be no more backward glances, no more voices from the past to haunt him. He will now move forward in the barren land of the present, void of sound.

When, the day after the revival, the boy, under the power of a compulsion, tries to baptize Bishop in the fountain in the park, Rayber vows that he will "cure" him of his obsession "or know the reason why."[116] The cure devised by Rayber is to take Francis Marion Tarwater back to Powderhead to confront what he had done. It is at this exact time that Rayber recalls his attempt to drown Bishop at the beach, and the "cure" he devises involves spending the night at Cherokee Lodge on the edge of a lake with the boys. In the darkest depths of Rayber's heart, he knows that it would be impossible for Bishop to drown if Tarwater tried to baptize him in a public place, but it may well not be impossible for him to drown if baptized in the middle of a lake. Even if he repressed this knowledge, while signing the guest book, Rayber has a premonition "that if he wished to save himself, he

[114] Ibid., 415.

[115] Ibid.

[116] Ibid., 422.

should leave at once, that the trip was doomed."[117] Regardless, he continues to move forward. As the boys follow him, the owner of the lodge, the woman at the desk, witnesses Tarwater's face as he receives another snapshot revelation while looking at Biishop: "The woman was startled by the expression on his face. He seemed to see the little boy and nothing else, no air around him, no room, no nothing, as if his gaze had slipped and fallen into the center of the child's eyes and was still falling down and down and down."[118] Having witnessed this snapshot already ourselves, we know exactly what is going through Tarwater's mind and when the woman tells him, "Whatever devil's work you mean to do, don't do it here."[119]

It would seem that Cherokee Lodge is the place chosen for the Devil's work by Rayber, who suggests drowning three times and then suggests baptizing—anything to get the boys in the water. The violent culmination that ensues is inevitable. The last snapshot we see of Bishop is through Rayber's eyes through the window of his room in the Cherokee Lodge. Having turned Bishop over to Tarwater, Rayber has fallen into a deep sleep. He awakens.

> He got up and went to the window. The boat with the two of them in it was near the middle of the lake, almost still. They were sitting there facing each other in the isolation of the water, Bishop small and squat, and Tarwater gaunt, lean, bent slightly forward, his whole attention concentrated on the opposite figure. They seemed to be held still in some magnetic field of attraction. The sky was an intense purple as if it were about to explode into darkness.[120]

Darkness falls. Rayber waits by the window "with serenity," an "observer."[121] The window frames blackness—an overexposure. When the drowning takes place, it is under the veil of darkness. Rayber, hearing aid attuned, hears Bishop bellow and collapses when he realizes "there would be no pain."[122] Tarwater, on the other hand, has a great deal of pain in store

[117] Ibid., 426.
[118] Ibid., 427.
[119] Ibid.
[120] Ibid., 454.
[121] Ibid.
[122] Ibid., 456.

for him as he, overcome with spiritual hunger, makes his way back to the holy ground of Powderhead. He clings to his perceived victory. The fact that he accidently baptized Bishop as he drowned him only bothers him a little bit. He moves through the final scenes of this drama clinging to a corkscrew bottle-opener that Rayber had given him, "his talisman"—"it promised to open great things for him."[123] He holds this artifact or a relic of the visible country as a kind of ritual to ward off any more appearances of the "invisible country." There are no more snapshot revelations in this last section of the book, however. God is going to deal with this defiant young man as He did with Jonah. Tarwater's "whale" arrives in a lavender car wearing a lavender handkerchief. Instead of being swallowed by the beast, Tarwater is brutally raped by the beast and left naked in the woods, his hands tied with the lavender handkerchief. When he regains consciousness, he burns the "evil ground" upon which he finds himself and "moves forward" on the "road home, ground that had been familiar to him since his infancy but now looked like strange and alien country. He knew that he could not turn back now. He knew that his destiny forced him on to a final revelation. His scorched eyes...looked as if, touched with a coal like the lips of the prophet, they would never be used for ordinary sights again."[124] He has crossed over. His feet may be treading the actual, but his "scorched" eyes are now and will continue seeing the Marvelous.

O'CONNOR, PHOTOGRAPHS, 2012

In the summer of 2012, I attended a seminar[125] held in Milledgeville, Georgia, the home of Andalusia, where Flannery O'Connor lived most of her life. Dr. William Sessions, editor of O'Connor's recently published prayer journal, conducted a session in which he read excerpts from that journal. In the question and answer part of that assembly, I asked Dr. Sessions if O'Connor had an interest in photography. He said, "No, I don't think she did." He paused a moment, then he said, "Now that I think of it, every time my wife and I went to visit Flannery [which was often], she took a picture of us as we arrived." The key here is that she took the same picture of William Sessions and his wife embarking from the various vehicles owned

[123] Ibid., 467.
[124] Ibid., 473.
[125] Avis Hewitt, "Archiving O'Connor," Grand Valley State University.

by them over a number of years. In her accumulated pictures of the Sessions, seasons passed and the husband and wife aged. These pictures might present themselves as a study when assembled by O'Connor, the amateur photographer. Jane Rabb, in the introduction to her anthology *Literature & Photography*, writes that from mid-nineteenth century on, "many authors became amateur photographers. They just didn't publicize their avocation."[126] O'Connor's behavior in the case of the Sessions' photographs opens for us a window to her creative process. What did she see as she studied the images of her friends over the passage of time?

O'Connor uses the very real personage of Francis Marion Tarwater, a prophet for modernity, as a conduit between the reader and the Divine reality. Tarwater is named after an American Revolutionary War military officer generally considered to be the father of guerrilla warfare because of his unconventional methods in battle. Tar-water, a mixture of pine resin and water, is advocated as medicinal by Irish Bishop of Cloyne, George Berkley in *Sins*, his last philosophical work, in 1744. Berkley's philosophy was popular after WWII because of the way he analyzed perception. Berkley believed that God provided phenomena for the elucidation of His people. These two elements, historical reality and the perception of Divine reality, are combined in O'Connor's main character and are illustrated by the verbal snapshots that we "see" through his eyes. The photograph serves as the medium to unite these seemingly disparate components. John Updike writes in his unpublished essay "All in the Family," "Always we are aware, in looking at photographs that something lay beyond the edges, in the dimensions of both space and time. Unlike the older, more humanly shaped arts which begin with a seed and accumulate their form organically, photography clips its substance out of an actual continuum."[127] In using the photographic snapshot to inform her pictorial technique in *The Violent Bear It Away*, O'Connor has chosen a medium that carries within itself a dual purpose. It represents at once the moment frozen and the continuum from which that moment has been lifted. The awareness of that continuum is what O'Connor manipulates in the novel. The "something [that] lay be-

[126] *Literature & Photography: Interactions 1840–1990*, ed. Jane Rabb (Albuquerque: University of New Mexico Press, 1995) xxxix.

[127] John Updike, "All in the Family" (unpublished), *Literature & Photography: Interactions 1840–1990*, ed. Jane Rabb (Albuquerque: University of New Mexico Press, 1995) 527.

yond the edges" of her verbal snapshots, does, in fact, lay beyond the "edges of both space and time." It is the something that Merton calls "illusion," that Hawthorne calls the "Marvelous," and that O'Connor calls the "invisible country." We are able to "see" that country just as God has always revealed it to his people—in snapshot moments that are fragmented but that seem to be part of some great invisible continuum that is both accessible and yet beyond human understanding.

Chapter 5

A "Turn in a Different Direction": The Short Story Collections

It was as if a blind boy had been turned so gently in a different direction that he did not know his destination had been changed.
("Parker's Back")[1]

I often ask myself what makes a story work, and what makes it hold up as a story, and I have decided that it is probably some action, some gesture of a story that is unlike any other in the story, one that indicates where the real heart of the story lies.[2]

It has always amused me that Flannery O'Connor, who has been instrumental in shaping the American short story into the form we recognize today, received a B- in her freshman composition class entitled "The Short Story" at Georgia College for Women in 1942. I wonder what her instructor thought when O'Connor's first book of short stories was published thirteen years later in 1955. In her lectures to young writers, O'Connor clearly outlines structure and elements of good short stories that include a "gesture" or an "action" that indicates the "heart of the story." These moments (often called "moments of grace") have kept readers speculating since the stories first appeared in publication. Thus far, I have considered the type of pictorial writing specific to O'Connor in the novels and how she purposefully utilizes it as a sort of sign language. As she has stated, she is speaking to the hard of hearing, and she is determined to make her message clear. Just as the signs in American Sign Language carry within them a history of American life (the sign for girl indicates a bonnet ribbon, the sign for boy, a cap), the artistic mediums or techniques chosen as templates for O'Connor's emblematic expression expand the range of messages emanating from her emblematic pictorial pauses. The short stories differ from the novels in that she varies her technique. While the novels are virtual galleries of pictorial mo-

[1] Parker upon seeing an illustrated man in Flannery O'Connor's "Parker's Back."

[2] Flannery O'Connor in *Mystery and Manners*, 111.

ments, the short stories showcase one or two signs that reverberate throughout the story as a whole. The gestures at the heart of some of the stories exactly replicate the elements of those in the novels, and these are the short stories we will consider in this chapter.

"A GOOD MAN IS HARD TO FIND"

One such pictorial moment occurs in "A Good Man Is Hard to Find." At the beginning of the story, the grandmother attempts to paint a visual picture of her version of the Old South during a family car trip through Georgia and into Tennessee.[3] The first spot of interest is Stone Mountain which, bears the largest Civil War Memorial in *bas relief* blasted on to the side of the mountain. In 1915, Stone Mountain was the site of the revival of the KKK. Organizers were inspired by the release of D. W. Griffith's *Birth of a Nation* and gathered at the site to restore this group that had begun to die out across the South. The family car, which has already carried them 55,890 miles over the years, seems now to be embarking on a journey into the past, or rather the *remembered* past. The grandmother tries to conjure "the good old days" for her grandchildren by painting a picture with her words. First, she fills in the details of the landscape: "Stone Mountain; the blue granite that in some places came up to both sides of the highway; the brilliant red clay banks slightly streaked with purple; the various crops that made rows of green lace-work on the ground. The trees were full of silver-white sunlight and the meanest of them sparkled."[4] The children are unimpressed by this landscape and go back to reading their comic books. The grandmother tries another tactic to draw them in to her re-creation: "'Oh look at the cute little pickaninny!' she said and pointed to a Negro child standing in the door of a shack. 'Wouldn't that make a picture now?' she asked and they all turned and looked at the little Negro out of the back window. He waved."[5]

As the trip progresses, she states, "'Little niggers in the country don't have things like we do.... If I could paint, I'd paint that picture,' she said."[6]

[3] This is similar to Nathanael West's Tod Hackett in *The Day of the Locust.* I discussed how O'Connor is influenced by this technique in chapter 2.

[4] O'Connor, *Collected Works,* 139.

[5] Ibid.

[6] Ibid.

When the children go back to their comic books, the grandmother tries again:

> "Look at the graveyard!" the grandmother said, pointing it out. "That was the old family burying ground. That belonged to the plantation."
>
> "Where's the plantation?" John Wesley asked.
>
> "Gone With the Wind," said the grandmother. "Ha. Ha."[7]

As the family car moves across Middle Georgia, and as the grandmother attempts to recreate the past, O'Connor has provided a filmic panorama that passes by outside of the car windows.[8] It begins with an establishing shot of the natural landscape over which looms Stone Mountain, an "appropriate" gateway to the past. This one image embodies both a glorified exhibition of the Civil War generals and the horrific activities of the KKK. Materializing in the dust and framed by the doorway of a shack is an African American child. He is viewed by the grandmother and children looking backward out of the rear window of the car. The *studium* of that photographic moment is the historical significance of that child juxtaposed with Stone Mountain. The *punctum* is the wave. The child's wave at the family places the scene in the family's present even though the grandmother tries to freeze the child in the past by calling him a "pickaninny."[9] By painting a picture of the child, the grandmother would dehumanize him and turn him into a representation: a picture of himself, styled as a pickaninny. The fact that the child waves back at the grandmother establishes his existence in the present and causes the wistful past to begin dissolving. In fact, by answering her grandson's question about the whereabouts of the "plantation" they are seeking with the words "gone with the wind," the grand mother reveals that all she really knows about the antebellum past is what she has learned from a movie. She has never actual seen a plantation like those in the film.

[7] Ibid.

[8] This is accomplished in a way similar to the car-window montage that occurs with Hazel Motes in *Wise Blood*.

[9] Robin Bernstein writes, "The pickaninny was an imagined subhuman black juvenile who was typically depicted outdoors, merrily accepting (or even inviting) violence" (Bernstein, 34).

This panoramic journey has taken us from the real past (the Civil War, the Ku Klux Klan) to the representational past (the monument, "pickaninny," and the film) to the reality of the present: the child's wave. It is a visual depiction of the way the "iniquity of the fathers" [will be visited] "on the children, to the third and the fourth generation"[10] We witness the grandmother in the process of passing on the legacy of racism inherited by all Americans. The materialization of the child waving from the doorway hovers over The Misfit's statement, "She would have been a good woman, if it had been somebody there to shoot her every minute of her life"[11] at the end of the story. Readers may wonder when they reach this statement whether the sins of the grandmother could have really been that bad. The image of the African American child looms. It does not fade, and it is the gesture that, as O'Connor said, indicates "the heart of the story" to American readers.

Probably one of the most enigmatic images that appears in O'Connor's fiction is found in the middle story of *A Good Man Is Hard to Find*, "The Artificial Nigger." The chipped and worn plaster figure, essentially a lawn jockey, materializes at the end of the story, unlike the "pickaninny" figure, which appears very near the beginning of the initial story in the collection, indicating an illumination of the events that have come before it. The story "glows" from the very first sentence, "Mr. Head awakened to discover that the room was full of moonlight."[12] The story is constructed as a stylized version of American Romance as set out by Hawthorne in his *Mosses from an Old Manse*, and O'Connor uses this mode to usher her readers into the Romantic realm of "glimmering shadows that lay half asleep."[13] Of course, as always, she writes with a satirical pen, but the elements are there. As we examine Mr. Head's bedroom through the gauze of "miraculous moonlight," we see first a defunct alarm clock sitting on top of an "overturned bucket" located at the foot of the bed. Time, it would seem, has been suspended. Mr. Head has been transformed into a "Vergil summoned in the middle of the night to go to Dante, or better, Raphael, awakened by a blast of God's light to fly to the side of Tobias....The slop jar out of the shadow made snow-white in the moonlight, appeared to stand guard over him like a

[10] Numbers 14:8 (English Standard Version).

[11] O'Connor, *Collected Works*, 153.

[12] Ibid., 210.

[13] Hawthore, 1.

small personal angel."[14] He is our hero who, viewed through a "kind of spiritual medium," sits in an "edifice" (his bed) that has "not quite the aspect of belonging to the material world."[15]

As Hawthorne writes his introduction to the *Mosses,* he contemplates the sermons that must have been written in the old manse by the many clergymen who have occupied the house before him. In her story, O'Connor contemplates the one sermon that Mr. Head has been preaching to his grandson, Nelson, in anticipation of their trip to Atlanta. "It was to be a lesson that the boy would never forget. He was to find out from it that he had no cause for pride merely because he had been born in a city. He was to find out that the city is not a great place. Mr. Head meant him to see everything there is to see in a city so that he would be content to stay at home for the rest of his life."[16] Hawthorne's narrator is also traveling. Moving further into the purview of Romance, he leads his readers along a meandering river whose domain is inhabited by the ghosts of Indians and Civil War soldiers. Ghosts exist in the O'Connor story as well. Mr. Head and Nelson make their way under waning moonlight to a train stop where "under the useless morning moon the tracks looked white and fragile. Both the old man and the child stared ahead as if they were awaiting an apparition"[17] When they board the train, Mr. Head and Nelson begin take on ghost-like characteristics themselves. "'I heard you,' the boy muttered. 'It's no use use in you yelling,' and he sat down and turned his head to the glass. There he saw a pale ghost-like face scowling at him beneath the brim of a pale ghost-like hat. His grandfather, looking quickly too, saw a different ghost, pale but grinning, under a black hat."[18] The presence of apparitions suggests that we have left the sphere of the natural and have wholly and completely entered the miraculous orb where anything can happen. The story of Mr. Head's and Nelson's journey begins.

Why does O'Connor so clearly fashion this particular story in the recognizable elements of the American Romance tradition, particularly when her hero falls far short of expectations? Mr. Head is no guide, no teacher. He is not Vergil or St. Raphael, but, in fact, as the story progresses, becomes

[14] O'Connor, *Collected Works,* 210–11.
[15] Hawthorne, *Mosses from an Old Manse,* 1.
[16] O'Connor, *Collected Works,* 212.
[17] Ibid., 213.
[18] Ibid., 214.

an uninitiated wanderer like his grandson, and yet, in his wanderings filled with confusion and lack of direction, he is led to his destiny, to the overarching image that dominates the story. His quest has taken him into the unknown, the unexperienced. He does not know real fear—not just the fear of embarrassment. He has publically rejected his grandson to protect himself. He may never outlive the consequences of this action. He is a hero that has been undone. "They [Nelson and Mr. Head] stood gazing at the artificial Negro as if they were faced with some great mystery, some monument to another's victory that brought them together in their common defeat. They could both feel it dissolving their differences like an action of mercy."[19] The boy turns to Mr. Head and says, "Let's go home before we get ourselves lost again."[20] Miraculously, when they return home and jump off the train, "the moon, restored to its full splendor, sprang from a cloud and flooded the clearing with light."[21] In fact, the two heroes have fulfilled their quest and they return home redeemed. In the moment they stood before the image, they "felt the action of mercy" and, in that moment, they recognized themselves as part of a long line of sinners in need of salvation.

"The Artificial Nigger," which features a lawn jockey as a visual image, is placed in the middle of O'Connor's first short story collection, *A Good Man Is Hard to Find.* Three African American figures in three different stories are central to a metanarrative that operates in the short story collection. The first story in the collection features the grandmother wistfully looking back at the "pickaninny" as she and her family speed headlong to their own deaths. The lawn jockey appears as an instrument of redemption for Nelson and Mr. Head in the middle story. In the last story of the collection, Sulk emerges as a savior of Mr. Guizac's refugee cousin. O'Connor uses the narratives to imbue the actions of the white characters with a historical context. The lawn jockey represents a figure that is historically both static and mobile. Many jockeys in the 1800s actually were black, in part because they were slaves, but also because they knew and raised horses. Pellom McDaniels has written a book about Isaac Burns Murphy, who was a legendary black jockey.

[19] Ibid., 230.
[20] Ibid.
[21] Ibid.

> He made it a profession. He was able to command a salary—rather a few contracts making on average of $10,000 a year, which would be equal to about $350 to $400,000 in today's terms. So what he was able to do was spend his money on items that made him a consumer. So he had a shotgun collection. He and his wife owned property in Chicago. They were able to take these vacations in this off-season that allowed him to spend his money and spend time with family. (NPR interview, 2016)

This profession was open to African Americans until the 1890s, when white jockeys became jealous and began violently inhibiting them in races. In 1893, the black jockeys were outlawed. This history adds another perspective on the image that appears in front of Nelson and Mr. Head. The lawn jockey represents not only repression and slavery, but also the ability to rise, to overcome, to flourish, and eventually to converge. O'Connor, writer of American Romance in the fashion of Hawthorne, chooses to elevate this object. In fact, the object is central to the story.[22]

In the "The Artificial Nigger," O'Connor sets the stage for Romance by opening the story in moonlight. As the curtains of night are drawn back, we see Mr. Head's bedroom through the window frame. Mr. Head awakens "to discover the room was full of moonlight."[23] The narration moves from one object to another, painting a picture that is at once actual and "Marvelous" in the Romantic tradition. The nature of these objects reflects the nature of Mr. Head himself, either because they are his choices or he has crafted them himself. After this illuminated beginning, the story takes place in the heat of the day, and when, at the end of the story, the central object—the "artificial nigger," or the lawn jockey—appears, it is not suffused with Romance. It is what it is, a common yard ornament. Part of the interpretative text of this object is the fact that it is common. It is a slice of the popu-

[22] In the preface to *The House of the Seven Gables,* Hawthorne writes about how the writer of Romance weaves the "marvelous" into the fabric of the story. He suggests that the Romantic writer must "mingle the Marvelous rather as a slight, delicate, and evanescent flavor, than as any portion of the substance of the dish offered to the public." He notes that the writer might want to alter the atmosphere of the story by mellowing the lights, for example, to "enrich the shadows of the picture" he or she is painting (1).

[23] O'Connor, *Collected Works,* 103.

lar culture. It is mass-produced. O'Connor underlines this by writing that it is "not possible to tell if the artificial Negro were meant to be young or old; he looked too miserable to be either. He was meant to look happy because his mouth was stretched up at the corners but the chipped eye and the angle he was cocked at gave him a wild look of misery instead."[24] This is not the gently illuminated object in a Romance. It is "cocked" like a gun. It is cutting edge. We have entered the realm of Pop Art, art that casts a critical eye on contemporary, mass-produced culture. In this short story, O'Connor has extended the Romantic technique of first illuminating objects to give them resonance. She submits the lawn jockey to the flat examination performed by the Pop Artists of her day. The way Nelson and Mr. Head respond to the image after their perilous journey turns the artificial nigger into a symbol that resonates across cultures and across time. The story ends in the moonlight just as Nelson and Mr. Head arrive home. After this day, Mr. Head has a new understanding of God's forgiveness and mercy. This is the "Marvelous" in this story.

In the last story of the collection, "The Displaced Person," a photograph provides the turning point for the plot of the short story. Mrs. McIntyre, owner of a dairy farm, surprises Sulk, one of her Negro hired hands, studying a photograph clutched in his hands. When she questions him as to why he is not in the field working, he automatically hands the photograph over to her. "It was a photograph of a girl about twelve in a white dress. She had blond hair with a wreath in it and she looked forward out of light eyes that were bland and composed. 'Who is this child?' Mrs. McIntyre asked."[25]

It is a photograph of Mr. Guizac's cousin, dressed for her confirmation, and it sets off the culminating chain of events in the short story. Mr. Guizac is a WWII refugee brought by the church to work as a hired farm hand currently employed by Mrs. McIntyre. Upon investigation, she discovers that Sulk has been paying Mr. Guizac three dollars out of each paycheck in order to bring his young cousin (photograph) to a better life America. For this, the girl, who is now four years older than in the picture, will marry him. The photograph and its implications shake Mrs. McIntyre to her very core, and "as soon as she got into the house, she lay down on her bed...and pressed her hand over her heart as if she were trying to keep it in

[24] Ibid., 229

[25] Ibid., 311.

place."[26] O'Connor uses a concrete art object—a statue—to illustrate the *punctum*, or what about the photograph has pierced her heart.

The image that occupied Mrs. McIntyre's mind as she lay on her bed was the angel over the Judge's grave. This had been a naked granite cherub that the old man had seen in the city one day in a tombstone store window. He had been taken with it at once, partly because its face reminded him of his wife and partly because he wanted a genuine work of art over his grave. He had come home with it sitting on the green plush train seat beside him. Mrs. McIntyre had never noticed the resemblance to herself. She had always thought it hideous, but when the Herrins (former hired help) stole it off the old man's grave, she was shocked and outraged. "When the Herrins left, the angel left with them, all but its toes, for the ax old man Herrin had used to break it off with had struck slightly too high. Mrs. McIntyre had never been able to afford to have it replaced."[27]

The blond girl in the photograph held by a black hand has perforated Mrs. McIntyre's heart and has brought back memories of a past that was already dead on the day the Judge spotted the statue in the store window. It is not a past that she particularly thinks is beautiful—but it belongs to her. It is part of the package that she earned when she, at thirty, married the seventy-five-year-old Judge for his alleged money, but that has been steadily chiseled away since the Judge died bankrupt three years later and left her only the mortgaged house and land. She has had to depend on hired "white trash" for help in running the farm. Like the grandmother, the grandeur of the past is what Mrs. McIntyre still worships, regardless of the fact that it is all an illusion, all false. The photograph of the little blond white girl represents a past as well, but a past founded in reality. The photo was taken before the girl spent three years in a concentration camp and before she would desperately marry a stranger in order to come to America to start a new life. Mrs. McIntyre disregards any of this reality and clings to a world that she has created for herself. The little island of the farm, like the toes of the Judge's statue, represents the wholeness of what she has lost. The photograph recalls a historical moment, the little girl's confirmation. By juxtaposing the photograph with a statue on a grave, O'Connor has encapsulated Mrs. McIntyre's desire to freeze the moment before little girls were marched off to concentration camps and before a black man could contemplate mar-

[26] Ibid.
[27] Ibid., 312.

rying a white woman and to dwell in that space indefinitely. It is in this way that Mrs. McIntyre saw the drama of her entire life in the confirmation picture. In "The Displaced Person," O'Connor superimposes the image of a tombstone angel on to the image of a young girl in the mind of Mrs. McIntyre, who must hold her heart to prevent the transformation is taking place. The grandmother and Mr. Head are transformed, but it could be argued that Mrs. McIntyre is not. Because of a stroke, she is doomed to spend her earthly life speechless. She loses her farm and no one comes to see her "except the old priest" who comes weekly and "explains the doctrines of the Church."[28] She has succeeded in freezing the moment, but at great cost.

A Good Man Is Hard to Find features three major images that fulfill the criterion of this study. They occur in stories at the beginning, the middle, and the end of the book, and they all highlight African Americans as agents of change. Toni Morrison has commented extensively on the purposes associated with the appropriation of African Americans in *Playing in the Dark*. She writes:

> A writer's response to American Africanism often provides a subtext that either sabotages the surface text's expressed intentions or escapes them through a language that mystifies what it cannot bring itself to articulate but still attempts to register. Linguistic responses to Africanism serve the text by further problematizing its matter with resonances and laminations. They can serve as allegorical fodder for the contemplation of Eden, expulsion, and the availability of grace. In other words they give the text a deeper, richer, more complex life than the sanitized one commonly presented to us.[29]

Utilizing African Americans as O'Connor does in these three stories could prove troublesome. However, except for the "pickaninny," who is a literary creation, O'Connor's peripheral black characters in this book have developed characteristics and lives that are distant but that suggest an existence beyond the boundaries of the story in an attempt to present them as somewhat dimensional. Many discussions of O'Connor and her portrayal of black characters exist throughout scholarship on her work. Let it suffice that

[28] Ibid., 326–27.

[29] Morrison, 66.

racism is a topic for another study. This work is about technique and we will leave it there.

EVERYTHING THAT RISES MUST CONVERGE

Technique plays a large role in *Everything That Rises Must Converge,* O'Connor's last collection of short stories, but in a way that is different than anything else. In a letter to Sister Mariella Gable on May 4, 1963, O'Connor writes that she has enough stories for a collection, but, she notes, "I appreciate and need your prayers. I've been writing eighteen years and I've reached a point where I can't do again what I know I can do well, and the larger things that I need to do now, I doubt my capacity for doing."[30]

Throughout the next, and last, year of her life, O'Connor worked on constructing this final collection of her stories. These stories, along with the manuscript for *Why Do the Heathen Rage?*, reveal an author experimenting...pushing the boundaries of what she has known into new areas of artistic expression. If O'Connor had lived longer, these works might have been labeled transitional. Where the stories in *A Good Man Is Hard to Find* are united thematically and held together by a tight arc, the stories in the second collection are tied together by artistic style or technique. Each story revolves around one resonating image: a hat, a bull, the woods, a water stain, a gun, a telescope, hell/heaven, a tattoo, and Judgment Day. The entire collection, framed by its covers, is a composition, a collage of images. The juxtaposition of these images causes a friction, a tension that works to hold the whole together. Using a compilation of images and juxtaposing them as a sort of sign language was almost *de rigueur* as part of the art milieu of the early sixties when O'Connor was writing these stories.[31]

Everything that Rises Must Converge ends with a story, "Judgment Day," which is the final version of the title story in her MFA thesis entitled "The Geranium." The geranium has been removed so that there is no distraction from her message about the final judgment that will meet all hu-

[30] *Habit of Being,* 518.

[31] Definition of Pop Art: 1. "use of existing imagery from mass culture already processed into two dimensions" from "advertising, photography, and other mass media sources" 2. "emphasis on flatness and frontal presentation" 3. "techniques imply the removal of the artist's hand" 4. "delving into areas of popular taste and kitsch" 5. "contemporary subject matter" (Livingstone, 1)

mans after death. The "sweet moral blossom" that O'Connor presents to us at the end of this volume is the story of the great friendship and love that had grown between Tanner, a white man, and Coleman, a black man, in the midst of all the surrounding "human frailty and sorrow."[32]

"PARKER'S BACK": A BREAKTHROUGH

James J. Napier writes about the "final achievement" of Flannery O'Connor's last three stories in *Everything That Rises Must Converge*, which give proof of a talent that, even as death approached, was able to put a stamp of meaning on her last efforts."[33] The narrative of O. E. Parker and his Sarah Ruth is the last story by Flannery O'Connor, written and revised in last three weeks of July 1964. Regina O'Connor, her mother, had "set up a table and electric typewriter by her bedside," and Flannery "[devoted] twenty-two hours a day to resting up for writing."[34] The tattoo on Parker's back represents the culminating development of her pictorial technique. By framing this one tattoo (low culture) of the Byzantine Christ (high culture) with Parker's very human body, O'Connor, in one pictorially stylized gesture, reaches across time, class, and culture to mesh the finite and the infinite. In this one act, she upends cliché, evokes fifteenth-century symbolism, and uses the eyes of the tattoo as a *punctum* which lifts the veil to a Divine reality. Parker carries this revelation to the fallen world by serving as canvas, receptacle, and emissary of the Divine. Choosing a human being as an image-bearer and mixing his blood with the ink used to create the image is a stylistic breakthrough into new artistic territory for O'Connor.

If we view this short story as O'Connor's final missive to the world, then I think there are three elements of the story that need to be considered in reference to this study of her pictorial text. These can be framed in three focus questions:

[32] I would like to note here that Coleman is a much more dimensional African American character than any that appeared in *A Good Man Is Hard to Find.* James J. Napier, in his article "Flannery O'Connor's Last Three: 'The Sense of an Ending,'" writes that the stories in this collection "reveal a readiness to portray black characters more confidently, to have them speak more revealingly, and move a little closer to the center of her fictional stage" (21).

[33] Napier, "Flannery O'Connor's Last Three," 21.

[34] Gooch, *Flannery*, 365.

1) Why did O'Connor choose to style her last pictorial image in the form of Byzantine mosaic?

2) Why did O'Connor decide to make her last image a tattoo?

3) Why, when she previously almost virtually neglected the topic, does she address the institution of marriage in "Parker's Back"?

WHY BYZANTINE MOSAIC?

As I have with other works in this study, I will first look to Hawthorne as a stylistic influence on O'Connor's "Parker's Back." In fact, there are a number of ways in which this story parallels Hawthorne's *The Scarlet Letter.* However, the most obvious comparison is, of course, the power that emanates from an image borne on the human body. The scarlet letter changes Hawthorne's Hester Prynne both internally and externally, and directly affects those with whom she comes in contact. "Walking to and fro, with those lonely footsteps, in the little world with which she was outwardly connected, it now and then appeared to Hester—if altogether fancy, it was nevertheless too potent to be resisted—she felt or fancied, then, that the scarlet letter had endowed her with a new sense. She shuddered to believe, yet could not help believing, that it gave her a sympathetic knowledge of the hidden sin in other hearts."[35]

The letter imbues Hester with a Divine sense. It has powerful spiritual properties that have made her sympathetic as she passes among her fellow men. Rather than shying from people because of her own sin, she is empathetic with the sins of others. Parker is compelled by the image that he carries as well. An awareness of a supernatural power comes over him and he begins to sense its bidding in the same way that Hester does. Her letter becomes as permanent to her as Parker's tattoo is to him. Both characters are defined and impelled by the images they bear.

Artistic creation is at the center of both stories. Hawthorne presents Hester as an artist who creates images with her needle. These embellishments are not just hers alone, but she is able to earn a subsistence living because of them. Her art begins to adorn everyone in the community. O'Connor presents Parker as an artist who is in the process of making his body into a collage of illustrations. In a very real way, Parker represents an

[35] Hawthorne, *Scarlet Letter*, 60.

"embodiment" of O'Connor's own style. When she has Sarah Ruth say to Parker, "At the judgement seat of God, Jesus is going to say to you, 'What you been doing all your life besides have pictures drawn all over you?'"[36] she might be thinking about answering a similar question when she herself appears at her final judgment.

Parker, like Hester, has an audience for his artistic arrangements. He is the talk of the pool hall, and his tattoos earn him sexual favors. Parker really has a pretty enjoyable life even though, as time moves on, he begins to feel a lack or emptiness that spurs him into adding yet another tattoo. So far, the composition or collage of images that is framed by his body is just not exactly right. It does not match his vision. Both Hester and Parker express themselves using a kind of sign language, a narrative composed of images. Throughout her career as a writer, this has been O'Connor's language as well, and it becomes important, then, to heed the properties of the last image she leaves with us, a Byzantine mosaic of Christ's face.

Even though Barry Moser decided to feature Parker's tattoo as a Byzantine painting rather than a mosaic in his cover illustration for Sarah Gordon's book *The Obedient Imagination*, O'Connor makes it very clear that the tattoo Parker receives is a mosaic version of the Byzantine Christ.

> "You found what you want?" the [tattoo] artist asked.
>
> Parker's throat was too dry to speak. He got up and thrust the book at the artist, opened at the picture.
>
> "That'll cost you plenty," the artist said. "You don't want all those little blocks though, just the outline and some better features."
>
> "Just like it is," Parker said, "just like it is or nothing."
>
> "It's your funeral," the artist said, "but I don't do that kind of work for nothing."
>
> "How much?" Parker said.[37]

[36] O'Connor, *Collected Works*, 663–64.
[37] Ibid., 667.

The distinction between a mosaic and a painting is crucial to the interpretation of this image. At first, when paging through the book of tattoos, Parker seems to be having a difficult time choosing the picture of "God" with which he hopes to "bring Sarah Ruth to heel."[38] He looks at all of the renderings of Christ—"The Good Shepherd, Forbid Them Not, The Smiling Jesus, Jesus the Physician's Friend, but he [keeps] turning rapidly backwards and the pictures became less reassuring."[39] Suddenly Parker hears...nothing. He hears silence as if, O'Connor writes, "silence were a language itself, GO BACK."[40] "Parker returned to the picture—the haloed head of a flat Byzantine Christ with all-demanding eyes. He sat there trembling; his heart began slowly to beat again as if it were being brought to life by a subtle power."[41]

The picture is chosen. Parker's fate, just like that of Hazel Motes and Francis Marion Tarwater, is sealed. He becomes "Christ-haunted." For Hazel, Jesus stalks him "from tree to tree in the back of his mind, a wild ragged figure motioning him to turn around and come off into the dark where he might be walking on the water and not know it and then suddenly know it and drown."[42] Tarwater sees "the bleeding, stinking, mad shadow of Jesus" who will not let him rest. In "Parker's Back," the Christ image is different in that it is stationary. Parker, like Hawthorne's minister wearing his black veil, or Hester wearing the scarlet "A," will carry his Byzantine Christ in this world and into the next. The properties of the Byzantine mosaic art form demand this kind of service.

Because the mosaics existed within the architectural framework of the Byzantine church, there was a "hierarchy of receptacles within which the pictures could be arranged."[43] "The mosaics exist in curved receptacles require the art pieces to be constructed using small uniformly shaped cubes, fitted together in a close network whose lines run in form-designing curves. The tension of these curves mirrors the tension of the rounded receptacles. In this way the spatial character of middle Byzantine mosaic expresses itself

[38] Ibid., 665.

[39] Ibid., 667.

[40] Ibid.

[41] Ibid.

[42] Ibid., 11.

[43] Otto Demus, *Byzantine Mosaic Decoration: The Aspects of Monumental Art in Byzantium* (New Rochelle, NY: Caratzas Brothers, 1976) 11.

even in the technical procedure."[44] The receptacle or niche encloses the space in front of the picture and, in fact, that space becomes "included in the picture."[45] The beholder is able then to walk into that location and to exist in the same space "in which the holy person or icon exists." He becomes enclosed "in the grand icon of the church; he is surrounded by the congregation of the saints and takes part in the events he sees."[46] The mosaic artist planned on the art piece being lighted from an outside source in the church so he designed his mosaic in the way best to reflect that light into the space shared by the beholder and the icon. He went to great lengths, plastering and replastering his space to take advantage of light disseminated by a nearby window. The icon and the beholder share the same source of light in the present. Light is not included in the actual design of the icon for this reason. The prototype of the icon is placed and designed in accordance with the light source. Consequently, the mosaic artist choses the cubes with which he is going to construct his mosaic for their reflective, radiating surfaces. Gold especially was selected to "produce a rich coloristic effect but also to light the spatial icon,"[47] particularly at night when the light emanated from candles and lamps. It was at night that the golden halos around the heads of the icons really came to life.

Parker's back, "almost completely covered with little red and blue and ivory and saffron squares,"[48] becomes a traveling receptacle which houses an iconic mosaic. The first thing Parker does when the tattoo is finished is to drink a pint of whiskey and to go in search of his companions at the pool hall. Having been absent for a time because of his marriage, upon entering the building, one of his old cohorts slaps him on the back yelling "Yeyyyyyy boy! O. E. Parker!"[49] Feeling isolated and uncomfortable in his new body, Parker tries to slink off into a corner, but his old buddies demand to see his new tattoo.

> And while Parker squirmed in their hands, they pulled up his shirt. Parker felt all of the hands drop away instantly and his shirt

[44] Ibid., 13.
[45] Ibid.
[46] Ibid., 13, 111.
[47] Ibid., 35.
[48] O'Connor, *Collected Works*, 668.
[49] Ibid., 671.

> fell like a veil over the face. There was a silence in the pool room which seemed to Parker to grow from the circle around him until it extended to the foundations under the building and upward through the beams in the roof.
>
> Finally someone said, "Christ!"[50]

The pool hall has become holy ground with the appearance of the Byzantine mosaic. O'Connor has replicated the experience of the Byzantine church in a pool hall, a place where nonbelievers might congregate. The beholders share the space with an icon. Parker, in an attempt to reanimate as his old self, sans image, and not the uncomfortable new self, lunges into the middle of the group and "like a whirlwind on a summer's day" begins a fight that rages until he, like Jonah, is tossed out into the alley by his old mates. A calm comes over the pool hall, and Parker, from his position on the ground in the alley, now that the catharsis has passed, contemplates another image of which his body is also the receptacle—his soul. In his reverie, his soul appears to him as a "spider web of facts and lies that was not at all important to him."[51] He had never really worried about his soul before. He probably never gave the idea of its existence a second thought, but, now, as he sat in the silent alley, the eyes of the icon "that were now forever on his back" were demanding that he attend to his soul. In this one gesture, with this one image, O'Connor has put in operation the doctrine of images that evolved during the "iconoclastic controversy of the eighth and ninth centuries."[52]

Does the prototype—i.e., the mosaic Christ—become or encompass some of the power of the archetype—i.e., the Christ? The exhibition of the power of the Byzantine Christ tattooed on Parker's back seems to indicate that O'Connor agreed with the theory that recognizes the archetypal power

[50] Ibid.

[51] Ibid., 672.

[52] Demus, *Byzantine Mosaic Decoration,* 5. Otto Demus writes, "The relation between the prototype and its image, argued Theodore of Studium and John of Damascus, is analogous to that between God the Father and Christ His Son. The prototype, in accordance with Neoplatonic ideas, is thought of as producing its image of necessity, as a shadow is cast by a material object, in the same way as the Father produces the Son and the whole hierarchy of the invisible and the visible world" (5–6).

in the prototype. In this theory, the "world itself becomes an uninterrupted series of 'images' starting with Christ and moving down to man, objects, and finally to prototypes of the Godhead created by artists." In this way the image becomes identical with its prototype, "and the worship accorded to the image is passed through the image to its prototype."[53] Therefore, Parker does not have just a prototype of Christ on his back—he HAS Christ on his back. It is impossible for him to disobey the directives of those all-powerful eyes. In this way, Parker, as image-bearer, differs from Hester as image-bearer. The letter may compel her, but she is not commanded by it. O'Connor has taken inspiration from Hawthorne but has moved forward to make her image-bearer her own creation—God's own creation.

It would seem, then, that O'Connor could not have selected an image from any other time that would have wielded the power that the Byzantine Christ does. In a way different from her other stories, in "Parker's Back," Christ becomes an actor *mise en scene* on the stage of this story. He is present in actuality. Parker, the bearer of Christ, suffers, and in a certain way, he does die, as many of O'Connor's characters do, at their moment of grace. When Parker insists on an exact replica of the mosaic, the tattoo artist warns him, "It's your funeral." With the completion of the tattoo, the old man that he was is gone, but a new man lives on, bearing Christ permanently on his body and who is controlled by the demands of the all-encompassing eyes. Taking note of Parker's behavior in response to the eyes tattooed on his back, we begin to realize why O'Connor chose tattoo as her pictorial medium in this last story.

WHY TATTOO?

Again, *The Scarlet Letter* may have been O'Connor's inspiration for the tattoo. Arthur Dimsdale reveals that he, too, is the bearer of a scarlet letter. His, unlike Hester's needlework letter, has been hidden but is etched directly on his chest. "Now, at the death-hour, he stands before you! He bids you look again at Hester's scarlet letter! He tells you, that, with all its mysterious horror, it is but the shadow of what he bears on his own breast, and that even this, his own red stigma, is no more that the type of what has seared

[53] Ibid., 6.

his inmost heart! Stand any here that question God's judgment on a sinner? Behold! Behold a dreadful witness of it!"[54]

This etching of the image directly on the body makes Parker's tattoo more in tune with whatever Dimsdale has done to make a scarlet "A" appear on his chest. Hawthorne gives us two endings for the image-bearers. Dimsdale collapses and dies after tearing away his "ministerial band" and revealing what has either been tattooed by himself or by some supernatural hand. Hester, however, lives on bearing her scarlet "A" for the rest of her life in the way that we can assume Parker will as well. It would seem that dying at the moment of grace is the easier of the two. It is the living on that takes forbearance and courage.

The tattooed image of Christ was one that occurred to O'Connor as she was writing the manuscript for *Why Do the Heathen Rage?*, the novel she left unfinished when she died in 1964. In that manuscript, there are ten pages that describe photographs taken by the main character, Walter Tilman. Walter is trying create a pictorial reality that contradicts the lies that he has written to Oona Gibbs, a woman with whom he corresponds and who has decided to visit him. In order to dissuade Oona from visiting, he has decided that a compelling visual text must be employed to convey a message that will strongly oppose the written narrative of his letters. He wants to repel her rather than attract her without admitting that he has lied to her. He chooses photographs to accomplish this because the mere nature of photography would make it seems as if the viewer were seeing truth—seeing what really happened. As the reader accompanies Walter on his photo shoot, she is able to witness the assemblage of framed texts that, not unlike O'Connor's cartoons, speak with voices of their own. It was upon reading these pages of this manuscript in the spring of 2012 that I realized my ideas about the purposeful design of pictorial pauses in O'Connor's work were feasible and, in fact, verifiable by using the manuscript to show the way O'Connor was thinking as she constructed her novels and stories.

It is within the frame of one of Walter's photographs that we first meet O. E. Parker, or at least his prototype. Gunnels, a farm hand whose body is covered with tattoos, tells Walter that he would like a photograph of the image of the Christ tattooed on his back so he can look at it, as it is not the particular Christ Gunnels had chosen in the tattoo parlor. This questioning

[54] Hawthorne, *Scarlet Letter*, 161.

the Christ choice firmly disappears in "Parker's Back," where the particular chosen Christ is everything. Walter agrees to take the picture, and when he looks at the Christ image through the camera lens, a passion begins to arise within him. He haphazardly snaps the picture and moves away from the tattoo. It takes "a fresh satanic breeze" to chill the passion that he experienced. This small passage has many of the tropes that we have been tracing in this study. In the process of constructing his pictorial story, Walter has viewed, framed in a camera lens, the image that stops him and throws him off balance. It is the face of Christ. This is the first time in O'Connor's writings, published or in manuscript, that we are presented with the power of the prototype.

O'Connor translates this idea to "Parker's Back." O. E. Parker was just 14 "when he saw a man in a fair tattooed from head to foot."

> Except for his loins which were girded with a panther hide, the man's skin was patterned in what seemed from Parker's distance—he was near the back of the tent, standing on a bench—a single intricate design of brilliant color. The man, who was small and sturdy, moved about on the platform, flexing his muscles so that the arabesque of men and beasts and flowers on his skin appeared to have a subtle motion of its own.[55]

Why is Parker so moved at the sight of the tattooed body? Maybe for the first time he is seeing the naked physical body in all of its glory displayed in public. Foucault describes the body as "the inscribed surface of events,"[56] and the body that stands before Parker, who never thought "there was anything out of the ordinary about the fact that he [Parker] existed,"[57] is inscribed in a way that makes a visual language that Parker can understand. Lees and Sharpe write that "although the styles of tattoo vary, Western tattoos, in particular, literalize this vision of the body as a surface or ground onto which patterns of significance can be inscribed."[58] Parker, "or-

[55] O'Connor, *Collected Works*, 657.

[56] Michel Foucault, "Nietzsche, Genealogy, History," *The Foucault Reader*, ed. Paul Rabinow (London: Penguin, 1991) 204.

[57] O'Connor, *Collected Works*, 658.

[58] Frances Mascia-Lees and Patricia Sharpe, *Tatoo, Torture, Mutilation, and Adornment: The Denaturalization of the Body in Culture and Text* (Albany: State University New York Press, 1992) 147.

dinary as a loaf of bread," is absolutely able to "read" the language of the illustrations. Much has been written about Parker's "loaf of bread" ordinariness. O'Connor does not apply this image lightly. In *The Violent Bear It Away,* the image of a stale forgotten loaf of bread is the only image that stops young Tarwater in his tracks and reminds him of his uncle's words, "Jesus is the bread of life."[59] Through the "texture of [Parker's] ordinary life," the "mystery of existence"[60] will be revealed.

Parker interprets the illustrated man[61] textually as having a "single design of brilliant color" with "an arabesque of men and beasts and flowers on his skin" which appear "to have a subtle motion of its own."[62] Clearly what Parker sees is "a body *image,* the seductive spectacle of a pattern engraved on human skin"[63] For Parker, it is a template. Making his body into a work of art is a way to bring some meaning to his life. Remember, he is 14, the age at which many young men experience a passage rite. There is certainly an aura of a sexuality surrounding the tattoos. After being tattooed, Parker is able to attract girls that were not interested in him before. He joins the navy and continues to add tattoos as he travels from port to port. All in all, the self-image he creates by this method of body adornment seems to have paid off, except that when a new tattoo is about a month old, "a huge dissatisfaction would come over him and he would go off and find another tattooist and have another space filled up."[64] Finally, when there is no more tattoo space left on the front of his body, he decides to desert from the navy, he meets Sarah Ruth, and his life again changes. It is in order to please Sarah Ruth that he chooses to have the Byzantine Christ tattooed on his back.

[59] O'Connor, *Collected Works,* 342.

[60] O'Connor, *Mystery and Manners,* 133.

[61] In 1951, Ray Bradbury published a book of eighteen short stories entitled *The Illustrated Man.* The premise of this book is that by firelight, the man's tattoos would begin to move and would tell a story. I have no evidence that

O'Connor was even aware of this book, but I like to think that it might have been in her lexicon of popular culture.

[62] O'Connor, *Collected Works,* 657.

[63] Andre Bleikasten, "Writing on the Flesh: Tattoos and Taboos in 'Parker's Back.'" *The Southern Literary Journal* 14/2 (Spring 1982): 8–18, 11.

[64] O'Connor, *Collected Works,* 659.

Theological analysis of this story is well documented by a variety of O'Connor scholars. Earlier, I considered the appropriateness of the choice Parker made by picking the Byzantine mosaic; now, for the purpose of this study, I am going to examine the physical process of tattooing and how the physicality of the medium can be elevated until it is almost religiously symbolic. The application of the Byzantine Christ by using the medium of tattoo accomplishes O'Connor's purpose, which is to illustrate Parker's body as a "temple of the Holy Spirit,"[65] as are the bodies of all believers, and to ready him to become one of God's prophets like Hazel Motes and Francis Marion Tarwater. He will only become like these forbearers in some ways. In many ways, Parker is O'Connor's most accessible "everyman" prophet. Unlike Hazel Motes and young Tarwater, he is not socially inept. He is "Yeyyyyy boy! O. E. Parker," formerly traveler of the seven seas and frequenter of pool halls. By making Parker identifiable to her readers in this way, O'Connor is bringing her readers into the presence of the icon. Parker, as receptacle, as Divine emissary, is just a "good old boy" with whom the reader could identify. In fact, any one of us in O'Connor's audience could become receptacles for the icon, and that, I believe, is O'Connor's point. The process of tattoo itself becomes representative or metaphoric of how the mundane and or ordinary can be elevated to the Divine.

TATTOO PROCESS

Step One: Cleansing/Purging: The body must be cleansed, shaved, and disinfected. A ritual cleansing is often part of a redemption or purification process.[66] For old Tarwater and for Hazel Motes, the cleansing is a "burning clean." The young Tarwater is immersed in the lake during the baptism ritual.

Step Two: Template: The tattoo artist will first begin by drawing an outline, a template, or a cartoon of the tattoo on the skin using the tattoo machine with needles attached. Each of O'Connor's prophets is granted a template, but none of them choose at first to follow it. Old Tarwater clearly outlines the destiny, replete with tasks, for his great-nephew. Hazel Motes's

[65] 1 Corinthians 6:19–20 (King James Version).

[66] In 2 Kings 5:8–10, Elisha tells Naaman to cleanse himself in the Jordan River seven times and he will be healed of leprosy.

mother and grandfather do the same for him. Parker has Sarah Ruth, because

> what Sarah Ruth represents is precisely what Parker lacks and what he must submit to in order to become a Christian. It takes Sarah Ruth's ruse to make him acknowledge his calling, that is to say to make him admit that he is being called—no more free to call himself, to name himself than to sign his body. And it takes her "ice-pick" eyes to pierce and disrupt his fantasy world, and to prepare him for the "all-demanding" eyes of Christ.[67]

Step Three: Pain: Cleanse again. Next the artist will begin shading the design using larger needles. Bleeding will probably occur.[68] Hazel Motes blinds himself with lye. Young Tarwater is raped. Parker's newly tattooed back is pounded, first in a pool hall brawl, and then by Sarah Ruth. Parker seems to have had the easiest time of it in this preparatory step. Again, a pounding is more reader-accessible. Again, Parker is our "everyman."

Parker's choice of image and the act of tattooing itself brings about a profound change in his life. As noted, this procedure mirrors the prophet-making operations visited on O'Connor's other "ordinary as a loaf of bread" men-turned-prophets. This metamorphosis is accomplished for all of them when the pictorial is used as the portal across which the veil between the visible world and the invisible is momentarily lifted. The compelling image in this story is anchored by and mired in Parker's very physical human body and this is why, I think, the necessity for the existence of Sarah Ruth comes into the story.

WHY SARAH RUTH?

With the exception of Dame Van Winkle, Sarah Ruth Cates Parker is possibly one of the most maligned wives in American literature. She is attacked in almost every critical article for her looks as well as for her behavior. Jill P. Baumgaertner describes her as "one of the plainest women in literature, bony and judgmental,"[69] and Richard Giannone calls her "aggressive,"

[67] Bleikasten, "Writing on the Flesh," 15.

[68] Jonah was swallowed by a whale. Esau wrestled with an angel. Peter was crucified. The list goes on....

[69] Baumgartner, *A Proper Scarring*, 48.

"henpecking," and "skinny, bossy, and [so] indifferent to [Parker's] sexual stance that he marries her to meet the challenge of her libidinal coldness."[70] Avis Hewitt attributes some of this disparagement on the fact that "O'Connor labels Sarah Ruth through Parker's eyes as 'plain.'[71] Is plain wrong?," Hewitt asks. "Plain means clear, distinct, and evident to the eye or ear, straightforward, unadorned without obstruction."[72] Sarah Ruth is plain in the way that Miller's Elizabeth Proctor is plain or that Morrison's Sethe is plain, and really, wasn't the "termagant" Dame Van Winkle justified in her complaints about Rip and his infernal laziness? Furthermore, I contend that we only have Parker's word for her plainness. One can only imagine how a woman would look that he might not think was plain, given his penchant for self-adornment. Sarah Ruth "did not smoke or dip, drink whiskey, use bad-language, or paint her face, and God knew some paint would have improved it, Parker thought."[73] Plainness does not defer O'Connor from the creation of memorable female characters, as none of O'Connor's women are *femme fatales*. Actually, none of her male characters are much to look at either. So why are Sarah Ruth's looks of such concern to her critics? The reality is that some of the things that have been written about Sarah Ruth would not be written now in this era of political correctness. That is not to say that plain women do not suffer the "slings and arrows" of social criticism. It is to say that these kinds of remarks are now disguised in social and academic repartee, but the sentiments are still existent.

Sarah Ruth's demeanor, as perceived by Parker, is reminiscent of the girl in O'Connor's PhD cartoon. The plainness of the PhD girl with glasses is deliberate and also critically celebrated. Her little dot eyes, unlike those of any of the other characters in the panel, look out directly at the viewer and could well be described as "ice-pick" eyes, just as Sarah Ruth's are. Again, Sarah Ruth's critics all mention the "ice-pick" eyes and how she uses them

[70] Richard Giannone, "Dark Night, Dark Faith: Hazel Motes, the Misfit, and Francis Marion Tarwater," *Dark Faith: New Essays on Flannery O'Connor's The Violent Bear It Away*, ed. Susan Srigley (Notre Dame, IN: Notre Dame University Press, 2012) 222.

[71] O'Connor, *Collected Works*, 655.

[72] Avis Hewitt, "Jolted to Life by Her Touch," paper presented at the "Startling Figures: A Celebration of the Legacy of Flannery O'Connor Conference," Georgia State College & University, April 13–16, 2011, 1.

[73] O'Connor, *Collected Works*, 655.

to keep Parker away from his religious vocation. Andre Bleikasten, however, addresses Sarah Ruth's looks in a positive rather than a negative way. He attributes the attraction that "a man like Parker" has for Sarah Ruth, "the sort of sallow, dried-up country girl whom under normal circumstances he would have not looked at twice," to her "*otherness.*" This is not "the alluring otherness of a gaudy *dopplegange*r," Bleikasten writes, "but the radical otherness of the Law, whose fiercely uncompromising representative she turns out to be."[74] Marshall Bruce Gentry points out that "Sarah Ruth is one of the most authoritarian figures in O'Connor's works, exceeded, if at all, only by Hazel Motes' mother."[75] O'Connor's stories are filled with strong, often strident female characters and Sarah Ruth is exactly what Parker needs. His love for her introduces some discipline into his American Romantic Hero-like existence. When he is very young, he lights out for the territories like Huck Finn, he moves from woman to woman, escaping the entanglement of marriage like Natty Bumpo, and when he is finally snagged, he is still a lazy barfly like Rip Van Winkle. But what makes Parker different is Sarah Ruth. He falls in love with her, and it is she who guides him to his great destiny. For her, he stops drifting and philandering. He begins to hold a job, and when he loses it, she talks with his employer and regains it for him. He is going to become a father and he will need her help in fashioning that role. It is for her that he has the Byzantine Christ tattooed on his back. Because of her, his destiny is secured. One of the difficult things about not dying at the moment of grace, as is the case with many O'Connor characters, is just that—not dying at the moment of grace. Living on, living on in a community of believers, living on in a marriage, is extremely difficult and O'Connor addresses this in her last story.

WHY MARRIAGE?

Marriage has not been a factor in the lives of O'Connor's characters. We were given a fictional version of marriage comically juxtaposed with a reality version of marriage in her master's thesis story, "The Crop," which we

[74] Andre Bleikastein, "Beginnings and Endings in Flannery O'Connor." *Mississippi Quarterly: The Journal of Southern Cultures* (Winter 2005–Spring 2006) 59 (1–2): 177–186, 13.

[75] Marshall Bruce Gentry, *Flannery O'Connor's Religion of the Grotesque* (Jackson: University Press of Mississippi, 1986) 80.

looked at briefly in chapter 1. In "The Displaced Person," readers are treated to a private display of love-making featuring a cigarette butt that takes place between Mr. and Mrs. Shortly within the frame of marriage. "When the cigarette got the proper size, he would turn his eyes to her and open his mouth and draw in the butt and then sit there as if he had swallowed it, looking at her with the most loving look anybody could imagine. It nearly drove her wild and everytime he did it, she wanted to pull his hat down over his eyes and hug him to death."[76]

There is a bedroom kiss between Ruby and Claud Turpin in "Revelation," and when Ruby sees her vision, Claud is included in it too. In *Why Do the Heathen Rage?*, Mrs. Tilman is managing the farm and her unruly children while overseeing the care of her stricken husband. In no other story of O'Connor's does marriage play any kind of a role until her last, "Parker's Back." This story begins with the words "Parker's wife...." Within the fractious marriage that follows can be found an exhortation for the community of believers. Avis Hewitt makes a convincing argument that for believers, "prospering in God calls for connecting eros and agape."[77] O'Connor represents Sarah Ruth as the person to make this connection for Parker when she describes the very first meeting of the couple.

> Without warning a terrible bristly claw slammed the side of his face and he fell backwards on the hood of the truck.
>
> Parker's vision was so blurred that for an instant he thought he had been attacked by some creature from above, a giant hawk-eyed angel wielding a hoary weapon. As his sight cleared, he saw before him a tall raw-boned girl with a broom.[78]

Sarah Ruth, standing there with her broom, becomes heaven and earth to him as her "immediate function in the story is to discipline the unruly male, to cure him of his extravagant fantasies and make him conform to accepted standards of cultural order, and that, in this role, she performs a socializing or ('civilizing') task often assigned to women in American literature."[79] She demands to see the hand that he claims he has broken, and her

[76] O'Connor, *Collected Works*, 291.
[77] Hewitt, "Jolted to Life by Her Touch," 3.
[78] O'Connor, *Collected Works*, 656.
[79] Bleikasten, "Writing on the Flesh," 13.

"hand was dry and hot and rough and Parker felt himself jolted back to life by her touch. He looked more closely at her. I don't want nothing to do with this one, he thought."[80] Almost before he knows it, he has married her. He is as unable to resist marrying Sarah Ruth, as he is unable to resist the all-encompassing eyes on his back. He is destined to meet and marry her. As we have stated before, it is for her that he selected the Byzantine Christ.

The meeting of Parker and Sarah Ruth seems to have been inspired by that between Hester Prinn and Arthur Dimsdale in Hawthorne's *The Scarlet Letter.* Meeting in the woods after they have not been alone together for seven years, Hester offers Dimsdale an escape, a way to accept God's forgiveness and to start over. Even though in chapter 18, he cries, "I seem to have flung myself—sick, sin-stained, and sorrow blackened—down upon these forest leaves, and to have risen up all made anew, with new powers to glorify Him that hath been merciful! This is the better life! Why did we not find it sooner?"[81] Of course, they never find the "better life." Dimsdale cannot accept his own humanness and dies. Hester lives on bearing her emblem.

After the original jolting to life, O'Connor does not offer this way out to her two lovers. They must live on and be married. Death is not an option. If a prophet is to live in a community as a participant in the human condition, in order to truly love God, he or she must, as Hewitt argues, love the human beings who live with him and around him. Parker has made a commitment to Sarah Ruth before witnesses, and I, for one, do not believe O'Connor, the writer of "A Stroke of Good Fortune," would have him desert his wife and child. The apostle Paul emphasizes the gravity of making the marriage vows when he writes in his letter to the Ephesians, "Husbands, love your wives, even as Christ also loved the church and gave himself for it."[82] He writes further, "For this cause shall a man leave his father and his mother, and shall be joined unto his wife, and they two shall be one flesh. This is a great mystery: but I speak concerning Christ and the church."[83]

In the last events of the short story, we find the beginning of the true marriage that never could exist between Hawthorne's ill-fated lovers. Their star-crossed romance provides O'Connor with a starting place upon which

[80] O'Connor, *Collected Works*, 657.
[81] Hawthorne, *The Scarlet Letter*, 129–30.
[82] Ephesians 5:25 (King James Version).
[83] Ephesians 5:31–32 (King James Version).

to construct a marriage that is part of the tapestry in the Divine reality and in the reality of the fallen world. O'Connor infuses each event with a double consciousness of its simultaneous importance in both realms. The series of events is as carefully modeled and constructed as Walter Tilman's photographs in *Why Do the Heathen Rage?*

Parker's mind is so occupied with his marital struggle that while he is plowing his employer's field, a tree in the middle of it seems to

> reach out to grasp him. A ferocious thud propelled him into the air, and he heard himself yelling in an unbelievably loud voice, "GOD ABOVE!"
>
> He landed on his back while the tractor crashed upside-down into the tree and burst into flame. The first thing Parker saw were his shoes, quickly being eaten by the fire; one was caught under the tractor, the other was some distance away, burning by itself. He was not in them. He could feel the hot breath of the burning tree on his face. He scrambled backwards, still sitting, his eyes cavernous, and if he had known how to cross himself he would have done it.[84]

On the earthly plain, Parker, obsessing about bringing Sarah Ruth "to heel," crashes his employer's tractor into the very tree she told him to avoid. On the heavenly plain, Parker has experienced a violent encounter with the holy and his shoes have consequently been blasted off his feet. He is standing on Holy ground in the presence of a burning tree. There can be no denial of the hand of God as initiator of the following events.

Parker flees to the city in order to get a tattoo of "God," which he figures will make Sarah Ruth begin to respond like his previous women have responded to his tattoos. "'She can't hep herself,' Parker [says]. 'She can't say she don't like the looks of God.'"[85] A "still small voice" directs him on the choice of the iconic Christ. As the tattooist imprints the prototype onto his back, Parker imagines "how Sarah Ruth would be struck speechless by the face on his back and every now and then this would be interrupted by a

[84] O'Connor, *Collected Works*, 665.

[85] Ibid., 670.

vision of the tree of fire and his empty shoe beneath it."[86] At the moment of the imprinting of his emblem, Parker has a foot, as it were, in both realities. His imaginings are punctuated by powerful visions. When the tattoo is finished, Parker is afraid to look at the image he is now bearing.

> The artist took him roughly by the arm and propelled him between the two mirrors. "Now *look,*" he said, angry at having his work ignored.
>
> Parker looked, turned white and moved away. The eyes in the reflected face continued to look at him—still, straight, all-demanding, enclosed in silence.[87]

Using two mirrors to look backward and forward at the same time, Parker, for the first time, contemplates his body of illustrations as a cohesive creation, a work of art that has been made whole by the addition of the Christ imprinted on his back. This double-mirror moment could be construed as Parker's taking a Lacanian measure of himself by looking at his mirror image, or it could be construed as a Romantic moment as Parker looks at both the actual and the imaginary. I cannot help but think that this is O'Connor's own way of looking "backward and forward at the same time." She is looking at her own body of work that is now at its finish by using Parker as her medium, her metaphor. With the imprinting of the face of Christ onto Parker's body, Parker himself is superseded as the artist. His body becomes God's creation in line with the Divine Plan. In Parker's case, however, this transcendent moment ends, and he makes his way out of the door to drink a pint and a half of whiskey and to start a bar fight, to get thrown out into the alley, where he contemplates the state of his soul, and decides to return home to Sarah Ruth so that she can sort it all out for him. And sort it out she does, but not in the way Parker had hoped.

On the drive home, Parker feels "a stranger to himself," like he is "driving into a new country." This dreamlike car trip marks a transcendent moment for Parker. He is on a new road. He will never travel this way again. Even in this "new country," however, quite a bit of the "old country" is still with him as far as his marriage is concerned. "He made as much noise

[86] Ibid.
[87] Ibid.

as possible to assert that he was still in charge here, that his leaving her for a night without word meant nothing except it was the way he did things. He slammed the car door, stamped up the two steps and across the porch and rattled the doorknob. It did not respond to his touch. 'Sarah Ruth!' he yelled, 'let me in.'"[88]

She has locked him out. She evidently does not respond to "the way he did things." Parker starts to turn away from the door, "a tree of light burst[s] over the skyline," and Parker falls back against the door "as if he had been pinned there by a lance."[89] Parker cannot escape confrontation with Sarah Ruth and is held fast in both realities. Sarah Ruth forces him to say his whole name to gain entry. It is the name of a prophet—two prophets—Obadiah Elihue. When he whispers the name, his "spider web soul bursts into a perfect arabesque of colors, a garden of trees and birds and beasts."[90] Again, this moment of transcendence does not last long. It is important to note that in this story there are many transcendent moments, and each one brings Parker closer to an awareness of his destiny. However, he still has his marriage to mend.

Sarah Ruth the wife is angry about his night out "without a word." This, in itself, in her mind, might be enough to account for the broomstick bashing. To her, the tattoo is just a tattoo. What she sees is a man, the father of her unborn child, who, after losing his job, stays out all night and comes home smelling of whiskey and sporting a new tattoo that he calls "God." Of course, Sarah Ruth, daughter of a "Straight Gospel preacher," is horrified by the tattooed image on Parker's back. For her, God is "a spirit. No man shall see his face."[91] Here we are again in the fifteenth-century quarrel over images. Sarah Ruth "voices not only the letter but also the spirit of the biblical tradition. Hers is the invisible and unrepresentable Lord of the Hebrew people, hers the stern law engraved on Moses' tablets, hers the religion of the Book and the Word and the Name, the religion of the Father."[92] If Parker is going to navigate in the community of believers, he will have to in some way deal with these disagreements. He must begin in his own marriage. The last scene, with "Obadiah Elihue—leaning against the

[88] Ibid., 672.
[89] Ibid., 673.
[90] Ibid.
[91] Ibid., 674.
[92] Bleikasten, "Writing on the Flesh," 15.

tree, crying like a baby," reveals that Parker finally bears an image that marks his rite of passage. He has passed from childhood to manhood. His life will be filled with pain, more broom bashings, certainly, but he will be a light bearer, a receptacle, an emissary.

Conclusion

When Sarah Ruth confronts Parker with the statement, "At the judgement seat of God, Jesus is going to say to you, 'What you been doing all your life besides having pictures drawn all over you?,'" I think it is a question O'Connor is asking about her own life and work. Sensing that she, herself, is soon to appear at the judgment seat of God, she looks backward at her life's work—creating images—and makes an assessment. That assessment is "Parker's Back." The use of the frame, the composition within the frame, and the message of artistic medium are all pictorial elements that this study has attributed to O'Connor's stylistic technique. "Parker's Back" exhibits these elements in their final translation.

The Frame

O'Connor has framed her pictorial moments with recognizable frames. The frames of the single-panel cartoons consist of either thin black lines or a black interior which is bordered and framed by the white of the page on which the cartoon appears. Though the panels do not seem impenetrable, there is a definite designation of inside and outside. She plays with the idea of frame, at times, by having her characters look out into the reader's reality and speak directly to them, as is the case with the PhD cartoon. Pictorial pauses in *Wise Blood* are framed, though the frames may not always be the traditional mirror or window that we have become accustomed to in literature. The framing objects range from the deserted Motes house to the "rat colored car." In the last scene where we see Hazel Motes dead on the bed, O'Connor experiments with removing the frame and encases the *vanitas* pictorial within Hazel's dead human body. In *The Violent Bear It Away*, O'Connor returns to the traditional literary frames as it becomes important for the photographic moments to be clearly contained so that the revelations of the Divine will seem simultaneous with real life in the stopped motion of the verbal snapshot. In "Parker's Back," the frame again becomes the human body, but it is not a lifeless body—the soul having been transubstantiated. Parker's is a body full of life and mobility. His spiderweb of a soul has been long unattended, but he becomes the bearer of the Christ—the real Christ, as would be requisite with the choice of the Byzantine mosaic. Parker's Christ-laden human body is the image O'Connor wants to leave with us in her last story. Christ resides in this imperfect vessel. All of the other images have been leading up to this one last illustration.

The Composition within the Frame

O'Connor emphasizes the importance of the compositional arrangement of figures and objects within her visual tableaux in *Why Do the Heathen Rage?*. She spends ten pages having Walter Tilman arrange and rearrange the people and objects encased in his photographs in the way that they can best convey the visual story he wants to tell. Composition, in this way, drives story and meaning. The cartoons all have captions that convey messages and that appear under the single panel. Often the messages which are ambiguous and clichéd are clarified by how the characters are arranged in the panel. This was particularly true of the PhD cartoon. The idea of the caption is significant in *Wise Blood*, where O'Connor choses the *vanitas* still life as mode for conveyance of meaning. Some manner of *momento mori* is understood by the reader because of the *vanitas* selection. In choosing abject and cast-off objects to fulfill the requirements of the *vanitas* form, O'Connor reaches backward to embrace and bring forward standard and tradition implications into the world of the present. The pictorial frames that enfold the women of *Wise Blood* hold compositions that exhibit assemblages of fragments of the contemporary world that include slogans and commercial advertising. What is inside that frame joins with the voice of the narrative on the outside to display a full and complete image of the character and her place, both in the novel and in the modern world. The pristine white borders of the snapshots evoked by the pictorial pauses in *The Violent Bear It Away* define the snapshot as a medium of the instant. In this novel, real events are frozen and held up close for contemplation. The flash and the understood presence of the accompanying negative are key to O'Connor's revelation of the existence of a Divine reality operating in tandem with the current reality.

Then, there is Parker. Parker exhibits a receptivity to both countries, the visible and the invisible. He is able to travel in both spheres for much longer that the snapshot moment. His awareness of the Divine reality extends for lengthier periods of time when compared with those of the young Tarwater. Parker's body is the canvas for a multitude of images that portray his adventures in the experiential world. O'Connor continues to work with comic-upended clichés in this story, particularly those dealing with the human condition. Cartoonish templates are still present, particularly in the husband and wife bashing scenes that were very popular in mid-twentieth century single-panel cartoons as well as on television. Ill as she was when she wrote "Parker's Back," Flannery O'Connor never lessened the power of her stylistic technique, and she never lifted her finger from the pulse of American culture. Does the collection of tattoos on Parker's back qualify as what the art world would label as assemblage? Parker, the artist, feels that it does not, and it is not until he acquires the image of the Byzantine Christ that all of the other images move into place. The selection of the Byzantine made of mosaic pieces is crucial to the compositional completeness of the design that is Parker and the design that is the work of Flannery O'Connor. With the choice of the Byzantine art form, the pictorial tableau expands to include the viewer for the first time. We are all Parkers. We are all in the presence of the icon as created by the artist, Flannery O'Connor.

The Message of the Medium

The stylistic mediums chosen by O'Connor with which to construct her textual pictorials also provide an accompanying voice to the comprehensive message. The linocut used for the cartoons is reproducible and reprintable. The actuality of gouging a cutting tool deep into linoleum to make a character reveals the hand of the artist in the primitive yet compelling final prints. Painting techniques that reflect the classical past as well as the avant-garde present provide levels of association while still adding even more voices to the choir that is meaning. Instantaneity and presence are the contributions of the snapshot medium selected for *The Violent Bear It Away*. Then we come to Parker and his tattoos. Choosing tattoo as her final medium enabled O'Connor to literally combine the blood of the Christ icon with Parker's human blood in an almost ritualistic engraving rite. Parker will bear the icon permanently. He will take it to his grave, just as his creator will do.

The strong statement that "Parker's Back" makes is, in part, O'Connor's coming to terms with her own participation in an "age of reproduction."[1] Parker's scenario mirrors the development of Flannery O'Connor's pictorial text, all rendered as a result of reproduction. To begin with, the undergraduate cartoons, made from linocuts, were printed in a newspaper that was disseminated across the college campus. The painted

[1] Walter Benjamin, "The Work of Art in the Age of Mechanical Reproduction."

and assembled pictorials in *Wise Blood* were recognizable to her audience because of the fact that art pieces are not only viewed in museums and galleries, but also in photographs in art books and brochures. This distribution of art to the masses, Benjamin writes, makes it available "for a simultaneous experience."[2] The introduction of the camera expands the space upon which experience can occur. That photographic experience was mimicked in *The Violent Bear It Away* in a way that would enable a modern audience understand the mechanics of Divine Revelation. The conventions of Byzantine mosaic provide for its reproductive or incarnational capacity—the prototype of the icon still carries some of the "aura" of the original.

Flannery O'Connor's lecture to young writers, which now appears in *Mystery and Manners*, entitled "The Nature and the Aim of Fiction," offers an explanation of her beliefs about good writing. Her own words can be applied to end this study of the development of her pictorial technique. O'Connor has faithfully and painstakingly, to the last, served as the image-bearer in order to open both the realm of reality to her readers as well as to imagistically create an awareness of the Divine realm by selecting "every word for a reason, every incident for a reason, and [arranging] in a time-sequence for a reason. [A writer] demonstrates something that cannot possibly be demonstrated any other way than with a whole novel."[3] Applying the pictorial is O'Connor's way of accomplishing this. To her, technique "is something organic, something that grows out of the material, and this being the case, it is different for every story of any account that has ever been written."[4] "The beginning of human knowledge is through the senses," she writes, and that is why she works so diligently to engage the senses by means of visual art. That she opens both realms to the reader is very important to O'Connor. Fiction, according to O'Connor, "is a plunge into reality and it's very shocking to the system."[5] The "sense of mystery" is "deepened by contact with reality" and the "sense of reality is deepened by contact with mystery."[6]

On these pages I have tried to create an assemblage in the manner of the one featured in *Everything That Rises Must Converge*. My creation is re-

[2] Benjamin, *Illuminations*, 234.
[3] O'Connor, *Mystery and Manners*, 75.
[4] Ibid., 67.
[5] Ibid., 78.
[6] Ibid., 79.

plete with cartoons, reproductions of classical painting, filmic montage, Cubist assemblage, artistic combines, collage, Coca-Cola commercials, snapshots, and tattoos. I have tried to color the composition with narrative that will spur associations and levels of understanding about Flannery O'Connor, the artist. Entering into the pictorial pauses in her narrative and examining the style and technique she applied allows us in some way to briefly come in contact with the "mystery," the "miraculous," and the truthfulness that is the nature of her art. *At the judgment seat of God, Jesus is going to say to you, "What you been doing all your life besides have pictures drawn all over you?"*[7]

[7] Sarah Ruth to Parker in Flannery O'Connor's "Parker's Back."

Bibliography

Aascia-Lees, Frances and Patricia Sharpe. *Tattoo, Torture, Mutilation, and Adornment.* Albany: State University of New York Press, 1992.

Armstrong, Nancy. *Desire and Domestic Fiction.* New York: Oxford University Press, 1987.

Asals, Frederick. *Flannery O'Connor: The Imagination of Extremity.* Athens: University of Georgia Press, 1982.

Auerbach, Erich. *Mimesis.* New York: Meridian Books, Inc., 1959.

Bacon, Jon Lance. *Flannery O'Connor and Cold War Culture.* Cambridge, UK: Cambridge University Press, 1993.

———. "A Fondness for Supermarkets: *Wise Blood* and Consumer Culture." *New Essays on Wise Blood.* Edited by Michael Kreyling. Cambridge, UK: Cambridge University Press, 1995.

Bahktin M. M. *The Dialogic Imagination.* Edited by Michael Holquist. Translated by Carl Emerson and Michael Holquist. Austin: University of Texas Press, 1981.

Barthes, Roland. *Camera Lucida.* Translated by Richard Howard. New York: Hill and Wang, 1980.

———. *Mythologies.* Translated by Annette Lavers. New York: Hill and Wang, 1972.

———. *S/Z.* Translated by Richard Miller. New York: Hill and Wang, 1974.

Baudrillard, Jean. *Simulations.* Translated by Paul Foss, Paul Patton, and Philip Beitchman. Los Angeles: Semiotext[e], 1983.

Baumgaertner, Jill P. *Flannery O'Connor: A Proper Scarring.* Wheaton, IL: Harold Shaw Publisher, 1988.

Bearden, Romare. "Rectangular Structure in My Montage Paintings." *Leonardo* 40/3 (2007): 291–300.

Benjamin, Walter. *Illuminations.* Translated by Harry Zohn. New York: Schocken Books, 1968.

Bieber Lake, Christina. *The Incarnational Art of Flannery O'Connor.* Macon, GA: Mercer University Press, 2005.

Bleikasten, Andre. "Writing on the Flesh: Tattoos and Taboos in 'Parker's Back.'" *The Southern Literary Journal* 14/2 (Spring 1982): 8–18.

Brooks, Peter. *The Melodramatic Imagination: Balzac, Henry James, Melodrama, and the Mode of Excess.* New Haven, CT: Yale University Press, 1976.

Bruggenann, Walter. *The Prophetic Imagination.* Minneapolis, MN: Fortress Press, 2001.

Brumbaugh, Anne M. "Sources and Cues in Advertising and Their Effects on the Activation of Cultural and Subcultural Knowledge on the Route to Persuasion." *Journal of Consumer Research* 29/2 (September 2002): 258–69.

Burger, Amy. "Preserve the pink: How to enhance the retro bathroom's charm." *St. Louis Post-Dispatch*, September 2, 2011. http://www.stltoday.com/lifestyles/home-and-garden/preserve-the-pink-how-to-enhance-the-retro-bathroom-s/article_4de41549-fd74-5dd6-b963-eda7f95c94ca.html.

Capobianco, Ken and Jay Cantor. "An Interview with Jay Cantor." *Journal of Modern Literature* 17/1 (Summer 1990): 3–11.

Capp, Al. *In Search of the Perfect Woman...Li'l Abner: Dailies. Volume 16. 1950.* Princeton, NJ: Kitchen Sink Press, 1993.

The Cartoons of Flannery O'Connor at Georgia College. Milledgeville: Georgia College, 2010.

The Cartoons of Flannery O'Connor at Georgia College. Edited by Marshall Bruce Gentry. Milledgeville, Georgia College, 2010.

Cook, Alstair. "George Price on Marriage and Other Disasters." *The World of George Price*. New York: Beaufort Books, 1988.

Curtiss, Mina. "Manet Caricatures: *Olympia*." *The Massachusetts Review* 7/4 (Autumn 1966): 725–52.

Del Giudice, Marco. "The Twentieth Century Reversal of Pink-Blue Gender Coding: A Scientific Urban Legend?" *Archive of Sexual Behavior* 41 (2012): 1321–23. doi:10.1007/s10508-012-0002-z.

Demus, Otto. *Byzantine Mosaic Decoration: Aspects of Monumental Art in Byzantium*. New Rochelle, NY: Caratzas Brothers, 1976.

Derrida, Jacques. *The Truth in Painting*. Translated by Geoff Bennington and Ian McLeod. Chicago: University of Chicago Press, 1987.

Di Renzo, Anthony. *American Gargoyles: Flannery O'Connor and the Medieval Grotesque*. Carbondale: Southern Illinois University Press, 1993.

Donahoo, Robert. "O'Connor and *The Feminine Mystique*: The Limitations That Reality Imposed on the Subject of the Feminist Business: Re-Reading Flannery O'Connor." In *On the Subject of the Feminist Business: Re-Reading Flannery O'Connor*. Edited by Teresa Caruso.

Dos Passos, John. *The 42nd Parallel: Volume One of the U.S.A. Trilogy*. New York: Manner Books, 2000.

Driggers, Stephen G., Robert J. Dunn, and Sarah Gordon. *The Manuscripts of Flannery O'Connor at Georgia College*. Athens: University of Georgia Press, 1989.

Ebert-Schifferer, Sybille. *Still Life: A History*. New York: Harry N. Abrams, 1998.

Eisner, Will. *Graphic Storytelling and Visual Narrative*. New York: Norton & Company, 1996.

Eliot, T. S. *The Waste Land: A Norton Critical Edition*. Edited by Michael North. New York: Norton & Company, 2001.

Foucault, Michel. "'Nietzsche, Genealogy, History." *The Foucault Reader*. Edited by Paul Rabinow. London: Penguin, 1991.

Frank, Joseph. *The Idea of Spatial Form.* Newark, NJ: Rutgers University Press, 1991.

Freud, Sigmund. *The Uncanny.* Translated by David Mclintock. NewYork: Penguin Books, 2003.

Friedan, Betty. *The Feminine Mystique.* New York: Norton & Company, 1997.

Friedman, Donald. *The Writer's Brush: Paintings Drawings, and Sculptures by Writers.* Minneapolis, MN: Mid-List Press, 2007.

Frye, Northrup. *The Secular Scripture.* Cambridge, MA: Harvard University Press, 1976.

Gale, Steven H. "Seventy-Five Years of 'The New Yorker' Cartoons: A History." *American Periodicals* 11 (2001): 95–130.

Gentry, Marshall Bruce. *Flannery O'Connor's Religion of the Grotesque.* Jackson: University Press of Mississippi, 1986.

———. "O'Connor as Miscegenationist." *Flannery O'Connor in the Age of Terrorism: Essays on Violence and Grace.* Edited by Avis Hewitt and Robert Donahoo. Knoxville: University of Tennessee Press, 2010.

———. "Wise Women, Wise Blood." In *Wise Blood: A Re-Consideration.* Edited by John J. Han. NewYork: Rodopi, 1994.

Gerald, Kelly. "The Habit of Art." In *Flannery O'Connor: The Cartoons.* Edited By Kelly Gerald. Seattle, WA: Fantagraphics Books, 2012.

Gerberg, Mort. *Cartooning: The Art and the Business.* New York: William Morrow & Company, 1989.

Giannone, Richard. "Dark Night, Dark Faith: Hazel Motes, the Misfit, and Francis Marion Tarwater." In *Dark Faith: New Essays on Flannery O'Connor's The Violent Bear It Away.* Edited by Susan Srigley. Notre Dame, IN: Notre Dame University Press, 2012.

Gooch, Brad. *Flannery: A Life of Flannery O'Connor.* New York: Back Bay Books, 2009.

Goodwin, James. *Modern American Grotesque: Literature and Photography.* Columbus: Ohio State University Press, 2009.

Gordon, Sarah. *Flannery O'Connor: The Obedient Imagination.* Athens: University of Georgia, 2000.

Gottlieb, Carla. "Picasso's 'Girl before a Mirror.'" In *The Journal of Aesthetics and Art Criticism* 24/4 (Summer 1966): 509–518.

Greenberg, Clement. "Collage." In *Art and Culture.* From *Art News.* Last modified September, 1958. www.shareecom.ca/greenberg/collage.html.

Hagermann, Meyly Chin. "Hemingway's Secret: Visual to Verbal Art." *Journal of Modern Literature* 7/1 (February 1979): 87–112.

Hawthorne, Nathaniel. *The Blithedale Romance.* Edited by Seymour Gross and Rosalie Murphy. Norton Critical Editions. New York: Norton & Company, 1978.

———. "The Gentle Boy." *Tales and Sketches.* Edited by Roy Harvey Pearce. New York: Literary Classics, 1996.

———. *The House of the Seven Gables.* Edited by Robert S. Levine. Norton Critical Editions. New York: Norton & Company, 2006.

———. *The Scarlet Letter and Other Writings.* Edited by Leland S. Person. Norton Critical Editions. New York: Norton & Company, 2005.

Hefernan, James. *Museum of Words: The Poetics of Ekphrasis from Homer to Ashbery.* Chicago: University of Chicago Press, 2004.

Heidegger, Martin. "The Thing." In *Poetry Language and Thought.* New York: Harper Collins, 1971.

Hemingway, Ernest. *A Moveable Feast.* Restored edition. New York: Scribner, 2009.

Hewitt, Avis. "Jolted to Life by Her Touch." Paper presented at the Startling Figures: A Celebration of the Legacy of Flannery O'Connor Conference, Georgia State College & University, April 13–16, 2011.

Hokinson, Helen. *There Are Ladies Present.* Boston: E. P. Dutton & Co., 1952.

Horkeimer, Max and Theodore Adorno. *Dialectic of Enlightenment (Cultural Memory in the Present).* Edited by Gunzelin Schmid Noerr. Translated by Edmund Jephcott. Stanford, CA: Stanford University Press, 2007.

Irigaray, Luce. *The Sex Which Is Not One.* Ithaca, NY: Cornell University Press, 1985.

Iskin, Ruth E. "The Light of Images and the Shadow of Technology: Lacan, Photography and Subjectivity." *Discourse* 19/3 (Spring 1997): 43–66.

Jackson, Gregory S. "A Game Theory of Evangelical Text." *Critical Inquiry* 39/3 (Spring 2013): 451–85.

———. *The Word and Its Witness: The Spiritualization of American Realism.* Chicago: University of Chicago Press, 2009.

Kahane, Claire. "The Revision of Rage: Flannery O'Connor and Me." *The Massachusetts Review* 46/3 (Fall 2005): 439–61.

Kyle, Jill Anderson. "Cezanne, the 'Plastic,' and American Artist/Critics." *Cezanne and American Modernism.* New Haven, CT: Yale University Press, 2009.

Laughlin, Clarence. "The Camera's Methods of Approaching Reality." *College Art Journal* 16/4 (Summer 1957): 297–306.

Livingstone, Marco. *Pop Art: A Continuing History.* New York: Thames & Hudson, 2001.

Lytle, Andrew. *The Velvet Horn.* New York: McDowell, Obolensky, 1957.

The Magic of Things Still-Life Painting 1500–1800. Edited by Jochen Sander. Frankfurt, Germany: Stadel Museum, 2008.

Maritain, Jacques. *Art and Scholasticism with Other Essays.* Minneapolis, MN: Filiquarian, 2007.

Martin, Karl. "Flannery O'Connor's Prophetic Imagination." *Religion & Literature* 26/3 (Autumn 1994): 33–58.

Martin, Michael, Interview with Pellom McDaniels. *All Things Considered.* May 7, 2016. National Public Radio.

Mascia-Lees, Frances and Patricia Sharpe. *Tatoo, Torture, Mutilation, and Adornment: The Denaturalization of the Body in Culture and Text.* Albany: State University of New York Press, 1992.

Mason, Paul. "Men, Machines, and the Mincer: The Prison Movie." August 1998. http://usf.usfca.edu/pj//articles/Prison.htm

McCloud, Scott. *Understanding Comics: The Invisible Art.* New York: William Morrow, 1993.

McLuhan, Marshall. *The Mechanical Bride: Folklore of Industrial Man.* Boston: Beacon Press, 1951.

McNamara, Carol. *The lens of impressionism: Photography and painting along the Normandy coast, 1850–1874.* Ann Arbor: University of Michigan Museum of Art, 2009.

Merton, Thomas. *The Search for Solitude.* http://kickass.to/thomas-merton-journals-pdf-t7411598.html.

Mitchell, W. J. T. *Iconology: Image, Text, Ideology.* Chicago: University of Chicago Press, 1986.

———. *What Do Pictures Want?* Chicago: University of Chicago Press, 2005.

Morris, Wright. "The Camera Eye." *Critical Inquiry* 8/1 (Autumn 1981): 1–15.

Moser, Barry. "Working Backward: A Reflection on the Linoleum Cuts of Flannery O'Connor." *Flannery O'Connor: The Cartoons.* Edited by Kelly Gerald. Seattle, WA: Fantagraphics Books, 2012.

Napier, James J. "Flannery O'Connor's Last Three: 'The Sense of an Ending.'" *The Southern Literary Journal* 14/2 (Spring 1982):19–27.

O'Connor, Flannery. *Collected Works.* New York: Library of America, 1988.

———. *Letters of Flannery O'Connor: The Habit of Being.* New York: Farrar, Straus, Giroux, 1979.

———. *Mystery and Manners.* New York: Noonday Press, 1969.

———. "The Nature and Aim of Fiction." *Mystery and Manners.* New York: Farrar, Straus & Giroux, 1961.

Orvell, Miles. "Writing Posthistorically: Krazy Kat, Maus, and the Contemporary Fiction Cartoon." *American Literary History* 4/1 (Spring 1992): 110–28.

Parker, Dorothy. "Big Blonde." In *Stories.* New York: Wings Books, 1993.

———. "Preface." *Men, Women, and Dogs* by James Thurber. New York: Harcourt, Brace, & Co., 1943.

Parry, Albert. *Tattoo: Secrets of a Strange Art.* New York: Collier Books, 1933.

"PhD Cartoon." http://fantagraphics.tumblr.com/post/26647483189/flannery-oconnor-cartoonist.

Photography Changes Everything. Edited by Marvin Heiferman. New York: Aperture, 2012.

Piper, Wendy. *Misfits and Marble Fauns: Religion and Romance in Hawthorne & O'Connor.* Macon, GA: Mercer University Press, 2011.

Poe, Edgar Allen. *Complete Tales and Poems.* New York: Barnes and Noble Books, 1992.

"Polka Dots" http://www.vogue.it/en/encyclo/cinema/p/polka-dots.

Price, George. *The World of George Price: A 55-Year Retrospective.* New York: Beaufort Books, 1988.

Prown, Katherine Hemple. *Revising Flannery O'Connor: Southern Literary Culture and the Problem of Female Authorship.* Charlottesville: University of Virginia Press, 2001.

Rabb, Jane. "Introduction: Notes toward a History of Literature and Photography." In *Literature & Photography: Interactions 1840–1990.* Albuquerque: University of New Mexico Press, 1995.

Reiniche, Ruth. "An Untapped Legacy: Flannery O'Connor's Ruby in 'A Stroke of Good Fortune' and in the Manuscript of *Wise Blood.*" *Flannery O'Connor Review* 9 (2011).

Rhodie, Sam. *Montage.* Manchester, UK: Manchester University Press, 2006.

Robinson, Casey. *The Old Maid.* Directed by Edmund Goulding. 1939; Burbank, CA: Warner Bros. Pictures.

"romare bearden: empress" *metropolis: jazz, free jazz, & improvised music* http://metropolis.free-jazz.net/romare-bearden-empress/artist-portraits/7971/.

Rowell, Margit. *Objects of Desire: The Modern Still Life.* New York: Henry Abrams, 1997.

Rush, John A. *Spiritual Tattoo: A Cultural History of Tattooing, Piercing, Scarification, Branding, and Implants.* Berkley, CA: Frog Ltd., 2005.

Scott, Walter. *Essays on Chivalry, Romance, and the Drama.* London: Frederick Warne & Co., 1887.

Sessions, William. "Flannery O'Connor and Freud: The Meaning of Life in Death." Emory University. Aquinas Center, Atlanta. November 19, 2012. Lecture. http://www.youtube.com/watch?v=ReXP1W-pm8w.

Sheed, Wilfrid. "The Tragedy of James Thurber." *Slate* (September 18, 2003). http://www.slate.com/articles/arts/books/2003/09/blind_wit.html.

Shiff, Richard. "Seeing Cezanne." *Critical Inquiry* 4/4 (Summer 1978): 769–808.

Sicker, Phillip. "The Belladonna: Eliot's Female Archetype in *The Waste Land.*" *Twentieth Century Literature* 30/4 (Winter 1984): 420–431.

Smith, Mack. *Literary Realism and the Ekphrastic Tradition.* University Park: Penn State University Press, 1995.

Sontag, Susan. *On Photography.* New York: Farrar, Straus, and Giroux, 1973.

Stack, Frank. "Introduction." *In Search of the Perfect Woman...Li'l Abner: Dailies. Volume 16. 1950.* Princeton, NJ: Kitchen Sink Press, 1993.

Stavitsky, Gail. "Cezanne and American Modernism." *Cezanne and American Modernism.* New Haven, CT: Yale University Press, 2009.

Stein, Gertrude. "Pictures." *Writings 1932–1946.* New York: Library of America, 1998.

Steiner, Wendy. *The Colors of Rhetoric.* Chicago: University of Chicago Press, 1982.

Stewart, Jack. *Color, Space, and Creativity: Art and Ontology in Five British Writers.* Madison, NJ: Fairleigh Dickinson University Press, 2008.

Sykes, John D. *Flannery O'Connor, Walker Percy, and the Aesthetic of Revelation.* Columbia: University of Missouri Press, 2007.

Thurber, James. *Men, Women, and Dogs.* New York: Harcourt, Brace, & Co., 1943.

Trachtenberg, Alan. "Seeing and Believing: Hawthorne's Reflections on the Daguerreotype in *The House of the Seven Gables.*" *American Literary History* 9/3 (Autumn 1997): 460–81.

Updike, John. "All in the Family" (unpublished). *Literature & Photography: Interactions 1840–1990.* Edited by Jane Rabb. Albuquerque: University of New Mexico Press, 1995.

———. "Writers and Artists." *The Writer's Brush: Paintings, Drawings, and Sculpture by Writers.* Edited by Donald Friedman. Minneapolis, MN: Mid-List Press, 2007.

Voris, Linda. "Interpreting Cezanne: Immanence in Gertrude Stein's First Landscape Play, *Lend a Hand or Four Religions.*" *Modernism/modernity* 19/1 (January 2012): 73–93.

Votteler, Thomas. *Contemporary Literary Criticism: Excerpts from Criticism of the Works of Today's Novelists, Poets, Playwrights, Short Story Writers, Scriptwriters, & Other Creative Writers: 013.* Detroit: Gale Research Inc. 1979.

Waldman, Diane. *Collage, Assemblage, and the Found Object.* New York: Harry N. Abrams, 1992.

Watt, Ian. *The Rise of the Novel: Studies in Defoe, Richardson and Fielding.* Berkley: University of California Press, 2001.

Watts, Emily Stipes. *Ernest Hemingway and the Arts.* Urbana: University of Illinois Press, 1971.

Weisenburger, Steven. "Williams, West, and the Art of Regression." *South Atlantic Review* 47/4 (November 1982): 1–16.

West, Nathanael. *Miss Lonleyhearts & The Day of the Locust.* New York: New Directions, 2009.

Westling, Louise. *Sacred Groves and Ravaged Gardens: The Fiction of Eudora Welty, Carson McCullers, and Flannery O'Connor.* Athens: University of Georgia Press, 1985.

Wood, Ralph C. *Flannery O'Connor and the Christ-Haunted South.* Grand Rapids, MI: Eerdmans Publishing, 2004.

Wylder, Jean. "Flannery O'Connor: A Reminiscence and Some Letters." *The North American Review* 255/1 (Spring 1970): 58–65.

Yaeger, Patricia. "The Woman without Any Bones." *New Essays on Wise Blood.* Edited by Michael Kreyling. Cambridge, UK: Cambridge University Press, 1995.

Yeates, Susan. *Learning Linocut: A Comprehensive Guide to the Art of Relief Printing through Linocut.* Bedfordshire, UK: Authors Online Ltd., 2011.

Index